French Entré

Norm

Independent reviews of the best
restaurants and hotels in the area

second edition

The French Entrée series of travel guides provides independent reviews and opinions on the best local restaurants and hotels in the regions of France. Unlike many other guides, no charge is made and the reviews are the author's own opinions.

To see our complete range of travel books, menu guides and themed phrse books for independent travellers, visit our **www.aspectguides.com**

In the French Entrée series:
Bed and Breakfast in France (1-904012-04-3)
Brittany (1-904012-03-5)
Calais, Bolougne and the North of France (1-904012-00-0)
Normandy (1-904012-02-7)

Companion to Food and Drink in France (1-904012-05-1)
French Business Phrase Book (1-904012-10-8)
French Family Phrase Book (1-904012-09-4)
French Young Traveller's Phrase Book (1-904012-11-6)

French Entrée

Normandy

*Independent reviews of the best
restaurants and hotels in the area*

second edition

Patricia Fenn

Aspect Guides

Second edition published in Great Britain 2002
First published in 1991

Published by Aspect Guides, an imprint of Peter Collin Publishing
32-34 Great Peter Street, London, SW1P 2DB

British Library Cataloguing-in-Publication Data
A catalogue record for this book is available from the British Library
ISBN 1-904012-02-7

Design and production by Navigator Guides Ltd, Norfolk
Printed and bound in Italy by Legoprint

Every effort has been made to ensure that the information in this guide is
accurate and up-to-date and the advice is given in good faith. However,
neither the publisher nor the author is responsible for any problems or
disappointments encountered before or during your travels.

Contents

The French Entrée Difference

This book is part of the French Entrée series of guide books that provide individual and personal reviews of restaurants and hotels in a particular region of France.

Unlike many of our competitors, we do not make any charge to include establishments. This might seem like financial suicide, but it does ensure that you get a true review of the restaurant and, most importantly, the choice of restaurants and hotels is ours. Many of the best restaurants and hotels are not featured in other guides because the owners are already very busy and don't need to pay to get extra custom. But you'll find them in these guides – because they offer great food.

You can blame Patricia Fenn for having the original idea for this series of guides. And 20 years ago, this was an inspirational idea! Still, Pat and the fellow editors who compile these guides travel thousands of kilometres every year in search of great food and a great atmosphere. We hope you'll find the guide useful, or simply enjoy reading the travels around France.

www.aspectguides.com

Using this book

Prices:

Prices are in Euros; this subject is worth a short note. When updating this edition, most of the establishments had not yet decided on a tariff in Euros – true even a month before the change happened! In these cases, we have converted the (old) French-franc prices into Euros at the rate in December 2001. However, we also found that some establishments used the change to Euros to round-up their prices. (However, this type of price-increase seems to be true across many different types of service!)

Maps:

The area maps are to help the reader to find the place he wishes to visit on his own map. Each place is given a reference on the relevant area map, but they are not designed to replace a good touring map.

Telephone:

The (o) in brackets at the beginning of a telephone number should be used when dialling in France, but when making calls from outside the area, e.g. from UK, dial 0033 then the nine digits omitting the o.

The five digit number given in the address, eg. 62000, are the postal codes, which should be used in all correspondence.

Grading:

L, M or S in the margin stand for 'L' = Luxury, 'S' = Simple and 'M' for those in between.

☆ The establishment fulfils exceptionally well at least one of the author's criteria of comfort, welcome and cuisine.

Acronyms:

🛏 stands for Hotel; ⊠ for Restaurant and C for Chambre d'hôte in combination with 4 above, ie. 🛏 S, ⊠ L, etc.

   o.o.s. = 'out of season';

   stc = service and taxes are included.

Raison d'etre

The first Normandy book, part of the French Entrée series, was published in 1991. Further editions followed over the intervening years, but now in 2002 it is evident that there have been so many changes that only a new edition will do. This is it.

It is new in that every one of the entries have been re-visited by me and re-assessed, but not new in that it relies on seventeen years' experience of the region and on hundreds of letters from readers relating their experiences. These are one of the book's unique assets. On the day I visit, there might have been an unprecedented disaster in the kitchen, or the patron might now recognise me and make a special effort. Neither of these occurrences is typical, but a thick file of thumbs up or down fills in the gaps in between.

I have made plenty of exciting new additions and found some wonderful new restaurants and hotels. Sadly, some old faithfuls have bit the dust, and with a recession greatly fiercer than we in Britain seem to realise, and a general disinclination of the young to take over family businesses, I expect more to follow.

The aim of the book remains the same - to paint a comprehensive picture of Normandy's hotels, restaurants, scenery and diversions, and then to leave the reader to decide what is right for him. The assumption is that we all have different priorities at different times. Take the kids and we're talking budget. Take the bride and the sky's the limit.

Look elsewhere for a quick symbolised reference guide or one for a particular income group. Snatch up this one if you want to know exactly what's on offer before you make the choice.

Stars ☆

These are to point you in the right direction - to the bullseyes. Pick of the bunch, they are chosen because they fulfill superbly well at least one - and preferably all - of the over-riding criteria -welcome, good food, comfort and situation. Other entries may be there simply because there is none better in that particular town; the stars are there because they have been tried and tested and proved to be winners.

Entrée to the Entrées

Hotels and restaurants are graded into three categories: **L** for Luxury, **M** for Medium and **S** for Simple, but always the prime criterion for recommendation is value for money. Service with a smile scores top marks. Few chain hotels are included because (a) they are not difficult to locate without any help from me and (b) I happen to prefer a degree of individuality and owner management to even the most efficient plastic uniformity.

L - Luxury

To spend a night in an **L** hotel you should expect to spend around 80-112€ for the room and find it equipped with every necessity. Bathrooms will be luxurious, often offering a jacuzzi and certainly a bath as well as a shower. Look for the ones that have a Michelin star attached to their restaurant - anything in this category should take their food seriously, and not just charge a lot for superficial gloss. Often there will be cheaper, less luxurious rooms, and these are well worth investigating if you like the trappings - the comfortable salons, the good restaurant, the swimming pool, the smooth service - without wanting to spend too much on the room. Remember though that the extras will push up the bill - breakfast, drinks at the bar, wine with dinner. If it's a special occasion it's worth going for the hotel's best, and even at top prices - around 160€ - you will be doing a far better deal than in the U.K. where beds, not rooms, are charged for.

    L restaurants are another matter and every visitor to France should try and budget to sample them. Lunch menus offer particularly good value, with a talented chef cutting costs to rock bottom in order to fill his restaurant. There are several listed where a four-course meal need only cost around £15. When you get to the double Michelin stars, like La Bourride in Caen, you are talking about 53€ for dinner, but even here there is a lunch menu at 30€.

M - Medium

The **M** category covers the majority of hotels, safe and not too expensive. The cost should be between 32€ and 64€, and my selection is nearly always owner-managed, bringing in the personal touch which we all appreciate above gloss. Rooms will be well-equipped, usually with telephone, T.V., good hanging space and with any luck some efficient lighting (but this is France). They will have en suite bathrooms with bath or shower, and you should have a choice of twin or double beds and the use of a garage.

M restaurants range from the typical French bourgeois style, with draped curtains, well-upholstered chairs, patronne likewise, and a clientele of local worthies, businessmen during the week and families for the sacred Sunday lunch gathering, to the small but tasteful new venture of a young couple anxious to get established. In the first group you will probably eat traditional French dishes, prepared by a patron/chef who knows what his regulars like and is not over-keen to experiment; in the latter there may be a new Michelin star chef striving for recognition, who may well enjoy extending the range of established cuisine with new ingredients and ideas from other countries. There is excellent reliable value to be found in this category, where a meal should cost between 12.5 and 29€.

S - Standard

It is the S category that causes me most pleasure and most pain. Pleasure because we all like a bargain and there is great satisfaction in discovering one probably not listed in other guides, and pain because obviously short cuts are a temptation. With S hotels I have to be particularly careful - one bad meal you can forget, a night with bedbugs you can't There is a limit to just how simple you can get, so nowadays most people would expect en suite 'facilities', probably a shower not a bath for a price between 24€ and 40€. There are some winners in this category, relying more on the owners' welcome and good will than on the frills, and these are the ones that the faithful Brits return to year after year.

S restaurants can imply a simple bucolic meal served at scrubbed tables in a farmhouse, one dish in a brasserie, a crêperie, a salad bar, or a basic town restaurant often attached to a hotel, where the patron cooks, and his wife and family serve to a devoted bunch of regulars, who rely on his plat du jour. These last are the ones to make for with an appetite but not if you require finesse.

Tips for beginners

Maps and Guides

Good maps are essential and I must stress that those in the front of this book are intended only as an indication of where to find the entries. They should be used in conjunction with the appropriate Michelin maps: 231 covers all Normandy; 52, 54, 55 will deal with smaller areas. The red Michelin, apart from all its other virtues, has useful town maps.

Booking

Sunday lunch is the Meal of the Week, when several generations settle down together to enjoy an orgy of eating, drinking, conversation and baby-worship that can well last till teatime. You should certainly book then and on fête days. Make tactical plans and lie low, or it could be a crêpe and a bed in the car. French public holidays are as follows:

New Year's Day	France's National Day, 14 July
Easter Sunday and Monday	The Assumption, 15 August
Labour Day, 1 May	All Saints' Day, 1 November
VE Day, 8 May	Armistice Day, 11 November
Ascension Day	Christmas Day
Whit Sunday and Monday	

If you wish to book ahead and do not speak French, try and find someone who does to make a preliminary telephone call. If necessary, write in English and let them sort it out, but make sure when you get the letter of confirmation that you understand what you've booked. Many hotels nowadays will ask for a deposit. My method is to send them an English cheque; they then either subtract the equivalent from the bill or return the cheque. Make good use of the local tourist bureaux, clearly indicated in the centre of every town, where you will find English spoken. Let them do the booking for you if you have problems. This is the place to pick up maps and brochures.

Closing Times

The markets, like the rest of the town, snap shut abruptly for lunch.

I regularly get caught out by not shopping early enough; if it's going to be a picnic lunch, the decision has to be made in good time. From 12 noon to 14.30 and sometimes 15.00, not a cat stirs. At the other end of the day it's a joy to find shops open until 19.00. Mondays tend to be almost as dead as Sundays and it's likely to prove a grave disappointment to allocate that as a shopping day.

It does not pay to be casual about the weekly closure (fermeture hebdomadaire) of the restaurants. It is an excellent idea to ensure that not every restaurant in the same town is closed at the same time, but do check before you venture. Thwarted tastebuds are guaranteed if you make a special journey only to find the smug little notice on the door "fermé". 'Sun. p.m. and Mon.' are the most common and often it will take a good deal of perseverance to find a possibility open then.

The acronym *closed: o.o.s.* means closed out of season (usually from October to Easter).

Changing Money

Everyone has their pet method, from going round all the banks to get a few centimes advantage, to playing it the easy and very expensive way of getting the hotel to do it. It depends on how much is involved and how keen a dealer you are as to how much trouble is worth it. I change mine on the boat, where I have always found the rate to be very fair. If you get caught outside banking hours, the bureaux de change stay open late.

Telephoning

To telepone any of the numbers within Normandy shown in this book from England you should dial the international code 00, then the country code 33, then 2 followed by the number. If you are phoning within France you should insert 0 before the 2, and this the format I have used in the book, on the assumption that most of the reservations will be made when you are in France.

Bring Home

The list of Best Buys doesn't change much. Obviously wine, but not the more expensive varieties which are, surprisingly, cheaper in England. Be a lager lout and take as much as you can carry. Coffee is much cheaper; jams, plain chocolate, stock cubes are worth considering, as are electrical goods, ironmongery, kitchen gadgets, and glassware. Best of all are impulse buys in the markets.

Breakfast

A sore point. The best will serve buttery croissants, hot fresh bread, home-made preserves, a slab of fresh butter, lots of strong coffee and hot milk, with fresh orange juice if you're lucky. The worst - and at a price of around 8€ this is an outrage - will be stale toasted bread, a foil-wrapped butter pat, plastic jam, a cup of weak coffee and cold sterilised milk. Synthetic orange juice can add another 1.5€ to the bill. If you land in an hotel like this, get out of bed and go to the café next door.

Tipping

Lots of readers, used to the outstretched British hand, worry about this. Needlessly – bills are often stamped 's.t.c.' (service, taxes, compris) and it means what it says – all service and taxes included. The only exception perhaps is to leave the small change in the saucer at a bar.

Garages and Parking

Considerably older and wiser since I started travelling so often, I now have sympathy with readers who insist on a garage. I can only advise removing any valued belongings, however tiresome that may be, and taking out adequate insurance.

Chambres d'hôtes

Unlike previous French Entrées, there are no chambres d'hôtes in this book. They were so popular that an entire book *Bed and Breakfast in France* (ISBN 1-904012-05-1) had to be devoted to them. It's a good idea to mix and match - say use this book for hotels en route and the other for a base for a longer stay.

Reader Comments

I am, as always, grateful for your help - none of these books would have been possible without readers' help. If you have any comments or suggestions, please write to me:

Patricia Fenn, c/o Aspect Guides, 32-34 Great Peter Street,
London, SW1P 2DB,
email: comments@aspectguides.com

Please let me know your comments, favourable or otherwise, and stating if you object to being quoted. Alternatively, visit our new website (www.aspectguides.com) and submit your comments online. I do try and answer each letter personally but please be patient!

NORMANDY

Normandy is BIG. And diverse. Five départements ring the changes from rustic to sophisticated, seashore to city, tourist orientated to bosky bucolic, dusty plain to lush valley, gastronomy to take-away, Relais et Châteaux to chambres d'hôte, autoroute to farmyard track. Back your fancy or sample a medley.

Calvados is the département best known to British tourists, and the one that offers most variety within its borders. Its préfecture is Caen, three-quarters destroyed in the war but still a good choice for a short city break, combining culture (the superb Mémoriale museum for Peace, William the Conqueror's castle, two great abbeys, Gothic churches, university, more museums), with gastronomy (one of Normandy's pair of Michelin two-star restaurants and numerous others), a superb Sunday market, and proximity to ferry port and sea.

Deauville is a one-off, epitomising fin-de-siècle elegance, millionaires' studs and race meetings, designer shops, classy hotels, glamorous Parisian customers, miles of sand. The sand is the only one of these attributes that extends to next-door Trouville, but it has others. More en famille than naughty weekend, hotels that open year round rather than six frantic weeks like its neighbour, real fishermen unloading real fish into a real market patronised by real Frenchmen. Brassy, cheerful, colourful Trouville.

Honfleur is special. Without doubt my number one choice for a weekend 'away from it all', especially now that the elegant new Pont de Normandie connects it with Le Havre so speedily. So photogenic. Great for a stroll round the quays, and then another getting to know it better, and then another into the quiet twisting mediaeval streets. Too busy at summer weekends, too expensive on the surface but not if you know where to go, infinitely rewarding if you enjoy sitting in cafes admiring the view, both human and scenic.

Deviate a kilometre or two on either side of the autoroute that speeds across Calvados linking Normandy's two great cities Caen and Rouen to find another Normandy. Here is picture-postcard-land: brown and white Normandy cattle, authentically eyepatched, black and white Normandy cottages authentically thatched, time-warped hamlets, gnarled apple trees, green valleys, primitive farms, 'cider routes'. And Deauville is how far away? You must be joking.

Bayeux is another good choice for a short break. Better than ever now that its centre has been pedestrianised, it not only has the historic tapestry and cathedral to offer but a pleasant and animated character.

The Suisse Normande is an extension of Calvados southwards. Not really very Swiss but unmistakably different. The wide and wonderful river Orne cuts through deep escarpments and offers all manner of water-sports. It's all craggy peaks, green valleys, unspoiled villages, with a higher ratio of French to English tourists than that nearer the coast.

And of course there is the Calvados of the D-Day landings. Arromanches is full of ghosts, evoked by the wreck of Mulberry Harbour and the D-Day museum, but a visit there will make you thoughtful rather than sad.

Seine Maritime

Caen's age-long rival, head of Upper Normandy - Rouen. He who is tired of Rouen must be tired of life. Less shattered than Caen by wartime devastation, still blessed with street after street of enchanting mediaeval buildings (some skilfully restored admittedly), a superb cathedral and other distinguished churches, and a heart which it is easy to find and love, more restaurants than you or I could ever exhaust and a population that loves to sit outside and supply the typically Gallic atmosphere, it is a city that alone merits the journey to Normandy.

Head north for the typical Caux (chalk) landscape of rolling plains that drop abruptly into the sea. Beaches are pebbly, white rocks are familiar from many an Impressionist painting, rivers carve their way to the sea via fertile valleys. Here are some of France's premier fishing fleets - Fécamp, Le Tréport, Étretat, salty, breezy, colourful, where the fish has at least a chance of being fresh. Dieppe is the Channel port with most colour, good market, good shops.

As its name implies, this is the département of the Seine, whose banks are well worth following, on either side. La Bouille is an unexpected jewel dropped down from the thundering autoroute between high cliffs. A sunny lunchtime could not be better spent than in one of the waterside restaurants here, a stone's throw from the mammoth barges.

Take a bac across to Jumièges with its historic abbey ruins and then follow the almost circular loop of the river along the Route des

Fruits, where stallholders sell whatever their various fruit trees have most recently produced.

Eure

Eure takes up the river where Seine-Maritime runs out, via the fabled Les Andelys and the castle of Richard the Lionheart, Giverny and Monet's gardens are not far away, and great forests sheltering picturesque excursion towns like Lyons-la-Forêt. Nearer the estuary is Pont Audemer, built over rivulets of the river Risle and the little-known strange marshland of La Bribre. The river from which the département takes its name flows through unspoiled countryside, with good picnicking on its banks. The préfecture is Evreux, a lively city with ancient cathedral that survived the bombardment. Paris is only an hour or so away, so restaurants become more sophisticated.

La Manche

La Manche is not at all sophisticated. This is bucket 'n' spade territory, with golden sands and golden family holiday memories. Carteret has the lot, plus a picturesque river estuary and the Manche's only Michelin star. Granville is bigger, a real fishing port, with real fishy restaurants and a cheerful bustle down by the sea, while up in its Haute Ville the ramparts enclose another world, hushed and secretive.

Inland, the lanes, farms and hamlets remain resolutely rural. Even more so is the dramatically wild NW corner, where the Atlantic rollers pound against fearsome granite cliffs - the highest in Europe. You could be in Cornwall. Great for windswept walks.

To the north-east are to be found the delightful fishing villages of St. Vaast-la-Hougue and Barfleur, animated by yachtsmen, coloured by salty old characters on wobbly bicycles. More lovely walks. Further down the peninsula are the windswept landing beaches whose names are written in the history books. And let us not forget Normandy's No. 1 tourist attraction, on the border with Brittany. For centuries Mont St Michel has drawn pilgrims from all over the world, and it still does. La Merveille they call it and that about sums it up. Get there early or late to catch the magic, and witness the rushing in or out of the tides over the salt marshes - faster than a galloping horse.

Orne

Orne is the least tourist-orientated, the most elegant, the domain of the spa, the forest and the horse. The National Stud has been here since the beginning of the 18C, covering over 1,000 hectares, with ten different breeds represented. Other aristocratic creatures crop contentedly behind private white stud fences. In the early morning you can come across them at exercise, their breath steaming in the misty air, or perhaps later on in the day stepping out proudly in front of a trap. Their owners spend half the year in Paris and the rest here in large gabled houses or family chateaux The lovely Perche region, which deserves to be better-known, has given its name to a breed of horse, the massive Percheron.

This is a département for leisurely pursuits, untainted by tawdry commerce. Golf is big and getting bigger, and huntin', shootin', fishin' are everyday pursuits, with a sports shop in every small town displaying rod and gun. Where the Manche is pre-war old-fashioned, with kiddies in sunhats and dresses tucked in knickers, Bagnoles de l'Orne harks back to Edwardiana. Large hotels with white sugar icing facades house the 'curistes'. Ladies and gentlemen saunter round the lake to take the waters, all is green, peaceful and very refined. Alençon is the main town, famous for its lace, but some of the smaller towns have interesting specialities too. In lively little Mortagne it is the black pudding, important enough to have its own annual festival.

Markets

French markets are more than just a utility, they are part and parcel of the French scene, and everyone loves them. It is worthwhile making a special detour to visit some of the best, which will spill out of the main market square into neighbouring streets and ensure that the bars round the square are kept very busy indeed.

Take your time strolling round the colour and hubbub and experience the pleasure of buying from someone who knows and cares about his wares. The man selling you a kitchen knife will be an expert on knives and will want to know what you need it for; the cheesemonger will choose for you a cheese ready for eating today or in a couple of days' time, back home. Trust them. Choose for yourself the ripest peach, the perfect tomato and buy as little as you need and no more, so that you can buy fresh again tomorrow.

Principal Markets:

These are the market days supplied by the French Tourist Office, but please note that some of the markets only operate in the summer months, some are morning only, some afternoon only and some all day. it is worth checking locally before you set off.

Calvados

Sun: Cabourg, Caen, Clécy, Grandcamp-Maisy (summer only), Noyers-Bocage, Pont d'Ouilly, Port en Bessin, Tilly sur Seules, Trouville, Villerville.

Mon: Pont l'Evêque, St. Pierre sur Dives, Vierville-sur-Mer.

Tues: Balleroy, Bloville, Caen (rue de Bayeux), Courseulles, Deauville, Dives sur Mer (summer), Dozulé, Grandcamp Maisy, Mondeville, Ouistreham (bourg), Thury-Harcourt, Villers sur Mer, Villerville, Vire.

Wed: Arromanches (summer), Bayeux, Bernières, Bonnebosq, Cabourg, Caen (bd. Leroy), Creully, Evrecy, Isigny, Lisieux, (Hauteville), Luc sur Mer (summer), Méry Corbon, Orbec, Thaon, Trouville, Villers Bocage.

Thurs: Le Bony Bocage, Blangy le Château, Bretteville sur Laize, Caumont l'Eventé, Condé sur Noireau, Douvre, Houlgate, Lion sur Mer (summer), Livarot, Merville Franceville (summer), Le Molay Littry, Mondeville, Trouville.

Fri: Blonville (summer), Caen (pl. St Sauveur), Cambremer, Colombelles, Courseulles, Deauville, Langrune, Lisieux, Ouistreham (Riva Bella), Trevières, Villers sur Mer, Vire.

Sat: Amfreville, Arromanches (summer), Aunay sur Odon, Bayeux, Beaumont en Auge, Beuvron, Dives sur Mer, Falaise, Fleury sur Orne, Grandcamp Maisy, Honfleur, Isigny, Lisieux, Louvigny, Luc sur Mer, Ouistreham (bourg), St Sever, Touques, Troarn, Verson.

Manche

Sun: Octreville, Hauteville sur Mer (summer).
Mon: Carentan, Torigni, St James, Bricquebec.
Tues: Villedieu les Poêles, Cherbourg, Bréhal, Quettehou.
Wed: St Hilaire du Harcouët, La Haye du Puits, Marigny, St Pierre Église.
Thurs: Coutances, Cherbourg, St. Mère Église.
Fri: Les Pieux, Valognes, Picauville.
Sat: Avranches, Granville, Mortain, Périers, Barneville, Carteret Gavray, St. Lô, Montebourg, St Sauveur le Vicomte, St Vaast la Hougue.

Eure

Sun: Houlbec-Cocherel, Gisors, Evreux, Ezy-sur-Eure, Ferriéres-sur-Risle, Perriers, Pont de Arche, St Pierre du Vawray.
Mon: Les Andelys, Beaumesnil, Bourg-Achard, Gisors, Le Neubourg, Pont Audemer, Thiberville.
Tues: Beaumont le Roger, Beuzeville, Damville, Fleury, Gaillon, Montfort, Montreuil-l'Argillé.
Wed: Barre-en-Ouche, Breteuil, Étrépagny, Evreux, Garennes, Ivry-la-Bataille, Lieurey, Louviers, Le Neubourg, Le Nonancourt, Routot, St Georges-du Vièvre.
Thurs: Brionne, Conches-en-Ouche, Evreux, Lieurey, Lyons-la-Forêt, Pacy.
Fri: Bec Hellouin, Broglie, Cormeilles, Gisors, Pont Audemer.
Sat: Bernay, Bourgtheroulde, Charleval, Evreux, Ivry-la Bataille, Louviers, Mainneville, Quillebeuf, Rugles, Verneuil.

Seine-Maritime

Sun: Angerville-l'Orcher, Biville, Criel, Darnétal, Gournay, Grand Couronne, Harfleur, Le Petit Quevilly, Rouen, Sotteville, Ste. Etienne-du-Rouvray, St. Nicholas d'Aliermont.

MARKETS

Mon: Bolbec, Buchy, Cany-Barville, Harfleur.

Tues: Bellencombre, Beuvreil, Bois Guillaume, Bonsecours, Boos, Dieppe, Duclair, Elbeuf, Foucarment, Francqueville-St.-Pierre, Goderville, Gournay, Grand-Quevilly, Harfleur, Petit-Quevilly, Rouen, Sotteville, Ste. Adresse, St. Etienne-du-Rouvray, Le Tréport, Yerville.

Wed: Bacqueville, Bihorel, Bosc-la-Hard, La Bouille, Canteleu, Dieppe, Gonneville-le-Mallet, Grand Quevilly, Harfleur, Lillebonne, Mesnil-esnard, Mont St. Aignan, Petit-Queilly, Rouen, St. Etienne-du Rouvray, Valmont, Veules-les-Roses, Yport, Yvetot.

Thurs: Bihorel, Criel, Dieppe, Elbeuf, Éretat, Fontaine-le Dun, Forges-les-Eaux, Harfleur, Londinières, Montivilliers, Pavilly, Sotteville, St. Etienne-du Rouvray, St. Saens.

Fri: Auffay, Bihorel, Blangy, Bois-Guillaume, Clères, Criquetot, Flainville, Gonfreville-l'Orcher, Gournay, Grand-Quevilly, Harfleur, Notre-Dame-de Gravenchon, Rouen, Ste. Adresse.

Sat: Aumale, Barentin, Bihorel, Canteleu, Caudebec, Dieppe, Doudeville, Elbeuf, Envermeu, Fécamp, Harfleur, Malaunay, Macourmel, Neufchatel, Petit Couronne, Petit-Quevilly, Rouen, Ry, St. Etienne du-Rouvray, St. Martin-de-Boscherville, St. Romain de-Colbosc, Le Trait, Le Tréport.

Orne

Sun: Alençon, Argentan, Céton, Courtomer, Domfront, Montilly, Mortrée.

Mon: Briouze; Remalard, Tinchebray; Vimoutiers (p.m.).

Tues: l'Aigle, Alençon, Argentan, Athis, Bagnoles de l'Orne, Nocé, Orival, Pervenchères; Soligny la Trappe (all day).

Wed: Damigny, Flers, Longny au Perche, La Mêle sur Sarthe, Le Theil sur Huisne, Ste. Colombe, Tessé la Madeleine.

Thurs: Alençon, Bellême, Bretoncelles, Céauce, La Ferté

Macé, La Ferté Fresnel, Le Merlerault, Messei,
Moulins la Marche, Putanges Pont Écrepin, Trun.

Fri: Argentan, Condé sur Huisne, Courtomer, Domfront,
Écouché, La Chapelle d'Andaine, La Forêt Auvray,
Tourouvre, Vimoutiers.

Sat: Alençon, Almenèches, Bagnoles de l'Orne,
Bretoncelles, Flers, Mortagne au Perche, Rânes, Le
Sap, St Georges des Groseillers, Sées;
p.m.: Carrouges, Gacé, Mortagne au Perche.

Norman food

Our Norman cousins are fishermen and dairy farmers by tradition and inclination. No surprise to find that Norman cuisine centres round the produce of the sea and the cow. Simple, fresh, local is the key. The Norman larder overflows with tender lamb from the salt marshes, thick yellow cream from the indulged Norman cow, with lobsters from the Cotentin rocks fit for the best tables in Paris and sole brought flapping from the Dieppe catch. Vegetables proliferate in this natural market garden (where they say a stick poked in the ground will burst into leaf overnight) and a surplus of apples and pears plop to the ground for want of picking.

The products of cow and apple - butter, cream, cider and Calvados - appear repeatedly (some might say monotonously) in the cooking. Sauce normande can literally cover a multitude of sins. At worst it can be merely cream sloshed indiscriminately, with no attempt to blend and enhance; at best an unctuous glossiness made by whisking the cream and butter into a cider sauce and used to coat, not drench, the vegetables or fish. The fecund Pays d'Auge gives its name to a sauce combining both cream and apple. The two most common bases are chicken and veal escalope, but turbot vallée d'Auge is a traditional dish for first communion celebrations around Étretat. The Caux area of Upper Normandy is potato country and you can expect to see them included in any dish labelled Cauchoise, along with the cream.

A familiar sight in the apple orchards is a fat pig happily rooting amongst the windfalls. When his time comes to be despatched by the local charcutier some of his more obscure parts will go into a variety of sausages, like the smoked andouilles from Vire, or the boudin noir, coloured with blood and enriched with cream - black pudding to you or me. The strong flavoured liver of the pig goes into terrines, along with the pork fat, their richness spiked with a lacing of Calvados. From Rouen comes canard rouennais. I don't know anyone in Normandy nowadays who sticks by the rules and smothers the duck so that its blood is retained but duck presses survive, which squeeze the bones to supply the juice to enrich the red wine and calvados sauce. The bird should be a special variety, half domestic, half wild and the Hôtel de la Poste at Duclair used to be famous for serving it in fourteen different ways.

Mussels breed abundantly along the coast and the tiny juicy variety from these cold northern waters have far more flavour than the inflated southern kinds. The Norman way of serving them of course is to add cream to the broth. If you see 'dieppoise' attached to a dish it will involve the baby grey shrimps hauled in at Dieppe. I prefer marmite dieppoise, a fish stew using white fish, shelled mussels and peeled shrimp and made piquant with spices (echoes of Dieppe's early eastern seafaring forays) to the overrated bouillabaisse made from the bony Mediterranean fish. Tarte aux pommes is the ubiquitous dessert, in legions of shapes and guises. Many is the slice of blackened cardboard pastry topped with thin leathery apple slices I've choked on in the interests of French Entrée. Tarte aux demoiselles Tatin is often found in Normandy but don't let them tell you its origins are local - it was in the Loire that the blessed Tatin daughters accidentally burnt and caramelised the sugar and turned the tart upside down to hide their carelessness.

Norman cheeses

Prime in all France are Norman cheeses. The northern grass is lushest and the bespectacled Norman cows that chew it are promotional poster clichés. To be true Norman they must be brown and white with a brown patch over at least one eye.

Many French will reject a cheese because it is not 'in season'; the date that the cows are put out to pasture and the length of time it takes to make the cheese comes into their consideration. Just as wine buffs know the soil and microclimate of every vineyard and how long the wine will take to age correctly, so will the cheese purist know at what season the grass sprouts, (not once but twice a year) and when the meadows break into flower. He will know about individual cheesemaking methods within an area sometimes no larger than a few fields.

There are really only four outstanding names to remember: Camembert, Pont l'Evêque, Livarot and the cream cheese loosely referred to by the name of the area from which most of them derive - Neufchatel. However, within these varieties there are many distinctions and its worthwhile remembering what to look for.

Camembert

There are around 2,000 brands of Camembert produced in France but of course no Camembert is as good as Normandy Camembert and the best of all is that which comes from the Auge country between the rivers Touques and Dives. Chalk and cheese is the difference between the commercial and the unpasteurised fermier. The best has an appellation V.C.N. (véritable Camembert de Normandie) and it's well worth any extra euros involved. Certainly the cheese is named after a village near Vimoutiers, where a monument stands to Marie Harel, generally credited with having 'invented' this delicacy in 1791 (but local lore has it that farmers' wives in the area had been perfecting its smooth creaminess for generations before). Napoleon III was presented with a cheese specially made for him in the village of Camembert in 1855 and he liked it so much that he kissed the waitress. Fifty years later a Monsieur Ridel designed the familiar little circular wooden box, so that the cheese could be packed and enjoyed at some distance from the farms.

Trust your nose when choosing the perfect Camembert, but it isn't easy to describe smells in cheesy terms -'Like the feet of a god' was one off-putting attempt. Correctly it should bulge but not run when cut, but British taste tends to prefer it riper than the French and I certainly like mine oozing a bit. Best seasons are late spring, autumn and winter.

Pont l'Evêque

Probably the oldest cheese in Normandy and still made almost entirely in the farms of the pays d'Auge, with commercial producers trying to emulate. Small, squat, soft and tender, with golden rind, it has a pronounced tang, should feel supple when pressed and smell 'savoury with some bouquet, as the king of the cheese-makers, Pierre Androuet, puts it. He also advises avoiding one with a 'cowbarn odour', which shouldn't be too difficult.

The generic name for the square cheeses of Lower Normandy is Pavé d'Auge. They are all at their best during summer, autumn and winter.

Livarot

Another cheese with a long history, probably devised, like so many good things, in a monastery. It has a stronger, spicier smell than Pont l'Evêque, due perhaps to its being aged in airtight cellars lined with hay. If you hear a cheese referred to as a 'Colonel' it will be Livarot, the five bands of sedge which enclose it evoking the five service stripes. Best seasons are late spring, autumn and winter.

Neufchâtel

The group of cream cheeses loosely termed Neufchâtel, after the town, come from north of the Seine in the pays de Bray. They make a tempting sight on the market stalls, in towns like Gisors, in their varying shapes and sizes - hearts, discs, obelisks. Look out for triple boudard, supposed to be the shape of the bung of a cider barrel, with a very pronounced fruity flavour. Its best season, like all these creamy cheeses, is late autumn.

My own weakness is for Brillat-Savarin, which comes from Forges-les-Eaux. This one not only looks but smells appealing, which is more than can be said for most, with a downy white rind and delicate creamy nose. It is not for the cholesterol-conscious - a triple cream with a wicked 75% fat content. An upstart little cheese, it was invented by the grandfather of Pierre Androuet between the wars.

Farms selling their own produce, cheese, cider and Calvados, can be identified by their green and yellow sign: Vente de Produits Fermiers. Following the indications in the pays d'Auge for the Route du Fromage makes a good excuse for an excursion, and penetrates deeply into the most gorgeously bucolic countryside. You can pick up leaflets at local tourist offices or from the producers themselves.

Good markets at which to enjoy selecting the perfect cheese are at St Pierre-sur-Dives on Mondays and Livarot on Thursdays.

Norman drink

Cider and Calvados are to the apple and to Normandy what wine and brandy are to Bordeaux. You cannot eat a cider apple - far too mouth-puckering - but you can see the trees throughout Normandy, wizened and bent with their load of tiny red apples. If you explore some of the side roads in the Auge region you will come across signs indicating Route du Cidre. There is one from Beuvron-en-Auge, which leads through delightful little villages set on hilltops above the sloping orchards, with dégustation cidre fermier signs on every farm gate. Quite an experience to sit in the farm kitchen at the scrubbed table and sample the golden liquid.

In autumn the presses go from farmer to farmer, each extracting from the neat glowing piles the juice which he will then mix with a proportion - usually about a third - of sweet apple juice to make his own blend of 'cidre bouché'. Left to ferment in the bottle, this is the champagne of cider. An everyday version, a kind of cider plonk known as 'petit bère', is made by adding a lot more water and passing the lot back through the apple pulp again.

Lovers of German Spätlese wines would appreciate that the best cider comes from the latest apples, with a touch of frost to concentrate the flavour.

Like wine-making there is a lot of judgement and a little luck in producing a good vintage, but perhaps in Normandy the farmers attach more importance to considerations like the moon being in the right quarter and the wind blowing from the right direction before perfect bottling can be achieved than would their aristocratic counterparts in Épernay.

Young Calvados is for stronger stomachs than mine. Not for nothing has the glass of the firewater offered between course been named a trou normand. It may well make room for more food but you can actually feel it burning the hole! However, a mature Calve, stored in oak for ten to fifteen years, is another matter - a smooth, golden, fruity and distinctly soothing digestif. Look for an appellation contrôlé label as an indication of quality - and don't drive afterwards!

Gardens

I must confess that, keen gardener though I am, I have hitherto adopted a take-em- or-leave-em attitude to French gardens. We are so richly blessed with superb gardens in England that those across the Channel seemed second-rate. Usually they were overformal, with stiff flowers in stiff rows in front of stiff hedges, and colours were chosen to contrast fiercely rather than blend seductively. Nowhere did I find the artful contrivance of the best English gardens, where the impression is that nature not the gardener made the choices. Border edges were precise and any clump that dared spill casually over was smartly reprimanded with the shears.

Only recently have I been persuaded to look again, so I cannot claim to be an expert or have a comprehensive experience of Normandy gardens, but some of those I did visit would alone merit the journey for the dedicated gardener. The Seine-Maritime département is particularly well-endowed, but brochures and maps for the whole region are freely available at tourist offices - and also see the French Entrée guide to Gardens of France.

These are my favourites, very different but both memorable:

Le Clos du Coudray

This is near the village of Loeuilly at the crossroads of the D6 and the D25, north of Rouen and beyond the pretty village of Clères. It has made wonderful use of the concept of treating the garden as a series of rooms, so that there is always a delicious surprise round the corner. There are trickling streams, lakes, arches, arbours, roses tumbling over specimen trees, a thatched cottage, pergolas, deep rich borders and cascades of flowers from May to October. Many of them are unusual and certainly new to me and the exceedingly good news is that you can buy a selection in the well-organised garden centre attached. Some seemed cheap, some (particularly the roses) expensive, compared with prices back home, but at least take a notebook and note the favourites. There is a good café if you want to make a day's outing, but allow a couple of hours minimum to do justice to the garden.

Le Clos de Coudray
  76850 Etampuis
  Seine Maritime
  tel: (0)23.35.34.196.85.
  Open: from Thursday to Monday from 10.00 to 19.00 in summer, from 10.00 to 17.30 from March 1st to April 15th and in November.
  Entrance: 5.5€

Les Jardins d'Angélique

These gardens are to be found NE of Rouen. Take the D42 direction Lyons la Forêt, exit at Montmain to the hamlet of Pigrard and the garden is on the right.

When their daughter Angélique died, Gloria and Yves Lebellegard decided that her most fitting memorial would be a beautiful garden, peaceful, serene, always changing, always growing. They have achieved their aim here. It is the kind of garden that you or I, given almost unlimited time, patience and dedication, might even imitate. There is nothing grand or commercial about this one, but the atmosphere is very special. Yves and Gloria are always on hand to show you round their treasures, not in a supervisory way, but more as fellow-enthusiasts. Yves' particular joy is roses, a passion which I share, so I learned a lot. Some of the names are the same, some quite different and he is keen to learn the English versions, so that he can buy from specialists like Peter Beale and Charles Austin. He is a gentle, kind man, who insisted that we ate our picnic in the shade of an arbour and then gave me some cuttings to take home. They will be the happiest of souvenirs.

Jardins d'Angélique
  Hameau du Pigrard
  76520 Montmain
  Seine Maritime.
  tel: (0)23.35.79.08.12
  open: from 1st May to 15th October every day except Tuesday, from 10.00 to 19.00. Entrance 3.2€

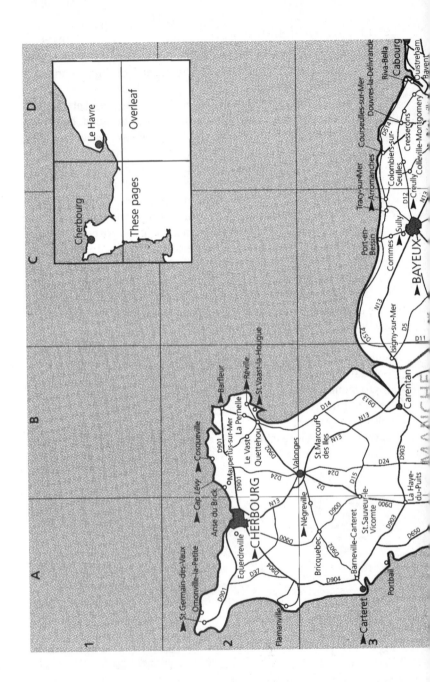

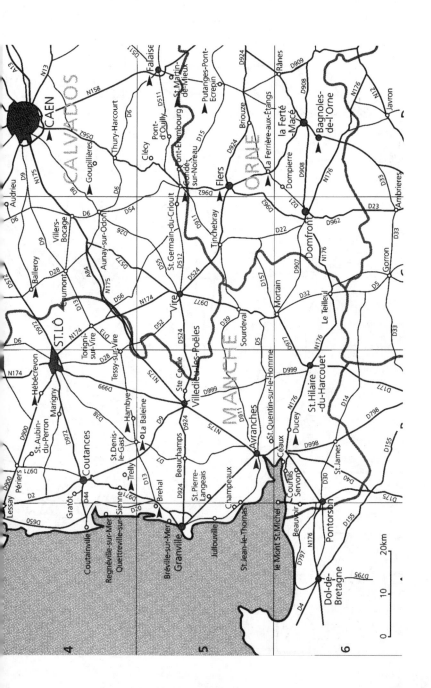

23

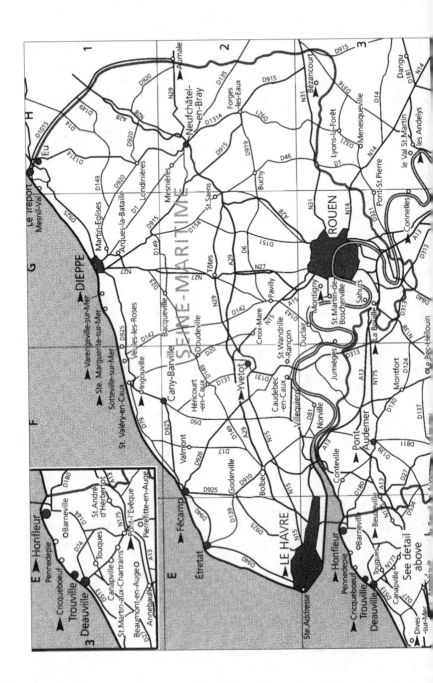

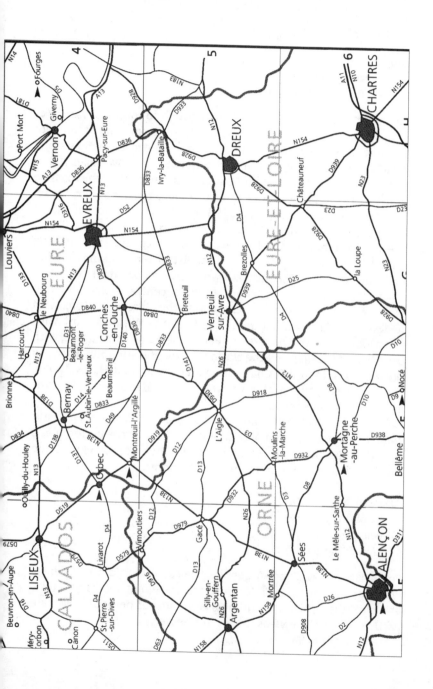

25

ALENÇON 61000, Orne

Map 6E
220km from Le Havre
Market: Tues., Thurs., Sat., Sun.

Just the right size for a town - large enough to contain a variety of shops, bars, restaurants, not so large that covering it on foot becomes a problem. Narrow, ancient cobbled streets, mellow stone courtyards, black Norman timbered houses, window boxes full of geraniums, pedestrianised centre, all guarded over by the massive Eglise de Notre Dame, a very agreeable place to pass an hour or so.

Lace has been manufactured in Alençon since 1665, in competition with the fashionable Venetian lace. You can still buy the local product in the Lace Museum, which shares a building with the town's art gallery. Alas, the art of lace-making is dying and now a scrap of the intricate work costs a good deal.

Alençon makes an excellent touring centre, from which to explore lower Normandy, especially the Perche region, with delightful little towns like Sées and Mortagne. Within a short drive in any direction are the forests - Perseigne, Écouves, Andaine, with the Alpes Mancelles and the National Park of Normandy-Maine to the west. Château d'Ô, Château de Médavy and les Haras du Pin, the national stud and stunning 18C château, are pleasant excursions to the north.

The problem is that I cannot find a hotel within the town that I could heartily recommend. Le Grand St. Michel, 7 rue du Temple, is probably the best bet, certainly central, but do not expect too much with a price tag of 23-41€ on the rooms.

Au Petit Vatel ☒ M

72 pl. du Cdt Desmeulles
tel: (0)233.26.23.78
closed: Sun. p.m.; Wed.

Popular for its cooking. A genuine welcome precedes every meal with a good deal of kissing for the locals. The dining rooms are pretty and pink, the cuisine is traditional Norman, but never dull. Fish are particularly good news, as too are the desserts.

Menus from 18.8€

Escargot Doré ⊠ M
183 av. Gien Léclerc
tel: (0)233.28.67.67
closed: Sun. p.m.; Mon. 17/7-7/8

An unpromising site on the outskirts of the town on the busy Le Mans nationale but at least it solves the parking problem. L'Escargot is a sprawling stone building, becoming quite smart nowadays.

Le Bistrot ⊠ S
21 r. Sarthe
tel: (0)233.26.51.69
closed: Sun. and Mon.; Aug.

This is the restaurant that Charles-Henry de Valbray (see below) recommends to his visiting friends and clients. It certainly has bags of atmosphere, a real bistro, decorated with old photos, and tin Ricard signs, with a lively bar.

The Menu du Marché, a mere 11€, featured all the old Parisianbistro favourites - tart à l'oignon, langue de boeuf with a piquant sauce or tête de veau, and crème brûlée to finish.

Great to see two young-at-heart newcomers to the town, but shame that one of them couldn't have helped out us starving tourists on a Sun./Mon. Menus from 11€.

☆ Château de Saint-Paterne
72610, St. Paterne. 3 km SE of Alençon on the D311 Chartres road.
tel: (0)233.27.54.71
Fax: (0)233.29.16.71
closed: 15/1-15/4.

St Paterne is not a particularly attractive suburb and seems to be becoming more and more engulfed in factories and road works.

All the more delightful then to find this oasis, set in 120 acres of woods, flowers, and the fruitful vegetable garden that supplies the kitchen with freshest and best.

The 15C château, reputed to have been the love nest of Henri IV, was inherited by its present owner Charles-Henry de Valbray, when he was in his early twenties. Perhaps if he had been older he might have been daunted by the task of restoring the crumbling building, finding furniture and fabrics and granting it a fresh lease of life as something between a chambre d'hôte and hotel. If it is the former I am quite prepared to cheat a little to include it in this hotel guide just because I'm doing my readers a favour, I'm prepared too conveniently to ignore the fact that half the property lies within the Sarthe département. You'll thank me for it.

Apart from the youthful energy that allowed C-H to tackle some of the more expensive construction tasks himself, he had other advantages - a brother who runs the successful Château de Briottières in the Loire (see 'Bed and Breakfast in France') who could pass on useful tips, an attic full of neglected treasures begging to be restored and put to good use, and, most of all, an inherent good taste which ensured that the natural elegance of the chateâu should be enhanced by his choice of curtains and furniture rather than drowned.

Perhaps a childhood spent under a Mediterranean sun influenced him in favouring bright cheerful colours - yellow for sun and blue for sea. Of his seven rooms I like best the cheapest - 88€, twin beds, feminine rose-spattered chintz, bath - and the most expensive - 128€, sunshine-yellow draped four-poster, elaborately pleated and swagged, French Revolution design curtains (which C-H admits are highly inappropriate in this aristocrats residence), antique bath, shower and loo - but all the rooms are spacious and have their own bathrooms.

Dinner is an occasion not to be missed. Eaten in the extravagant light of thirty candles, it is served by loyal local ladies, like the ever-smiling, invaluable, Marie-Denise who are only too willing to contribute to the renaissance of the chateau which was always the heart of the village that St. Paterne used to be. Four courses, aperitif, coffee and wine cost from 38€. There is a new eating experience at the Château, the Auberge du Château, which has been created out of a previously disused wing. The walls have been colour-washed in terracotta and the theme is Provence, an instant pick-me-up in northern France. The speciality will be tapas and it will be open to non-residents. I look forward to the first reports.

There is always something new to report on St. Paterne and this time it is not only the Auberge, but the gîte that C-H has arranged in a circular erstwhile pigeonnier by the entrance gate. It's charmingly conceived in bright colours, quite different from the elegance of the chateau furnishings. With a well equipped kitchen and bathroom, it would make a comfortable base for a longer stay. Rooms cost between 88€ and 176€ per night. A swimming pool is another welcome innovation.

Starred of course.

ALPES MANCELLES

To the south-west of Alençon lies a particularly attractive area little known to British tourists. Granite walls enclose the valley of the Sarthe, making a dramatic impression of rock, heather, and sparkling water, in contrast to the several forests - Perche, Andaine, Perseigne - which are alternative excursions in this lovely area.

The best-known, and recognised as one of France's prettiest villages, is St. Cenéri, 14 km SW of Alençon by the D101. The river is crossed by a picturesque stone bridge, and an 11th century Romanesque church stands guard above the gorge. Old stone houses are wreathed with many flowers to welcome the tourists who drive out at weekends to eat and drink at one of the cluster of bars and restaurants above the river. The Lion d'Or used to be called the Auberge des Peintures, because penniless painters would gather there and offer a painting (many of which still decorate the walls) to pay for their lunch.

LES ANDELYS 27700, Eure

Map 3H
40 km SE of Rouen
Market: Mon.

Les Andelys because there were originally two distinct areas, le Petit Andely to the west and le Grand Andely to the east. But who cares about that, or about any other part of the town than the bit that faces on to the river. Here the Seine is at its most magical. The river loops and curves dramatically, set in its chalky white escarpment The Gaillard Castle towers above and contributes considerably to the romantic scene.

This was the chosen site for the fortress built by Richard the Lionheart, Duke of Normandy, and subsequently King of England, in 1196, barring the way to Rouen from the French king, Philippe

Les Andelys

Auguste. So massive was its foundation, so formidable its site that it held Philippe at bay for seven years, by which time King John had succeeded to the English throne. Philippe assembled all his formidable resources and eventually the castle yielded to his battering.

A visit to the ruins is a must, whether you approach them by a long puff up the hill behind the Tourist Bureau or by car, 3 km via le Grand Andely. The view is literally breathtaking. Far below the curves of the Seine lie shining to left, to right and to centre; le Petit Andely nestles in the crook and the river barges passing slowly in and out of the range of vision, as though pulled by an invisible string, add animated perspective.

☆ La Chaine d'Or 🛏 ☒ L-M

27 r. Grande
tel: (0)232.54.00.31
Fax: (0)232.54.05.68
restaurant closed: Sun. p.m.; Mon., Tues lunchtime and Jan.
hotel closed: Sun. p.m.; Mon. and Jan.

The progress of the Chaine d'Or has been ever onwards and upwards since I first wrote about this auberge right on the banks of the Seine. M. et Mme Foucault have worked long and hard to achieve the success of a Michelin star in their restaurant and a Complet sign up more often than not in their hotel. They start off with an enormous advantage. The view over the Seine from some of the bedrooms and the restaurant is pure picture-book; Les Andelys is near enough to Rouen and indeed to Paris to provide an ideal weekend getaway, and the hotel and restaurant are both well-known and well-loved.

The eight bedrooms have been steadily upgraded over the years and although I may regret the passing of the faded old furniture and the fin-de-siécle decor, I have to concede that the plumbing is better than of yore. The cost is now between 70€ and 121e€ and there are two apartments at 125€. It is well worth paying for a room with a view if you can get hold of one.

The restaurant is the more important factor here, the tables by the windows are eagerly sought. The cooking is sophisticated - a croustillant filled with soft boiled eggs and asparagus tips, oysters in a champagne sauce, chocolate soufflé with a jasmine sauce - making the cheapest menu, at 26€, a bargain for such skilled presentation. Prices leap after this, so it is a good idea to consult the menu before committing yourself.

A star for a comfortable hotel, with good food and one of the best sites in Normandy.

If the restaurant is full or beyond your budget there is consolation at hand. There could hardly be a better picnic site than here by the river, where there are stone benches and shade. Or, almost opposite the hotel:

Mistral ⊠ S
    26 r. Grande
    tel: (0)232.54.09.00
    closed: Mon.; Feb and one week in Nov

So-called because the first owners came from Provence and their tiny restaurant/salon de thé is themed accordingly. The decor zips you down to the south immediately. Cloths are yellow provençal prints, walls are stark white and there is a little creeper-covered patio at the rear to make the most of every glimpse of sun.

Dishes are in character - a soupe de pistou (5.6€), an anchoiade 6.7€, sardines 6.4€; the 16.1€ menu includes a brandade, confit of goose that has cooked for five hours or a garlicky daube. See Val St. Martin.

ARGENTAN 61200, Orne

Map 5E
59 km SE of Caen
Market: Tues., Sun.

Once an attractive town, famous for its lace, but badly damaged during the Mortain-Falaise pocket action. Two fine churches survived, but needed extensive restoration. St. Germain dates from the 15th century and is bordered on its south side by the remains of the 14C castle of the dukes of Alençon. A fine Flamboyant porch opens on to the rue St. Germain. St. Martin is still under scaffolding. It's a sizeable town, with a good market in the main square, and plenty of bars and shops.

La Renaissance 🛏 ⊠ S
    20 ave. de la 2 me Division Blindée.
    tel: (0)233.36.14.20
    restaurant closed: sun p.m.; mon.

Excellent value here in a little restaurant near the station run by Monique and Olivier Lecocq. The menu (priced between 19.2€ and 39€) includes wine as well as dishes like fillet of beef in red wine sauce or a choucroute of fish.

Rooms with bath cost between 51€ and 74€.

ARROMANCHES 14117, Calvados

Map 3C
31 km W of Caen, 11 km E of Bayeux
Market: Wed.

This once sleepy little seaside town will forever be assured of a place in the history books as the site chosen for the sensational.Mulberry Harbour which made possible the 1944 landings - probably the most extraordinary feat of daring and maritime skills of the whole war. Not until you have visited the splendidly evocative museum and the new cinéma circulaire on the hill above the town, where the almost incredible story is related, can you possibly appreciate the concept and scale of the venture. Many caissons of the artificial harbour still protrude from the sea like a huge semicircle of basking whales. More are washed up on the beach, black and menacing, with the word 'Danger' painted on them - an understatement if ever there was one.

One cannot reprove Arromanches from profiting from its wartime fame and the part that the people of the town played in the landings. They are rightly enormously proud of their role and in 1994 gave the veterans a huge welcome. Now the tourists invade the little town, climb to the points d'orientation, and are strangely silent as it begins to dawn on them how it must have been. Hotels, restaurants and bars abound to cater for them.

The beach here is wide, wonderful and very animated. The tide recedes for several kms, leaving plenty of firm sand for walkers, joggers and more esoteric sports; the sand yachting looks just as much fun as wind surfing and a good deal less wet, and there is a fascinating machine called Speedsport - a three-wheeled buggy which careers along the sands powered by a parachute. One misty morning I drew the curtains and saw two horses trotting ahead of Boadicea-like chariots; their drivers, in characteristic backwardleaning stance, guided them towards the sea and in a moment they were lost in the greyness. Ghosts? Perhaps.

☆ La Marine 🛏 ⊠ M

Quai de Canada 14117
tel: (0)231.22.34.19
Fax: (0)231.22 98.80
closed: 15/11-15/2

Never growing too big for its well-known boots, the Marine remains a family-run hotel, in a prime position overlooking the sea and Mulberry, serving good food, especially fish. The rooms are not particularly large but are well-equipped and comfortable. Ours, 122, probably the best, boasting three windows overlooking the watery panorama, had peach curtains and flock wallpaper, lots of cupboard space and the usual appalling French lighting.

The restaurant, always full at summer weekends, is large and very pleasant, decorated in appropriate blue and green sea colours, making the most of its picture windows and the seascape they reveal. Cooking is reliable - nothing flashy but good quality, I recommend the second menu at 19.2€, which provided us with oysters, steak and dessert. Breakfasts are taken in the adjoining bar, which can get a bit smoky.

Private parking round the corner, a bit tight if you bring the Roller. We got locked out at 10.30 p.m. and had to rely on some guests to let us in, so make sure you take your key with you. 30 rooms at 58-64€ (worth paying for the ones with sea views). Menus from 16-33€.

If you want to sleep peacefully and eat well in an M category hotel overlooking the sea, La Marine would take a lot of beating. Starred for long-term reliability and reader-popularity.

See Tracy-sur-Mer.

AUDRIEU 14250, Calvados

Map 4C
13 km SW of Bayeux

Signed to the south of the N13 between Caen and Bayeux, on the D158

Château d'Audrieu 🛏 ☒ L

tel: (o)231.80.21.52
Fax: (o)231.80.24.73
closed: 15/12-14/2

A stunningly beautiful 18C château, perfectly symmetrical. It is set in immense grounds, surrounded by ancient trees and flower gardens and there is a heated swimming pool.

There is little trace today of the horrors and destruction of the Normandy landings when for six weeks the chateau was in no man's-land, attacked by British and Canadians from one side and by Germans from the other. 27 shells landed on the building, but the golden Caen stone resisted most of the blast.

Assuming that most customers for the L bracket can afford that little bit extra to pay for a really special room, I usually counsel going for nothing but the best but here the newly converted attic rooms at 126€ are probably the best value. If you really don't care a fig, the apartments cost up to 384€.

Cooking meriting a Michelin star from Alain Cornet, trained at Senderens, is something to remember. He uses local produce, from

Château d'Audrieu.

sea and market, and embellishes it with imagination and skill. Sea trout with juniper berries, tête de veau with andouille from Vire are examples. Menus start at 32€.

The same family have run the chateau for many years and many readers look forward to seeing them every year for their annual Normandy fix.

AUMALE 76390, Seine-Mar

Map 2H
22 km E of Neufchatel-en-Bray

The market in this centre of the dairy farming industry takes place on a sloping tree-lined square, hung about with many flowers. The town has many attractive boarded and timbered houses and an ancient market hall.

Le Mouton Gras
Aumale

Hotel du Mouton Gras 🛏 ☒ M

2 r. Verdun
tel: (0)2.35.93.41.32
closed: Tues; 23/8-10/9

One of the most attractive buildings of all - 17th century, classified, heavily beamed and set round a courtyard - houses this family-run hotel. Inside is predictably dark and cosy with lots of beams, copper pans, red check tablecloths and mock oil lamps. Josette Gauthier takes care of the hospitality while husband Jean concentrates on the cooking. The food is traditional Norman, in generous quantities. Menus start at 16€.

First and foremost this is a restaurant, but there are six comfortable rooms in a barn annexe across the courtyard which cost from 45€. Readers have approved of both food and beds, but objected to the high cost of wines.

Villa des Houx 🛏 ☒ M

av. Gén de Gaulle
tel: (0)2.35.93.93.30
Fax: (0)235.93.03.94

Don't be put off, as I nearly was, by the outside of the Villa des Houx. It looks huge, and is eccentrically timbered like a Disney pastiche of a Norman building, with gables, towers, balconies and whatever. In fact there are only thirteen rooms, all big and airy, with good bathrooms and excellent value for the standard of comfort, at 48-72€. Menus from 16-47€ are good value.

I think this would be an excellent place to stay, however. I would welcome reports.

AVRANCHES 50300, Manche

Map 5B
126 km S of Cherbourg
Market: Sat.

Sited on the main approaches to Brittany and Mont St Michel, Avranches is a popular overnight stop. Sadly, although it is a lively enough town with plenty of bars and brasseries down in the lower section by the caste, it has no outstanding restaurant to recommend.

In 1944 General Patton launched his victorious 3rd Army attack from Avranches and American soil was subsequently flown over to form a square for the Patton Memorial, which thereby stands on American territory.

On the Place Daniel-Huet, past the garden of the Sous Prefecture, is la plate-forme, where Henry II knelt in 1172 to do public penance for the murder of Thomas à Becket. There's a fine panorama of Mont St Michel from the terrace at the end of the square. Another good viewing point of the Mount and surrounding countryside, river Sélune threading through, is from the Jardins Publiques above the main town; the gardens are a blaze of all the unflower-like flowers so dear to French gardeners' hearts. Cannas, cacti, begonias, tortured into unnatural cohabitation, dazzle the eye with their strident orange, purple and fuchsia-pink. Gertrude Jekyll would have turned in her grave at the vulgarity, but the gardens are certainly a cheerful, cool retreat and the Avranchins are extremely proud of them. For connoisseurs of the bizarre, a visit to the basilica of St Gervais might prove interesting. There in the Treasury rests the skull of St. Aubert, holed by the reproachful finger of St. Michel, grown impatient at Aubert's dilatoriness in building the usual tribute to the saint on the summit of Mont Tombe, later Mont St. Michel.

La Croix d'Or ⍖ ☒ M

83 r. de la Constitution
tel: (0)233.58.04.88
Fax: (0)233.58.06.95

A 17C Relais de la Poste, now an extremely pretty little hotel. Lots of polished copper, oak armoires, big fireplace, set the tone in the flagged entrance hall and the stone walls of the dining room are relieved by the cheerful yellow and blue decor.

The son of the previous owners has now taken over and is all much more professional, bustling and, I imagine, prosperous. As this is the only restaurant worth considering in the town you can imagine how busy it gets. I did feel the friendly welcome was somewhat lacking - a complaint inherited from the former regime, but it was nearly lunchtime when I called.

Croix d'OR, Avranches

A lovely surprise awaits you behind the hotel. There is a burst of colour from the hydrangeas, hollyhocks, lavatera filling the courtyard, around which are set the 29 rooms. The temptation to do these up has mercifully been resisted, so that the prices remain very reasonable - 49€ for the smallest with shower and 58€ for one with two beds. They are a good size and simply but attractively decorated with flowery chintz fabrics, all looking out on to that lovely garden and assured of tranquillity. Menus start at 22€ (lunch only), then 16.8-40€. Demi-pension 45-57€ per person.

Le Jardin des Plantes 🛏 ☒ M-S

    70 pl. Carnot
    tel: (0)233.58.03.68
    Fax: (0)233.60.01.72
    closed: 24/12-2/1

As its name suggests, at the top of the town by the botanical gardens. The brasserie-style restaurant is certainly very popular and perhaps I am doing it an injustice in suggesting that the Croix d'Or is the only good restaurant in town. It's a busting friendly place, with a jolly landlord behind the bar who didn't turn a hair when I asked to see the rooms during the busy lunchtime period. Meals cost from 12.5€. The rooms are in an annexe at the rear and vary considerably. I was very impressed with the 78€ version - a big room with bath and a view of distant water. Others from 27€.

A good choice perhaps for a miserable day when all you want is company, good cheer and a plateful of something hot to cheer you up. Good for families too.

BAGNOLES-DE-L'ORNE 61140, Orne

Map 6D
39 km SW of Argentan
Market: Tues., Sat.

As the name suggests, a spa town, very well known for the treatment of circulation problems and *maladies des dames*. Very efficacious I was repeatedly told. 50% of the visitors are curistes from all over the world. The Brits are very fond of the place, admiring the turreted and beamed architecture of the style dubbed Anglo-Norman, and many of them are buying property there, some in the prominent Residence du Lac, an old palais in prime position overlooking the lake.

It's all very tidy, very green, very manicured, with an extremely short season. Most of the hotels close for at least three months of the year, but are booked well ahead for the summer. There are so many of them that it's hard to imagine them all full, but that is the case in July and August At other times of the year you have plenty of choice.

It is essential to pick fine weather in which to visit the little town. Given sunshine, it is very pleasant to walk around the central lake, sit outside the peach coloured casino with a drink in hand, or even take a ride in a calèche (pony trap). Alongside the lake you can hire ponies and horses and take off accompanied or solo. On pleasant weekends the Parisians pour into the town and the cafés and restaurants become lively and colourful; at other times the town can appear deserted and desolate. Most visitors eat in their hotels, so the restaurant scene is not good.

It's an excellent choice for a peaceful break, either overnight on a long journey or for a longer restful stay. Out of season the proprietors will be very pleased indeed to see you.

*Hotel Bois Joli
Bagnoles de l'Orne*

☆ **Bois Joli** 🛏 ⊠ M
72 Av. Philippe du Rozier
tel: (0)233.37.92.77
fax: (0)233.37.07.56
closed: Jan.

The exception to the shut-up rule. They may not have many guests but they do have practically the monopoly o.o.s., and they look after them very well indeed. The bedrooms are delightfully old-fashioned, with high ceilings and masses of space. Ours, with pale blue colour scheme, and overlooking the lake, is known as the Pompidou room, after a previous incumbent. Others, all in Empire style, all different, cost between 46€ and 100€. But the real surprise here was the food. Hotels with 20 bedrooms, 19 of them empty, tend to send the chef home and open a tin for the isolated diners. Not so at the Bois Joli. Our dinner was both imaginative and generous. Pigeon stuffed with foie gras, Norman sausages cooked in cider are the house specialities. The patron and his wife could not have been more accommodating. Menus from 16-40€.

Perhaps the Bois Joli's heyday was fifty or so years ago - the public rooms are a bit faded - but, like Bagnoles itself, it is a very good recommendation for a more elegant age. Starred for good value in both bed and board.

Lutétia 🛏 ⊠ M

Blvd. Paul Chalvet
tel: (0)233.37.94.77
fax: (0)233.30.09.87
closed: 15/10-15/3

See what I mean about the long winter in Bagnoles? I stayed in the Lutétia on a previous visit and loved the quiet tastefully decorated rooms, the luxurious bathrooms, the glassed-in terrace overlooking a pleasant garden, dotted with expensive recliners, and Madame Tramontana's benign supervision. I don't suppose any of that has changed but this time, on a spring visit, the hotel was firmly closed so I cannot personally vouch, and the arrow must go.

There are 30 rooms, from 67-81€, some in the annexe, some in the main building, which is a villa in a peaceful residential area not far from the town centre. If it's still as good as I remember it, this is excellent value.

Menus from 22-59€.

☆ Manoir du Lys 🛏 ⊠ M

Rte de Juvigny
tel: (0)233.37.80.69
fax: (0)233.30.05.80
closed: Sun p.m. and Mon o.o.s.; 1/1-15/2

3 km out of town, surrounded by the forest, on the D335, is this half-timbered manor house, which has earned consistent praise from FE readers. A great part of this must be attributed to the management, in the very capable hands of the Quinton family. As the car drives up, some member of staff will rush out to carry the bags and direct the driver to the car park, Madame Quinton or her daughter will be there at reception, and son Franck will be busy in the kitchen. The family are constantly improving the property. There is a tennis court and two swimming pools (one covered). In summer tables are set outside, and the feel-good factor is high.

The 23 rooms have a wide price differential - with prices starting from 61€. As they all have good bathrooms and are well equipped, I would counsel the cheaper ones, which are decidedly the best value.

Franck's cooking merits a Michelin star and the service in the pretty dining room is suave, so the cheapest menu, Le Petit

Normand, at 25€ is excellent value.

Fish appears on the more expensive menu - bass with a tomato mousse, monk fish roasted and served on a base of spinach and wild mushrooms - and the desserts get more adventurous, like a selection of apple-based dishes. Menus from 26€

Starred as a popular hideaway run by a caring family.

BALLEROY 14490, Calvados

Map 4C
16 km SW of Bayeux
Market: Tues.

Like a stage set, with one wide main street of weathered grey stone houses, all of a period, leading down to the focal point, the Chateau de Balleroy. It was built in the 17th century by Mansart for

Château de Balleroy.

Jean de Choisy, whose descendant, the Marquis of Balleroy, sold it to the late Malcolm Forbes, the American publishing tycoon.

Manoir de la Drôme ⌧ M
tel: (0)231.29.60.94
closed: Sun. p.m; Mon; Wed; Feb

My, how the Manoir has came on since readers first alerted me to the talent in this nice old stone house on the village outskirts. From simple delights to Michelin star in a very short space of time.

Menus start at 29€ (another considerable change!) and feature M. Leclerc's specialities, like three kinds of duck liver pâté, a fricassé of sole, again with foie gras and a wonderful chocolate tart with sweet red wine.

BARFLEUR 50760, Manche

Map 2B
28 km E of Cherbourg

Just one wide main street lined with granite houses leading down to the colourful fishing port. It makes a pleasant outing to drive here and walk round the harbour past flowery cottage gardens in the Cour Ste. Cathérine, to check out the plaque commemorating the departure of William the Conqueror in 1066 for the conquest of England, and to visit the 17C chapel at the harbour extremity. There's even a sandy beach here. Richard Lionheart also contributed to Barfleur's page in the history books by embarking from the port on his way to be crowned our king. You could extend the drive to visit the lighthouse at the Pointe de Barfleur, and climb the 365 steps to view the panorama which covers the whole of the east coast down to the cliffs of Grandcamp and stretching over the vicious rocks that guard the entrance to the harbour.

Hotel Le Conquérant ⇔ M
16 r. St. Thomas Becket
tel: (0)233.54.00.82
fax: (0)233.54.65.25
closed: 15/11-15/3

In the main street but calm and peaceful, thanks to an unexpected large and leafy garden at the rear, where it is most agreeable to sit and sup. Breakfast is served here whenever the weather permits. Otherwise it's around the inglenook fireplace in the cosy dining room.

The building is a 17C manor-house converted by the father of the present owner, Catherine Delomenéde and her husband Pierre. The sixteen bedrooms (two in the garden, with terrace) are comfortable and equipped with British TV. At 56€ I think they provide a superb base for exploring the region and would be high on my list of favourites.

Rooms are 32-72€, some with shower and wc. Menus from 12.5€ (crêpes).

☆ **Hotel Moderne** 🛏 ⊠ M
   Place du Gén. de Gaulle
   tel: (o)233.23.12.44
   fax: (o)233.23.91.58
   closed: Wed.; 14/7-30/9

This strange ochre-coloured building with oriental-looking dome, has had a new lease of life since the present owners, the le Rouliers, took over.

Evrard le Roulier is a fine chef who takes delight in the prime fresh ingredients available in his region, and the dining room not the bedrooms is the raison d'être for this establishment. It is large and airy and used by local gastronomes as well as tourists. The platter de fruits de mer is a wonder to behold, but more modest spenders should look no further than the 13.6€ menu - excellent value.

Nothing much seems to have happened to the eight bedrooms since I first stayed there ten years ago, a fact reflected in their price (38€ upwards). I would counsel sleeping at Le Conquérant and eating here.

'One of the best meals ever.' Ann Reiners. I would agree - new star.

BARNEVILLE-LA-BERTRAN 14600 Honfleur, Calvados

Map 3E
6 km SW of Honfleur

Even if you have no intention of staying in Barneville, take the pleasant drive west of Honfleur along the Côte de Grâce, then swinging inland on the D62 and D279 amid deeply rural and very green Norman countryside.

Auberge de la Source ⊨ ☒ S

tel: (0)231.89.25.02
closed: 11/11-15/2

There are no recommendable simple hotels in Honfleur and a town base can be noisy, so this little Logis de France could be a valuable asset. It is looking considerably smarter these days, under the jurisdiction of M. and Mme. Legeay, all freshly painted black and white, with the pretty garden well under control, and there are plenty of white tables and chairs under the trees from which to listen to the discreet tinkle of the stream from which the Auberge derives its name. A very peaceful spot to came home to.

There are sixteen rooms, mostly in the annexe building, comfortably equipped. Demi-pension is insisted upon but the cooking is good, so for those who do not fancy turning out in the evening, the deal is a good one. Prices for two people per day are between 64€ and 125€, for one they are 57€.

BAVENT 14860, Calvados

Map 3D
7 km SW of Cabourg by D513 and D95A

In other words, not in the village of Bavent at all but the other side of the main road. Look for the sign.

Hostellerie du Moulin du Pré ⊨ M ☒ L

Rte de Gonneville
tel: (0)231.78.83.68
fax: (0)231.78.21.05.
closed: Sun. p.m. and Mon. except July, Aug. and fetes; 1/3-15/3; Oct.

An interesting one. Plus points are the undeniable prettiness of the setting - a flowery garden with stream running through, old farm implements scattered on the lawn, fresh white paint, birdsong - and the interior - heavy beams, big log fire, cosy atmosphere, and the reliable cooking of Jocelyne Holtz. Not such good news are the prices and the fact that the rooms are pretty basic. I was wondering whether this should be the time, after many years inclusion, to forget about the Hostellerie. But rule no.1 is to take advice from the locals, who visit regularly and have ears to the ground, rather than the experience of an isolated occasion, and here they were unanimous. 'Isn't it rather expensive?' I suggested. 'Yes,' was the unanimous reply, 'but worth every franc.' So lie back and enjoy it.

The menu is likely to include items like bavarois d'avocat aux huîtres pochés, flan de langoustines au coulis de crustacés, soupe de fruits rouges, so you are paying for sophisticated expertise in the kitchen. Menus from 31-42€. Rooms cost 57€ with bath/shower and wc, or 45€ without a wc, but with a shower/bath.

BAYEUX 14400, Calvados

Map 3C
28 km W of Caen
Market: Wed.

I cannot think of any town that has changed so much over the past decade as has Bayeux. Pre-pedestrianisation, its one long main drag was a noisy, dangerous, fume-ridden nightmare, with pedestrians nervously proceeding Indian-style along narrow pavements, and drivers becoming increasingly frustrated. All that has changed and now it is possible to stroll, window shop, drink coffee, watch the world go by and appreciate this delightful town. Some of the side streets are beginning to get the message too and cafes are opening up in newly-cleaned stone, traffic-free enclaves.

One of the prettiest is near the square designated for parking for the Tapestry, where a little stone bridge crosses the river. Perfect for peaceful picnicking, with plenty of benches thoughtfully provided.

Otherwise there is a good crêperie, Le TriskeA, whose terrace overlooks the water-wheel that churns up the river, or an interesting Italian restaurant with the sensible asset of a heated terrace. On a blustery July day it meant that we could still enjoy the view and fresh air without a shiver.

The city had the good fortune to escape the devastation that removed so much character from other less fortunate Norman towns, by virtue of serving as a hospital town during the 1944 fighting and by being the first French town to be liberated. Restoration work of the town's treasures is constantly in progress. The old noblemen's houses and ancient smaller dwellings have been spruced up; iron balconies gleam with fresh paint and the grime-free Caen stone now glows a creamy gold.

The city's greatest asset is of course the tapestry of Queen Mathilde, housed in an erstwhile seminary in a quiet square, well signed from all directions. Try and get there early or late so that you don't have to crane over burly German shoulders or shuffle round in a slow Japanese gaggle. Don't even think of trying to polish it off in less than two hours and that's pushing it. I've never yet met anyone who did not rate the experience as less than wonderful.

On the first floor is a mock-up of every detail of the work and a clear description in English and French of what is going on. The critical scenes - Harold's oath, Edward's death, Harold's coronation, the Norman invasion, William's bravery, Harold's death - are all emphasised to make identification easy when you do eventually get to see the actual tapestry. Check the times of the showing of the 15 minute film to make sure you don't have a long wait for the English version. And then at last, suitably awestruck, into the dark passage where this priceless account of the customs, clothing, food, events of 900 years ago, recorded so vividly, awaits you. Don't miss the English moustaches!

Bayeux is fortunate in having another string to its cultural bow the magnificent Norman Gothic Cathédrale Notre Dame. Only the towers and crypt remain from the original church which was completed in 1077 by Odo, William's companion in arms who proved so turbulent that he met a sticky end at William's instigation. This is not the place for a lengthy description of its many virtues, but take it from me that a half-hour here will be well spent. Even the much denigrated bonnet which 19C 'improvers' thought would be a suitable cap for the central tower makes an unmistakeable landmark from within the town and from far and wide around it The cathedral is set in the oldest part of Bayeux, wed worth exploring to admire half-timbered houses and quiet courtyards.

Hotels and Restaurants:

Bayeux is an excellent choice for a base at any time of the year, with plenty to admire in indifferent weather, and fortunately its hotels and restaurants recognise the fact and stay open for most of the winter months.

☆ Hotel d'Argouges ⌨ M

21 r. St. Patrice
tel: (0)231.92.88.86
fax: (0)231.92.69.16
closed: july

Facing onto a huge square not far from the town centre and a Relais du Silence, the nice old 18C hotel particulier is approached through an archway. I like it better than ever, perhaps because the owners Marie-Claire and Daniel Auregan are so welcoming. There is an annexe next door, approached via a large garden, where the rooms are slightly cheaper than in the main building. There are 23 altogether, varying considerably, so it is worth discussing your preferences. Rooms cost from 50€. Secure free parking.

Readers have been very happy to stay here for a reasonable sum, enjoying the peacefulness in the town centre, so a star for first choice in this must-see town.

Le Lion d'Or ⌨ M ⊠ M-L

71 r. St. Jean.
tel: (0)231.92.06.90
fax: (0)231.22.)6.64
closed: 23/12-23/1

Now that the rue St. Jean is pedestrianised, this old coaching inn, set back in a courtyard, is quiet enough to rate as a Relais du Silence. It is Bayeuxe's best-known hotel and has been in the same family for many years. Its fortunes have varied over that time. I personally had my doubts about the justifiability of the Michelin star from way back and now I see that it has been removed. That can only be a good thing from the customer's point of view. No star is far preferable to an ill-advised one. The latter situation leads to complacency, the former, with luck, to a must-try-harder approach. I believe that this could be the case here. With several new hotels burgeoning in the town and surrounds the Lion d'Or must have realised that it can no longer rely on its faithful (largely British) clientele to go on supporting it without question. The daughter of the previous owner is now in charge and there is a revitalised atmosphere.

The decor previously disappointed - not my idea of what is appropriate for an ancient provincial inn anyway. Now all the bedrooms are being re-decorated and are pleasant and light. The dining room is still a bit pompous but the service is good and the cooking improving all the time.

Readers' views have varied in the past - old-timers disillusioned, newcomers still pleased to find such an atmospheric base in the centre of town. I believe that it is time to forget old triumphs and disasters and look at the Lion d'Or with fresh eyes.

26 rooms from 104€. 1 apartment available (price depends on season). Lunchtime menu is 17.5€ and evening menu is 24€.

Otherwise

Churchill Hotel (see Restaurant l'Amirauté) 🛏 M

> 14 r. St. Jean
> **tel:** (0)231.21.31.80
> **fax:** (0)231.21.41.66.
> **closed:** 15/11-1/3

Centrally situated, freshly decorated and sound-proofed, with benefit of good restaurant, integral to hotel but not under the same management. A good bet if you like to eat in but not extravagantly. There is a demi-pension arrangement

31 rooms 48-74€. 1 apartment 83-109€.

1'Amaryllis ⊠ M

> 32 r. St. Patrice
> **tel:** (0)231.22.47.94.
> **closed:** Mon. and Jan

Currently my number one choice in the town if good food is toppriority. L'Amaryllis is on the main western approach road to the town, opposite a big parking square, and therefore lacks the ambiance of the restaurants in the historic centre, but the cooking makes up for a lot.

Menus start at 15.7€.

La Rapière ☒ S-M

53 r. St. Jean
tel: (0)231.92.94.79
closed: Tues. p.m. and Wed. o.o.s.

The reverse of l'Amaryllis. Here the decor and atmosphere score top marks, with the cooking a touch patchy. However, over the eleven years since I first discovered this little restaurant, readers have been well-satisfied and if you stick to the charcoal grills and fish which are the house specialities, you can't go far wrong.

It's not really in the rue St Jean at all, but tucked away in an old courtyard. Stone walls, lace tablecloths, pink napkins, open fires, all contribute to a feeling of well-being, and the warm welcome helps. There is a 12€ menu but I would go for the next one up, at 22€, which buys nine oysters, an entrecôte steak, salad and dessert. Wines are reasonably priced.

Good marks on the whole but I fear the star must go since reports have not been unanimous.

l'Amirauté ☒ M

14 r St. Jean
tel: (0)231.21.31.80
fax: (0)231.21.41.66

There are numerous little cheap restaurants at the bottom of the rue St. Jean, with tables enticingly laid out on the pavement. If all you need is a sandwich and lots of passing-by interest, this is the place to head for. However anything more ambitious is fraught with hazards. I think I'm fairly proficient in the art of menu judging by now but the usual stroll up and down, judging the clientele, the food on their plates and the prices, let me down badly here and we ended up sadly disappointed with the kind of tasteless, badly presented food that alas is not uncommon nowadays in France.

All the more frustrating when just across the road is l'Amirauté, whose 9.3€ menu offers honest simple fare that is just right for an inexpensive lunch. 9.3€ bought terrine, omelette for me, poulet Vallée d'Auge for him, and a good apple tart. Of course there are far more ambitious menus up to 40€.

☆ La Table du Terroir ☒ S
42 r St. Jean
tel: (0)231.92.05.53.
closed: Sun. and Mon p.m.; 14/10-14-11

And now for something entirely different. In the rue St. Jean is abutcher by name of M. Bisson, famous locally for his charcuterie, terrines and sausages. No ordinary butcher though, since he has had the brilliant idea of cutting out the middle man and dishing up his products in his own restaurant Costs are kept to a minimum by using just one simple stone-walled room round the corner in the Allée d'Oranger, and the consumer benefits from the modest bill. Other restaurateurs must hate him.

You sit at long scrubbed tables and tuck into copious meat-based dishes. The French just love it, but it seems that the Brits have yet to discover the novelty. I don't know when M. Bisson does his butchering because he always seems to be in attendance in his little restaurant, but perhaps that's because it was brand new when I visited and he was still excited at his new venture. Can't blame him.

On the 9.6€ menu you can choose between juicy terrines or salad for starters, then a grill of whatever, then green salad or potatoes, then dessert or cheese. Bad luck vegetarians because even the salads are full of pâté de foie. The grillade comes hot (section of grilled meats) or cold (house charcuterie). How's that for value?

You don't have to stick to the menu. Well worth sampling is the house speciality - feuilléte Bayeusain, which is a kind of upmarket Cornish pasty made with flaky pastry and more meat than veg. Or paupiettes of ham braised in cider, or roast pork or, perhaps best of all, a gigot of pré salé lamb. Desserts understandably pale into insignificance but there is always a tarte maison. Starred for individuality and good value. Menu prices go up to 26€.

BEAUMESNIL 27410, Eure

Map 4F
12 km SW of Bemay
Market: Mon.

l'Étape Louis XIII ⊠ M-L

Rte. de la Barre
tel: (0)232.44.44.72
closed: Tues.; Wed.; (Tues only in Jul. and Aug.)

A special-occasion place, with the best cooking for miles around. The chef/patron Christian Ravinel,has been awarded his first Michelin star, confirming that his 16€ menu (weekdays) is a bargain. He relies mainly on local ingredients and recipes, but cooked and presented suavely and with no expense spared.

The Étape is as olde-worlde Norman as they come, with two pretty dark cosy rooms, luxuriating in a big log fire on chilly nights. A winter place I feel. More reports for a star.

Menus from 22€.

BEAUMONT EN AUGE 14950, Calvados

Map 3E
6 km W of Pont l'Evêque by D118
Market: Sat

A village sauvegardé, in other words protected. Very pretty, very peaceful, rather more dignified and aristocratic than other pretty Norman villages, more stately grey stone merchants' houses than black-and-white farmers' cottages. Its situation comes as a surprise.

Walk across the grassy square and suddenly the ground drops before you, disclosing a remarkable view of the Touques valley. A gap in the far distance reveals the sea and Trouville, 15 km away.

Auberge de l'Abbaye ⊠ M

tel: (0)231.64.82.31
closed: Tues.; Wed.; except July and Aug.; 3 weeks in Jan. 1/10-7/10

Not hard to find - this is a very tiny village and the auberge is bang in the centre. Like the village, it is very pretty and very old – 17C. A place for cold winter evenings I feel rather than summer lunches. Ceilings are low, supported by columns, beamed walls are painted red, giant twisted wine presses provide the decor.

Christian Girault's cooking is unrepentantly old-school. His 26€

menu revealed tartare de saumon, carrée d'agneau, cheese and good desserts of the classical persuasion. No fireworks but good ingredients, well-presented.

Menus from 27€ (with a choice). Good short wine list.

BEAUVOIR 50170 Manche, Pontorson

Map 6A
5 km S of Mont St. Michel by D976

Just a name on the main road south.

Hotel Beauvoir 🛏 ⊠ M
tel: (0)233.60.09.39
fax: (0)233.48 59.05
closed: 15/11-7&21

A pleasantly old-fashioned hotel which looks as though it has been catering for Mont St. Michel visitors for generations. Its virtue is that it does not regard this an excuse for a rip-off. The number of French people dining on the covered terrace testified to the regular value here (menus from 11€).

The rooms are fine, even if one regrets the flock wallpaper when a country print would have been more in keeping with the building's character. 18 of them cost from 54€ with bath, phone and TV.

LE BEC-HELLOUIN 27800, Eure

Map 3F
24 km SE of Pont Audemer
Market: Fri.

It's a lovely drive on the D130 through the Montfort forest, following the river Risle to the great ruined abbey of Bec-Hellouin. There's an extraordinary peaceful feeling to the village, like a cathedral close, even when it is thronged with visitors.

The abbey, founded in 1034, has strong links with England, as the commemorative tablet in the grounds will tell you. Duke William's friend and counsellor, Lanfranc, was Instructor at Le Bec and subsequently became Bishop of Canterbury. His secretary,

Gundulf, became Bishop of Rochester and architect of the Tower of London. There are guided tours of the abbey, generally in French, but the grounds are open to wander around, and those prepared to climb 210 steps up St. Nicholas Tower will be rewarded by a fine view of the Bec valley.

There are several crêperies in the village, which readers have recommended, a restaurant called Le Canterbury about which I have heard absolutely nothing and a famous old inn:

Auberge de l'Abbaye ⇔ ⊠ M

Pl. Guillaume le Conquérant.
tel: (0)232.44.86.02
closed: Mon. lunch; Tues. lunch; Jan.

Everyone takes a photo of the Auberge. It oozes charm, with ancient beams and rustic antiquity, in a perfect setting above a peaceful grassy square alongside the old church. I have been in and out of love with it for years - in because I'm a sucker for slanting squeaky floors, old fashioned flowery wallpapers, polished old family heirlooms, out because at times I felt (and readers agreed) that it was cashing in on its situation. I believe that it is reasserting itself,

Auberge de L'Abbaye

thanks to a refit of most of the rooms, the new entrance hall, and fresh paint around the courtyard where breakfast is taken in fine weather. Perhaps the jolt has been salutary and things are looking up. Always a good time to visit.

Some of the rooms are very pretty - I had no grumbles with my room, but one reader took issue with me when I described them as 'simple'. 'Simple my foot,' he wrote, 'I would call them basic.' As I say, they are in the process of being revamped, so care is needed when booking.

The food has certainly improved, with plenty of 'plats du terroir', like rabbit terrine, but is too expensive.

Rooms from 74€.

Menus from 15.5€.

BÉNOUVILLE 14970, Calvados

Map 3D
10 km NE of Caen

What was once a quiet village on the minor road leading to the sea is now surrounded by main roads and concrete, but it is still a good choice to stay near the ferry port.

La Glycine 🛏 ☒ S

11, Pl. Commando No 4
tel: (0)231.44.6).94
fax: (0)231.43.67.30
closed: Christmas to 10 January

The youthful M. and Mme Decker have worked hard at improving their investment in what was once just a wisteria-covered bar. An entry in Michelin is their reward. Readers have been well pleased with the value here. The 25 rooms cost from 46-69€ and menus range from 21.5-39€. There is no choice at this level but if you fancy the dishes of the day you're in luck, because they include ideas like a fricassé of mussels with rosemary, half a chicken in Vallée d'Auge sauce and a gâteau normand with caramelised cream. Good value.

BERNAY 27309, Eure

Map 4F
71 km S of Le Havre
Market: Sat.

I owe Bernay an apology. Not oneof the previous editions of Normandy has even mentioned the place. I did have my reasons. A preliminary glimpse from the main road which follows the railway line and sidings looked highly unpromising, giving me the excuse to skip this one and get on with something more interesting. Even when my home town was twinned with Bernay and I could ask local dignitaries what they could recommend, there was much head scratching but little inspiration. My loss, because when this time, determined that no stone (or bistro) should be left unturned, I did investigate further I discovered that it's not at all bad.

Maybe not worth a diversion, but if you should happen to findyourself nearby and in need of nourishment or a leg stretch, you could do far worse. I found it to be well provided with brasseries, three or four restaurants, two Logis de France hotels, and numerous bars.

The main shopping street is often traffic jammed. Much nicer is the pedestrianised rue Gaston Folloppe, fined with old beamed buildings and leading down to the little river Cosnier. Plenty of alternative eateries here, with seating outside when the sun shines. I thought the cocktail bar Le Piano looked interesting, with a huge range of drinks and J.P.Bernais' wine bar la Cour des Miracles, with 100 whiskies and 40 calvados on sale. Tucked away behind the shop, through the courtyard, is an unexpected little bistro, good for light lunches - salads, home-made foie gras, cheeses, with a welcoming log fire on a cold March day.

Too cold alas for us to sit outside in the cobbled street, we chose instead to eat inside at:

Le Lapin Gourmand ⌧ S

r. Gaston Folloppe
tel: (0)232.43.42.32.10
closed: Sun. Wed. and 15/7-15/8

Excellent value here in this little charcutier/traiteur. Something for everyone here, smart wine section next door to household necessities like Vim and dishcloths, take-away home-made charcuterie, plus eight simply-laid tables, all efficiently served by one efficient lady, wife of the patron/chef. You can order anything from the window display - quiches, terrines, ham, salads, home-made desserts, or choose something hot, freshly cooked - there is no set menu, it is all à la carte. Husband had a fat ham omelette and I enjoyed a large and lovely spinach and bacon salad. On the next table the parents, surrounded with their market shopping bags, tucked into steaks, while their children were blissfully into huge platefuls of golden crisp frites. Ideal for a cheap lunch, with or without the kids.

BEUVRON-EN-AUGE 14430, Calvados

Map 4E
30 km E of Caen, 15 km of Cabourg
Market: Sat. p.m.
Access: from Dozulé take the D85 then the D146 (or get pleasantly lost in the maze of country lanes).

If one had to select just one village to typify the Auge region Beuvron would be a strong contender. It not only has all the usual accoutrements of black-and-white timbered cottages, roses round the door, cider apple trees, black-and-white cattle, and farmhouses advertising their own cheese, but it centres on a superb example of ancient market halls. Far too good for animals and vegetables, it now houses a well-known Michelin-starred restaurant.

☆ **Le Pavé d'Auge** ☒ **M-L**
   tel: (0)231.79.26.71
   fax: (0)231.39.04.45
   closed: Mon.; Tues.; 24/11-28/12

Clever use has been made of the outstanding features of the heavily-beamed old market hall, so that one is impressed with its heritage but not over-awed. The Americans love it.

   Jerome Bansard gives them exactly what they want - a meal full of flavours, often composed from local recipes and local ingredients (like the fish which is especially good) without too many surprises.

   The cheapest menu at 20.8€ is available on Sunday evenings - useful when so many restaurants are shut altogether, and on

Saturday evenings, and lunch during the week. Otherwise it is 31€ or 39€. The wine is not cheap but there is a commendable range of half-bottles. Starred for excellent food in delightful surroundings.

Auberge de La Boule d'Or ⊠
Pl. Michel Vernughen
tel: (0)231.79.78.78
closed: Sun. p.m and Wed. (except in Jul. and Aug.); 15/12-10/2

Mme Duval proudly announces on her card that she has won the Grand Prix National de la Tripe, so I felt rather wimpish in ordering the poulet Vallée d'Auge instead. But it doesn't really matter - both dishes are typical of the region and both indicate the lack of pretension which is typical of this little restaurant. Nothing like so glamorous as its neighbour, le Pavé, but what it lacks in grandeur it makes up for in friendliness (and economy). Even in winter the interior is cheerful, with pink walls, pink napery, pink and green curtains and dark beams. We were served by the patron's niece, who had to keep rushing out to the street to reprove her son.

Just testing, I tried the only sophisticated dish on the 16e menu - the terrine de petits legumes au poisson. It looked good, but would have tasted better had it not been over-refrigerated. Husband did far better sticking to smoked ham - his plate overflowed with juicy mountain ham. My chicken was fine but his 'fish of the day', which turned out to be lotte, was better. Cheese board disappointing, tarte aux pommes unusually more like an English apple pie and none the worse for that. Menus from 15.5€.

I gather there are some rooms above the restaurant - all reports welcome.

N.B. The details supplied by the Boule d'Or state that the above are the closing days, but my notes say firmly that, because the weekends are so important, they close midweek. Best to ring and check.

There is another contender for Beuvron's culinary honours - la Forge, just opposite the Boule d'Or. Tablecloths are red check, food is cooked over the open fire. The reputation is that it is cheap, cheerful, smoky, fun, erratic, and that the patron is a 'character'. Any personal experiences?

BEUZEVILLE 27210, Eure

Map 3E
15 km E of Honfleur, 14 km N of Pont l'Evêque
Market: Tues.

Strategically sited, just off the autoroute, this small town makes an ideal staging post for basic shopping and, if you happen to be there on a Tuesday, a leg stretch round the market.

☆ **Le Cochon d'Or** 🛏 S ☒ M
pl. du Général de Gaulle
tel: (0)232.57.70.46
fax: (0)232.42.25.70
closed: Mon.; 15/12-15/1

☆ **Petit Castel** 🛏 M
tel: (0)232.57. 76.08
fax: (0)232.42.25.70
closed: 15/12-15/1

How good it is to see an old faithful not only continue to be faithful but to excel itself with unanimous reader approval. There have been many changes here, particularly in the last few years, but they have been wise ones. The Cochon d'Or is greatly gentrified since it used to be our stop off the night boat for that first magical taste of France - coffee and croissants served in a Gaulois fug. Catherine and Olivier Martin, daughter and son-in-law of the previous proprietors, have taken over the reins and now the restaurant is very smart, with deep rose walls, flowery curtains and chairs, expensive carpets. Notwithstanding, when we dropped in and hesitantly asked for two coffees, M. Martin responded, 'I cannot refuse you.' Well he could have done. Many have. But here is a man out to please and that is high in my list of desiderata for a hotelier.

The whole set-up - modest rooms in the Cochon with a modest price tag, more luxurious rooms across the road in the Petit Castel - is equally to my liking. You are on a budget but still like your rooms spotless and the welcome warm? It's the Cochon for you. You want something smarter with new bathroom and view over garden? Make for the Petit Castel, to sleep and eat breakfast, then dine at the Cochon. A free locked garage is another bonus.

The re-furbishing of the Petit Castel is now complete. The rooms have in common bright cheerful colours but otherwise are all different, so that you can specify double or twin bed, bath or shower, garden or road, and pay accordingly (but always assured of good value). In the Cochon the rooms are simple but infinitely better than many I've viewed at twice the price.

Best of all, because this all started off as a restaurant-with-rooms, rather than the other way round, the food has always been unusually good and is now better than ever, while prices have remained fair. It is good honest Norman cooking, unpretentious, copious and good value. That doesn't mean boring though. On the 16.1€ menu for example you can choose a tart filled with mild sweet onions flavoured with thyme for a starter, the fish comes in various guises, with a Dover sole costing a reasonable 13.1€, and the pâtisseries, even on the 11.7e menu, is much more interesting than average.

Starred for its convenient position near coast and ferry, gentil management, good rooms, great value.

Rooms 37€ with shower and no wc or 54e with bath, phone and TV in Cochon d'Or, from 42€ to 54€ in Le Petit Castel.

Menus at 14.2€, 19€, 26e, 32€ and 42€.

BÉZANCOURT 76220, Seine-Mar

Map H3
10 km SW of Gournay by D316 and D62

A hamlet in lovely wooded countryside.

Chateau du Landel 🛏 ⊠ M
   tel: (0)235.90.16.01
   restaurant closed: Sun. p.m.; 15/1-15/3

The 18C chateau was once a staging post on the pilgrims' route to Compostella. Now it is once again a peaceful relaxing haven for travellers.

It is the family home of M. and Mme Pierre Cardon who have converted the gracious rooms into a hotel with 17 individual bedrooms. Each room is totally different from its neighbour. You can choose a spacious luxurious example, dignified and elegant with brocade, or a smaller cheaper Mansard-window version, or a family

Chateau du Landel

suite. Ours was all pink and white, with the Toile de Jouy that the French love so much on walls, curtains and bed cover. This one had a well-fisted but tiny bathroom, others have larger bathrooms, smaller bedrooms and some have not yet been re-furbished, so if you get a chance to choose make sure you sort out your priorities. They cost from 80-160€.

The peacefulness is immediately striking as you approach the lovely building via a long drive. The grounds are extensive and delightful, the swimming pool is one of the best I have encountered in a hotel - large, well-heated and surrounded by plenty of expensive recliners - and there is a tennis court in excellent condition.

M. and Mme Cardon are still very much in evidence and not above making a bed or two when required but nowadays they leave the day-to-day running of the hotel and the cooking to their son Yves, who spent his childhood here. The 26€ dinner menu yielded haddock mousse, fillet of beef and a chocolate marquise, with a choice of one alternative dish in each of the three courses - admirably compact. The dining room is particularly attractive in winter when the huge log fire blazes in the vast chimney. However, fine weather would mean drinks on the terrace and a swim, so both options are delightful.

LA BOUILLE 76530, Seine-Mar

Map 3G
75 km E of Le Havre; 20 km W of Rouen
Market: Wed.

La Bouille is a well-kept secret for many visitors who never think that a turn off the autoroute just one exit short of Rouen and a mere 3 km diversion could bring such rich rewards. If once they would wind down the corkscrewing hill to the peaceful little mediaeval village tucked between mighty river and sheltering escarpment they would be forever hooked.

They would discover beamy Norman cottages, a crêperie or two, a chemist, three hotels and several restaurants, but La Bouille's unique claim to fame is its proximity to a wide and interesting stretch of the Seine, where great barges and container ships pass astonishingly nearby, up and down to the docks at Rouen and the refineries at Le Havre.

The Rouennais of course have discovered the picturesqueness ofthe settlement long ago, as did the 19C landscape painters. This is a favourite Sunday excursion. There's a charming drive along the river bank to take the ferry across to Duclair and a little red bac chugs across from La Bouille too, to Sahurs, where's there's a café/bar by the water's edge and a modest Logis (see p.222). But the No. 1 treat is to book a table for lunch at one of the excellent restaurants for which La Bouille is known. The weather, of course, makes all the difference, so they tend to be packed out when the sun shines and deserted at other times.

When the gourmands have gone home its a lovely place to stayon - peaceful, very near to the big city, which can be easily reachedby whatever route you fancy. The easiest is to rejoin the autoroute,the quickest is to hold your nose and avert your eyes from theproliferation of heavy industry while following the road nearest to theriver, via Moulineaux, Grand Couronne and Grand Quévilly, but the prettiest by far is to take the bac across the river and enjoy the little D51 for the first ten miles or so before it too gets immersed in the conglomeration.

St Pierre 🛏 M ☒ L

4 Pl. de Bateau
tel: (0)235.18.01.01
fax: (0)233.48.59.82
closed: Sun; Mon; 2 weeks in Oct.

When Bernard Huet was tragically killed in a car crash in 1995, heads were shaken and the end of the St. Pierre was prophesied. Bernard and Giselle had been such a good team - she up front, he taking care of the business side. Giselle has proved them wrong. The show must go on and she continues to welcome and advise, as tall, blonde, elegant and seemingly as cheerful as ever.

Just before Bernard died the whole of the downstairs area was redecorated. Out went the mauve and in came a more restful yellow and green - upholstery, carpet and curtains now in perfect harmony. The biggest change of all has been to the terrace, always La Bouille's prime viewing situation. Now there is a substantial sage green trellis arrangement, providing the base for climbing plants and dividing up the area most attractively. On fine days the forty covers out here are keenly contested for.

The new young chef is shaping up well, showing imagination as well as confidence. The food is sophisticated and elegantly served, using prime expensive ingredients, especially seafood.

This is primarily a restaurant-with-rooms, but the rooms are a very good deal at a reasonable price. Make sure you get one of the three better ones overlooking the front though. You can lie in bed and watch the great ships pass by your window as if drawn by an invisible rope. Furnishing is vaguely oriental, with cane providing the character.

Stop press: Giselle tells me she is retiring, so the star must go. Watch this space. Menus are 28e, 34€ and 48€ (for three courses, all available midweek). 7 rooms from 56€.

☆ Les Gastronomes ☒ M

pl. de Bateau
tel: (0)235.18.02.07
closed: Wed. p.m.; Thurs.; 13/12-27/12

A pretty little doll's house, one room down, one up, the latter with a view of the Seine if you crane a little. Rustic and cosy, with tables outside if it gets a bit too cosy in summer.

The brothers Marrière are in charge, one in the kitchen and one

Les Gastronomes

doing the welcome bit, both charming. Jacques' cooking gets better and better - traditional but with individual trimmings, skilful sauces, The wine list and the service are beyond reproach and the atmosphere has been specially praised by readers, so the star certainly stays.

Menus are 18€. 23€ and 36€.

La Maison Blanche ⊠ M

quai Hector Malot (0)235.18.01.90
closed: Sun. p.m.; Mon.; 16/7-5/8

'The new owners are young, friendly and efficient. Our room was good with a fine view and the food and service were excellent. We would definitely stay again.'

The old white house overlooks the river, with a pleasant interior decorated with old furniture and ancient faience. A good stop for tea, this one, with that panoramic view thrown in. Menus from 17.6€.

La Maison Blanche

BRÉHAL 50290 Manche

Map 5A
10 km N of Granville
Market: Tues.

A small market town at the junction of several roads, left as a backwater after being bypassed by the D971.

☆ **Hotel de la Gare** 🛏 ⌧ S
  1 pl. Ct. Godard
  tel: (0)233.61.61.11
  closed: Sun. and Mon. (except in Jul. and Aug.)

A little hotel (just nine rooms) in the centre of the town, with the friendliest atmosphere imaginable. One of my absolute favourites.

Responsible for the cheery atmosphere are the owners, Pierrette and Georges Coffre, who are particularly fond of English guests and are able to converse with them in their own language. Georges proudly showed me his garden behind the hotel. 'Who says we don't grow oranges in Normandy?' And there was living proof that indeed they do - tubs of citrus trees loaded with fruit. It's a calm green place to sit, take breakfast or a drink.

The rooms are very comfortable and will cost from 46€. The garage is free.

Georges is chef de cuisine and this is a case where demi-pension is a good idea, because his cooking is generous and way above average (45€ per person). Otherwise menus start at 14.4€ .

A star for just about everything, including universal reader-appreciation. 'The hotel is like a new pin, and M. and Mme Coffre and daughter are so friendly.' Hilary Cosgrove.

L' BRETEUIL SUR-ITON 27160, Eure

Map 5G
31 km SW of Evreux
Market: Wed.

The little town is almost surrounded by an arm of the Iton, forming a pool bordered by the public gardens. Adèle, daughter of

William the Conqueror, was married in the 11th century church here; the pillars in the transept date from William's reign, but the interior's most striking feature is the arcades in the nave, resting on twelve massive pillars built of grison, the red stone of the area. The Hôtel de Ville in the market square must qualify as the narrowest ever.

Le Biniou ⊠ S

> 72 pl. Lafitte
> **tel:** (0)232.29.70.61
> **closed:** Sun., Mon. lunch and p.m.; Tues. p.m.; 6/8-31/8

I am always delighted to discover the Binious of this world. Small, unpretentious, welcoming, in the market square - that's my recipe for my kind of restaurant. It specialises in fruits de mer, and 20e will buy a platter that should keep you busy for a happy hour or so, but if you're not in that mood catch the 12€ mid-week menu - fish mousse, steak au poivrre, tarte du jour, or the 17.6€ version - nine oysters, roast salmon, cheese, pineapple charlotte. You can't really go wrong.

LE-BREUIL-EN-AUGE 14130, Calvados

Map 3E
21 km S of Deauville. 9km N of Lisieux

On the main road, the D 579; if time is no object, the D48 from Pont l'Evêque to Lisieux is a much more attractive route. Le Breuil, which fills in the gap between the two roads, has little to recommend it except:

☆ Le Dauphin ⊠ M

> **tel:** (0)231.65.08.11
> **fax:** (0)231.65.12.08.
> **closed:** Sun. p.m.; Mon.; Nov.

The solid white building right on the road gives little indication of the pleasures within. The decor has been kept deliberately simple - white cloths, tiled floors, cane chairs, but the warmth is there, both in the comforting log fire (and Le Dauphin is at its best when it's a bit chilly outside) and in the welcome. Chef-patron Régis Lecomte has not allowed a royal visit (Her Britannic Majesty no less) to put him above welcoming his customers and to making a further round after they have finished their meal to check that all was comme il faut (and to collect their justified congratulations).

There is a photo of the Queen and a framed letter from Buck House saying how much she enjoyed her visit in 1987. All credit to whoever arranged the stop for having chosen exactly what I imagine was required - a typically Norman restaurant. I asked Régis why he thought he had been selected. 'Because I speak English I suppose', he disclaimed modestly.

Gratifyingly the prices have remained modest too. His 31e menu (not Sat.) is a snip for cooking of the very highest quality, well meriting the Michelin star. It featured one of the house specialities, a barbecue d'huîtres spéciales d'Isigny aux lardons, which I had to try. Basically grilled oysters, but given exactly the right timing, flavoured with plenty of garlic but always retaining the oysters' delicacy, set in a thin bouillon full of savours. I stayed with the fish for the next course, a paré de morue roti because cod has become my favourite fish since we have learned to cook it properly, and roast is a good way to do it, on a bed of spicy green lentils. Immaculate cheese board, then the tarte aux pommes by which all other tartes aux pommes should be judged - crispest pastry, melting apples, flavoured with lemon and served with a cinnamon ice cream. Perfection and worthy of two stars.

Menus at 31€, 35€ except Sat p.m.

LE BREUIL-EN-BASSIN 14330 Calvados

10 km SW of Bayeux on the D5

Le Château de Goville 🛏 ⊠ L

   Rte de Bayeux
   tel: 02.31.22.19.28
   fax: 02.31.22.68,74
   closed: Tues and Wed in winter (except by prior arrangement)

The château was one of my early favourites, when Jean-Jacques Vallée first converted his family home into a b.&b. He had always been in the habit of escaping from his busy career as a couturier on the Faubourg St. Honoré to relax in this lovely stone house in the peace of the Bessin countryside, but gradually came to realise its potential as a guesthouse. Its character was more chambre d'hôte than hotel, so reluctantly it had to be omitted from the guide. Now that he boasts no less than twelve bedrooms, it can legitimately feature here again - which is very good news because it is full of character and a very beautiful place to stay.

You either hate or love the daring decorative schemes. On my last visit my bedroom had royal blue panelling, curtains and drapes in black and rose voile, blue Bristol glass, black lacquered furniture, and I loved it. Even the conservative will appreciate the family-heirloom furniture, and enjoy the impressive style and Jean-Jacques' welcome.

The reaction to the over-the-top, defiantly different, Calvados possibility, so convenient for the delights of Bayeux, will, I suspect, be mixed. Not for the cautious or hide-bound, something special for the adventurous,

Rooms, obviously all different, cost from 88-120€. Menus (about which I would like some first-hand reports) cost from 24€ and are served in what used to be Jean-Jacques' antique shop next door.

BRÉVILLE SUR MER 50290, Manche

Map 5A
3 km N of Granville

The beach here is a joggers' paradise - windswept dunes as far as the eye can see; there's a golf course too, with good sea views. But personally I would give it a miss and head straight for Granville. As the hotel scene there is a bit bleak, I was forced to look around the neighbourhood and found one possibility here on the main Coutances road.

La Beaumonderie ⊨ ⊠ M-L
20 rte. de Coutances
tel: (0)233.50.36.36
fax: (0)233.50.36.45
closed: 15 days in Jan.

Newly opened as a hotel in 1995, this large Edwardian villa, freshly painted, is now looking very smart. As well it should - this is definitely the most up-market hotel in the area. Rooms are lovely, all twelve are different but tastefully furnished with luxury bathrooms. Everyone wants those with a sea view of course and they will set you back up to 141€, but there are cheaper ones (from 51-67€) at the front of the house, which is well removed from the road, behind a soothing garden.

There are two inestimable and rare assets here - a large heated covered swimming pool in the grounds, and a bar - Le Blues, described as the place to 'enjoy rare whiskies or home made cocktails round the fireplace at the English pub. Enjoy a wonderful plush atmosphere'. Well it's not that plush. The Orangerie restaurant I have not tried, but it has a lovely view towards the sea, and is given lots of character by an umbrella-like roof and a big open fireplace. Menus start at 25€. Demi pension is 28€ on top of the room price. More reports obviously needed, but this certainly fins the gap for a peaceful luxury hotel in this area.

BRIONNE 27800, Eure

Map 4F
28 km S of Pont Audemer, 76 km E of Le Havre
Market: Thurs.

Following the D39 along the left bank of the river Ride is a delightful way to approach the town, whose tourist attractions comprise a park on the river bank and the ruins of an 11th century keep, from which the hotel takes its name.

Auberge du Vieux Donjon 🛏 S ⊠ M

pl. Frémont-des-Essarts
tel: (0)232.44.80.62
fax (0)232.45.83.23
closed: Mon.; 15/10-10/11

Half-timbered, lots of flowers, pretty china, old beams, red ceiling in between, pleasant owners, inexpensive.

Serge Chauvigny's cooking continues to please most customers, though his prices have gone up alarmingly since I first wrote about him, leading to higher expectations and recently there have been mixed reactions. One reader rued the tinned veg (quite right too) and described the food as 'basic', the service as amateur, so the star will have to be suspended.

There are eight simple but comfortable rooms. Insist on one overlooking the courtyard because the ones in the front can be very noisy. The courtyard is a big attraction - most pleasant to sit here for breakfast, and dinner, or just to relax among the foliage after a hard day on the tourist belt.

'Every bit as good as your recommendation. We can recommend the plateau des fruits de mer on the à la carte menu at 35e for two people; the set menu at 26e is also very good. Our only criticism is that the breakfast was very frugal - one baguette each with packaged butter and jam. Otherwise your star classification very well justified.'
Michael Stubbs

Rooms are 43€, menus from 12.8€ (lunch); otherwise from 19€.

BRIOUZE 61220, Orne

Map 5D
17 km SE of Flers
Market: Mon.

A pleasant quiet little town with sloping market square.

Hotel Sophie 🛏 ☒ S
pl. Albert 1er.
tel: (0)233.62.82.82
fax: (0)233.64.97.01
closed: Fri. p.m.; 15/8-3/9

The kind of modest, good-value little hotel that is fast disappearin from France, partly because of high taxation and party because the children are not interested in the commitment involved in running a family hotel.

Here the patrons are aptly named M. and Mme Excellent. Didier is chef and cooks old-fashioned dishes like gigot, rosbeef, and côte de boeuf grillée. But, surprisingly away from the sea, the speciality at Sophie's is fresh fish. When there is an arrivée (delivery), it appears on all the menus from 11.2€ to 30€. For us it happened to be oysters and we weren't complaining.

Local popularity is a good indication of the value on offer here in the small dining room, red check cloths, lovely smells, and the bar to retreat to later.

The nine rooms are small and simple, with showers, perhaps not quite such good value at 40€, but the food is awaiting more reports for an star.

CAEN 14000, Calvados

Map 4D
107 km W of Le Havre. 119 km SE of Cherbourg
Market: every day from Tues. to Sun. but Sun. is the big day

Caen, capital of Lower Normandy, is a city of contrasts - the dismal post-war re-building and the magnificent monuments that survived, the grid of new streets and the winding alleys of the old, the antiquity of the abbeys and the castle and the youthful vivacity of the university in the city's heart.

Sad though it is to ponder that we shall never enjoy again the three-quarters of the buildings that crumbled in the wartime devastation, there remains enough of the old city to make a visit profitable. My advice would be to ignore the area south of the rue St. Pierre (apart from the excellent shops and restaurants), and to concentrate on two particularly attractive localities, never forgetting of course the abbeys and the castle, which is the focal point of the whole city. Just below it, in the paved Vaugueux area, the character is more fifteenth than twentieth century. The narrow cobbled streets and crazily-angled gabled houses have been carefully restored and a stroll around the antique shops and a coffee at a pavement cafe by the fountain makes a pleasant diversion.

Less touristy, less self-conscious, perhaps more typical of the 11th century Caen that has been lost, is the area to the north of the rue St. Pierre, where dignified patricians' houses, mediaeval beams and plaster, winding alleyways and a great leafy square, the Place St. Sauveur, deserve every visitor's attention. Turn up the rue Froide and wander at will, looking up as well as around. Interesting boutiques are springing up in these pedestrianised lanes, contrasting with the department and chain stores in the modern section, and some of the most rewarding restaurants have realised the appeal of the old buildings.

CAEN

Caen - Abbaye aux Hommes

The rue St. Pierre itself has been vastly improved by pedestrianisation and it is now a calm stroll, window-shopping, most of the way towards the Hôtel de Ville and one of Caen's great monuments, the Abbaye aux Hommes.

For all its reincarnations since the 11C, Caen is still first and foremost William's town. References to the great Duke of Normandy and his Queen, Matilda, crop up repeatedly in the names of shops, streets and of course in the two great abbey churches. The Abbaye aux Hommes was William's outward sign of repentance for the sin he committed in marrying a blood relation, against the wishes of the Pope. In fact his cousin Matilda had shown some reluctance to the idea of marrying a bastard, causing William to drag her by her hair around her chamber until she was convinced. Convincing the Pope he left to his Secretary, Lanfranc (see Bec-Helouin), who talked the pontiff into rescinding his prohibition of the match. It was a nice touch for the happy pair to build their spiritual memorials at opposite limits of the city, with the great fortified castle in the centre protecting them from their worldly enemies.

The monastery buildings, rebuilt in the 18C and now used as the Town Hall, protected the citizens of Caen during the bombardment of 1944; many thousands of them took refuge inside, and the complex was miraculously saved (as indeed was Matilda's abbey, the Abbaye aux Dames, though somewhat battered).

Only a slab before the high altar now marks the spot where William was buried. The tomb was ravaged once by the Huguenots in the 16C and again during the Revolution when his remains were thrown into the river. The dedication leaves no doubts about the priorities: 'Duke of Normandy, King of England'.

The building of his abbey began in 1077, romanesque, and was finished two centuries later, gothic, a striking contrast of styles within and without. Recently cleaned, the amber Caen stone is illuminated by light flooding through the three layers of windows, framed in graceful arches.

Matilda's abbey is less colourful, but impressive, as is her mausoleum inside.

Other points of interest are the capitals in the choir and the 11C crypt and the monastery, again rebuilt in the 18C; look out for the remarkable fountains in the lavatorium, the cloisters and the double staircase.

Just outside Caen, well marked from all directions, is the Mémoriale, the museum for peace. If that sounds less than rivetting, especially for those not excited about the war, be prepared to be enlightened, inspired and very moved. The latest technology is used to bring the events to life, wraparound screens show contemporary films taken by both sides, skilfully representing both points of view, with powerful sound effects. Some of the photographs are harrowing, particularly those of the youthful Norman freedom fighters about to be hanged for their resistance. Allow more time that you could imagine necessary. Open every day from 09:00 to 19:00. and until 21:00 in July and August

The best tip I can pass on concerning Caen is not to miss the market that fills the Place Courtonne and spills over on to the neighbouring quays. Sunday can be a difficult day to fill in northern France, especially when the sun is not shining, and a wander around the eclectic stalls that put on show so temptingly their offerings, literally from chalk to cheese, is a clever way to fill an hour or so. Cafés and bars in this area stay open to cater for market-day appetites.

Hotels: Oh dear. Keen though I am to suggest lodgings fit for this interesting city, which would make such a good base for a winter breakaway, I must admit the choice is slender. So slender that I am driven to include a chain hotel, since most of the rest are modern and characterless too. At least the Mercure has views over the yacht basin:

Otherwise

Hotel Mercure ⇥ ☒ M
r. de Courtonne
tel: (0)231.47.24.24
fax: (0)231.47.43.88

Big rooms, well equipped, practical, central. 110 rooms from 83€, menu 19.2€, with breakfast at 9.6€.

Holiday Inn - City Centre ⇥ ☒ M
pl. Foch
(0)231.27.57.57
fax: (0)231.27.57.58 R
closed: 15/7-15/8

This is the old Hotel Malherbe re-furbished. Once I had got over the appalling name I quite liked it and would now rank it as first choice in the city. Most of the rooms have pleasant aspects over the green expanse of the Hippodrome, perhaps ten minutes walk from the centre. Everything has been smartened up and the rooms are spacious and gracious. There is a restaurant, Le Rabelais, downstairs, where the food is not at all bad, and a New Orleans style piano bar.
92 rooms from 77-111€.

In vain did I search for a smaller, cheaper hotel to recommend. To re-cap the last edition's suggestions, La Moderne, 116 bd. Mar. Leclerc (0)231.86.04.23, , which had gone from top of my list to bottom, has now been refurbished and its central position scores highly, but the English theme is not for me. (40 rooms from 61-104€.) The Quatrans, 17 r. Gemare (0)231.86.25.57, scored as many thumbs down as thumbs up; although the rooms are pleasant, the patronne was not (36 rooms from 45€.)
Restaurants: Here the scene is brighter, with plenty of choice in all categories, including two-star Michelin restuarants.

☆ **La Bourride** ☒ **L**
15 r. du Vaugueux
tel: (0)231.93.50.76
closed: Sun.; Mon.; 20/8-4/9

I have followed Michel Bruneau's career with interest and delight, since, fresh from Le Manoir d'Hastings, he set up here in the picturesque Vaugueux area, setting unparalleled standards of excellence among the bars and fast-food outlets. The first macaron followed swiftly and now the second ensures that his tables are always full. So if you are planning a treat, make sure you book ahead. I can hardly fault the experience. I like the inside of the galleried restaurant as much as I like the venerable exterior, I like the intimacy of its scale - so tiny that you feel privileged (but never cramped); I like not being required to add a drink at the bar on to the bill - no pursed lips if you prefer to go straight to your table, I like the raised fire on cold winter nights and the gentle classical music that soothes rather than blasts. I like the amuse-gueules, a taste of the joys to come rather than a mass production job. And of course I like, very much indeed, the food.
Michel never loses sight of his Norman origins and there are

always plenty of regional delicacies on the menu. But with the touch of genius that makes you place your trust in the man, even if he offers you sausages. Which he does - charlotte d'andouille is one of his favourite specialities, and is guaranteed to convert even the most hardened sausage-phobe. If you wish to sample the definitive tripes à la mode de Caen, poule vallée d'Auge, or tarte aux pommes this is the time to order them. The only snag is that any subsequent encounters are bound to disappoint.

Quality like this does not come cheap. Unless of course you take in the mid-week (or Sat. lunch) menu, which is a true bargain. Otherwise it's 40 or a dizzying 98€. You could always order just one dish from the carte, if you have that kind of restraint, but at any level expect the wine to match the food in cost and standard.

Starred for some of the best cooking in Normandy.

☆ Le Carlotta ⊠ M
16 quai Vendeuvre
tel: (0)231.86.68.99
closed: Sun; 15 days in Aug.

Restaurants gastronomiques are all very well but my favourite kind of restaurant is the brasserie. I love them because they are so very French, so very flexible, so very full of character. You eat or drink what you want, when you want, without any kind of pretension or fuss. Sadly, like many other good things that one took for granted in France, the good ones are becoming rare. Brasserie is becoming synonymous with fast food outlet and a smoky, noisy den serving cheap microwaved food is not at all what I have in mind. Here in Caen is a gem, a paragon in the species. Carlotta in fact is so excellent that it breaks the usual brasserie rule that you don't have to book. Here, especially at lunchtime when the local businessmen settle down at their favourite tables, you would be asking for disappointment in assuming you could sit down immediately. But whether you book or whether you wait, it will be well worthwhile.

This is the very essence of brasserie-dom. Here are the leather banquettes, the art deco lights and murals, white napery, waiters in black suits and starched aprons, some even sporting moustaches.

The dishes are equally traditional - roast duck, beef tartare, tête de veau - plus wonderfully fresh fish, all served in portions to satisfy pre-Weightwatcher appetites. Mine could not handle the menus, admirable though they were: 15€ bought six oysters, roast veal and pâtisserie maison, or the Menu Affaires offers just two courses with wine for 19.2€. The hommes d'affaires looked very happy with their filet de boeuf and pâtisserie, washed down with honest red. No, I settled for a simple sole, which proved to be simply the best. Cooked in butter and served with potatoes mashed with garlic, parsley and lemon and a tomato stuffed with ratatouille for a very reasonable 13.6€. Save room if you can for the desserts and particularly the assiette gourmandes, a platter of nine different puds like profiteroles, pistachio sorbet, nougat glacé with cherry sauce, tarte Tatin. At 6€ too good a bargain to pass by.

Starred for lively, buzzy atmosphere, excellent honest cooking.

Le Boeuf Ferré ☒ M-S

10 r. des Croisiers
tel: (0)231.85.3fi.40
closed: Sat. lunch; Sun.

In one of the oldest, most attractive streets in Caen. To find it, turn up the rue Froide and take a right. The original Boeuf Ferré was so successful that it overflowed into a satellite next door. Same menu, different door, similar decoys, with raftered ceilings and stone walls. Both have a youthful, animated atmosphere (sometimes, with regrettable piped pop) and are particularly popular with local office workers at lunchtime. It is easy to see why the place is so well patronised. The 15.7€ menu offers excellent value - like a terrine of sea trout with chive cream sauce, then fresh salmon with sorrel, topped up with wickedly calorific profiteroles. The 19.2€has more choice and includes a complimentary Kir.

Le Pressoir ☒ M

3 ave. H. Chéron
tel: (0)231.73.3271
closed: Sun. p.m.; Mon.; Sat. lunch; 28/7-22/8

This attractive little restaurant near the hippodrome has gone from strength to strength since I first wrote about it and classed it as (S). It now has an entry in Michelin and the cheapest menu price has doubled at 20€. This is still good value, however, and the cooking continues to be gratifyingly unpretentious, with items like cassoulette of mussels, grilled beef, sole meunière. It's a charming little restaurant with an ancient cider press justifying its name, old copper utensils and authentically worm-eaten furniture.

Le Dauphin ☒ M

29 r. Gémare
tel: (0)231.86.22.26
fax: (0)231.86.35.14
restaurant closed: Sat. Sun. lunch
hotel closed: 16/7-5/8

The Dauphin does have rooms and it would be so helpful if I could recommend a central bed with a restaurant attached, but in this case the thumbs down have all been for the hotel part of the deal. Readers have agreed with my impression that they are too expensive for what they offer, somewhat dark and sometimes noisy. So we'll forget that bit and concentrate on the restaurant.

Robert Chabredier never forgets his Norman heritage. That said, his cooking is never dull and predictable. He uses seafood to stuff ravioli, his salt marsh lamb is meltingly tender and he sparks up the traditional apple tart with rhubarb. Go for the 15.5€ menu (not weekends) and you will be delighted. The building was once an old priory in the oldest part of Caen, close to William's castle. In its heavily restored reincarnation the rustic dining room has been retained and the atmosphere there is warm and friendly.

Le Gastronome ☒ S-M

43 r. St. Sauveur
tel: (0)231.86.57.75
closed: Sun; Mon.

A little restaurant in the road bordering the Place St. Sauveur. Excellent value on the 16€. menu.

Le Panier à Salades (R)S-M

24 r. Pierre Girard (0)231.34.22.22
closed: Sat. lunch; Sun.

I am always delighted to find a good salad restaurant in France, and this one is good enough to tempt the firmest carnivores. They need not be deprived of their meat because it comes in various guises here along with the greenery. There is a vast range of salads that should please every fancy, and better-than-average desserts, all served in a pleasant atmosphere in an art deco decor. Up to you how much you spend - it could be as little as 6.4€ or as much as a full menu elsewhere.

L'Assiette ⊠ S
2 pl. Fontelle
tel: (0)231.85.21.89
closed: Sun.

A cheap and very cheerful restaurant between the Hotel de Ville and the Palais de Justice, handy after a visit to the Abbaye aux Hommes. I like the fact that they change the menus every day selon le marché. There is a menu Terre and a menu Mer, starting at 13€. Good value and well recommended locally.

A late recommendation which I have not yet checked out but which sounds like the answer to many a prayer is a little hotel in the old quarter, the Hotel Cordeliers, 4 r. des Cordeliers (0)231.86.37.15. 15 rooms a mere 21-56€. Reports particularly welcome.

Otherwise

CAMBREMER 14340 Calvados

In the heart of the Pays D'Auge on the Route du Cidre.

Château Les Bruyères (HR)L
Route du Cadran
tel: 02.31.32.22.45
fax: 02.31,32,22.58
restaurant: open 14-Jul to 31-Aug; Sat lunch, Sun lunch from 7-Apr to 1 Jul and from Sept-Dec
hotel: closed from 31-Dec to 7-Apr. (I think I've got it right, but it's so complicated, best to check before embarking)

An imposing 19th century residence, set in an extensive 'parc', with thirteen rooms of differing standards, from 72-159€.

CANON 14270, Calvados

Map 4E
20 km SE of Caen on the D47. 6 km S of Méry Corbon off the N13

Deep in the Calvados countryside on the old coach route from Lisieux to Falaise, the château and, particularly, the gardens of Canon make a delightful diversion from the main tourist attractions of the region. Essential, though, to pick a fine day, when a stroll around the magnificent lakes, following the many streams and springs and admiring the rose gardens, set out in the 'English' style, can be best appreciated.

Around the 18C château (not open to the public) are the Chartreuses, a succession of flower gardens surrounded by ancient walls, on which apricots, figs and peaches flourish. Wander deep into the woods following the streams (bluebell time especially) and you will stumble upon neo-classical ruins, a Chinese kiosk and a temple.

The house and gardens were designed by an 18C lawyer who instigated the feast of the Bonnes Gens. Once a year the villagers chose from among their numbers a Bonne Mère, a Bon Vieillard (Good Old Man)and a Bon Chef de Famille and rewarded their virtues by a feast in their honour. Bonnes Gens is still the alternative name for Canon.

Open weekends and holidays from Easter to end of June from 14:00-19:00 and every afternoon, except Tues. from 1/8-30/9.

CAP LÉVI 50840 Fermanville, Manche

Map 2B
15 km E of Cherbourg

The D116 out of Cherbourg follows the coast closely until it reaches Fermanville where it carries straight on and ignores the pimple on the map that is Cap Lévi, the coast's northernmost extremity. That is the good news because very few cars bother to deviate. Unless of course their drivers already know about the wonderful coastal walks along the old coastguards' routes, or the uncrowded beaches to lie on, or the rocks to scramble over when the tide recedes, or the feeling of being almost out at sea among the passing cargo boats and the lighthouse's warning flash. There is a tiny harbour here but not much else, except the next entry.

La Lorette (HR)S
tel: (0)233.44.49.49
fax: (0)233.44.16.15

Named after the parish of Notre Dame de Lorette in Paris, which founded a children's summer camp here and built a chapel in pink granite. Before that the house was owned by a sea-captain; in the days when Cherbourg was an important port for ocean liners there must have been plenty of interest for him to train his telescope upon.

Nowadays the reincarnation is that of a six-bedroomed hotel, family-run, warm and friendly. They welcome all kinds – rambler, cyclists, families, weekenders, with equal enthusiasm. The dining room is particularly attractive, with a varnished boat acting as bar. Menus with lots of local seafood are 14.4€ or 22€, but you could settle for a crêpe or galette with no eyebrows raised.

Breakfast can be taken in bed, looking out onto the sea, or in the garden, with plenty of space for childish exuberance.

Rooms cost 32€ or 35€, all with showers and lavs.

'Pleasant reception, a good place for families, though the soundproofing not perfect. Owner lives in adjoining house with his own family. Simply-cooked seafood dishes very good.' Lesley Goodden.

CARENTAN 50500, Manche

Map 2B
50 km SE of Cherbourg; 69 km NW of Caen
Market: Mon.

The centre of the Manche dairy farming industry, a town of many squares too full of cars, a nice old church and some shady arcades, but nothing in the way of lively bar or brasserie.

An unsuspected whole new world is to be found if you follow the signs to Port de Plaisance. There, dominating the flat marshy landscape of the estuary of the river Douves, rises a forest of masts. The marina here shelters hundreds of boats during the winter. Take the opportunity of a gulp of ozone by taking a walk along the banks of the canal.

Auberge Normande ⊠ M

bld. Verdun
tel: (0)233.42.28.28
closed: Sun. p.m.; Mon.

The tendency was to shy away from the Auberge Normande when its last patron, the darling of local gastronomes, decamped for Honfleur, but now things have settled down under the new owners, the very rustic, very Normande inn has been smartened up and the bonus is that the cooking, if not still Michelin star-worthy, is very good.

The 21€ menu yielded oysters with scrambled eggs, gigot of salt marsh lamb, cheeses and dessert, with a trou Normand thrown in halfway through. There is a cheaper 15.8€ version. Worth a new look.

CARTERET 50270 Barneville-Carteret, Manche

Map 3A
37 km SW of Cherbourg
Market: Sat

I never thought Carteret could ever change. Its bucket 'n' spade, sun 'n fun, easy-going, family-friendly image seemed timeless and immutable. You don't go to Carteret for the latest trends, you go because you fancy an unsophisticated undemanding holiday, gilded with a touch of nostalgia for your own youth spent in similar surroundings.

The surroundings here are still lovely. The town is built on an estuary whose seaward curves beg for paint-brush or camera. The sandy beach is wide and wonderful especially at low water, with rocks and rivulets to add interest. Sheltering under the cliffs is a row of wooden beach huts where you might expect to see Mum and Dad sitting in deck chairs watching their offspring making sand castles, skirts tucked in knickers, floppy white beach-hats.

So far so little change; the new bit is at the other end of the town, where a new marina has been built and a promenade landscaped.

There are new shops, catering mostly for tourists, and the whole place seems to have extricated itself from its time-warp, which may or may not be a good thing. I still like it very much.

One change that is very good news is the arrival of a new hotel:

Hotel des Ormes
Carteret

☆ **Hotel des Ormes** 🛏 M
quai Barbey d'Aurevilly
tel: (0)233.52.23.50
fax: (0)233.52.91.65

This old house set back from the first new road by the marina had only been open seven months when I called, but already it was full, and when I had had a look round I could see why. The owner has cleverly decorated the ten comfortable rooms in light, bright and cheerful fabrics and paint, and they all have pleasant aspects over either the sea or the flowery garden at the rear. There is no restaurant, but the breakfast room and salon are also agreeable places to sit, should the weather rule out the peaceful garden. All the rooms have luxurious tiled bathrooms, with bath or shower, and cost from 79€ for a double with one bed to 99€ for a three-bedded room. Starred for the best accommodation in an attractive location.

Carteret

☆ The Marine ⊨ M ⊠ L
r. de Paris
tel: (0)233.53.83.31
fax: (0)233.53.39.60 R
closed: Mon lunch; Thurs lunch; 12/11-1/3

It has been many moons since the Marine was a simple family hotel, and the fifth generation of Cesnes are now in charge. Laurent was not content to take over in the kitchen without some impressive work experience in top kitchens elsewhere - Taillevent to name but one - and a Michelin star was his due reward. The hotel is so near the water that he could stick out a fishing-line from the terrace to provide the ingredients for the next meal.

Fish figures strongly on his menus, in guises to suit both new customers lured by the macaron and old faithfuls who might be disappointed to find too many changes. Plaice arrives with an original sauce derived from another Norman staple - Camembert -but langoustines are simply roasted to retain their natural flavour and juices. He's good at tripe too. For this standard of cooking the 25€ menu (not Sat p.m. nor Sun. lunch) is a tremendous bargain; otherwise the choices start at 31€. Small wonder that the restaurant is always full.

The 28 rooms likewise - you'll have to be quick off the mark to get one of the best views, overlooking the estuary. None of them is particularly large nor grand, either in the main hotel or in the annexe across the road, but they are comfortable enough, at 74-101€ (you pay for that view) and the breakfasts are good.

I must be fair to one discriminating reader and mention that she found the food disappointing and the service rushed, but the Marine has always been a lovely place to stay, with a drink on the west-facing terrace overlooking the estuary as the sun goes down guaranteed to be a holiday highspot. Now with the exceptional cooking of Laurent as a bonus, it is more desirable than ever. The star stays.

l'Hermitage 🛏 ⊠ M

Promenade de l'Abbé Lebouteiller.
tel: (0)233.04.96.29 / (0)233 04.46.39
fax: (0)233.04.78.87
closed: Sun; 1511-15/12; 3 weeks Jan.

The terrace of this long-established fish restaurant overlooking the water has been admirably smartened up recently, with tubs of manicured bay and window boxes, and immaculately laid tables, served by smart waiters. A game of musical chairs has to be endured to get a table here on a fine summer day, but it will be worth it. Inside is nowhere near so special - modern pine decor and not a lot of atmosphere in the large dining room. But the food in both sections is to be commended, especially the fresh and lavish plâteaux de fruits de mer, which have greatly pleased readers. Menus from 15€ but a single dish of beautiful fish for the same price is probably a better bet.

The really exciting news concerns the rooms that have been built above the restaurant You have to climb the hill behind to reach them, and will be rewarded by a superb view from their terraces. They vary in size and price, but all are ultra-modern, and exceptionally well equipped, with kitchenettes apiece (which should keep the cost down somewhat, although it is certainly not excessive at 40-80€).

'We stayed in a holiday flat behind the restaurant. These are beautifully equipped, bright, comfortable, spacious, wonderful view and would be ideal for a short, self-catering family holiday. The breakfast was walked up the hill on a tray piping hot. Excellent bathroom, bath, hot water, etc. Very quiet. Dinner superb in parts. Huge spider crabs, crunchy fresh and of unparalleled deliciousness and vast assiettes de mer. Vegetables awful, soggy chips, overcooked carrots, but good steak. Choose the fish dishes which are after all their speciality.' Tim and Alice Renton.

CAUDEBEC-EN-CAUX 76490, Seine-Mar

Map 2F
51 km E of Le Havre, 36 km W of Rouen
Market: Sat.

Things are looking brighter in Caudebec these days. Nothing can disguise the hideous re-building that took the place of the picturesque town that bordered the Seine pre-war, but pedestrianisation, flowers and fountains certainly help. It's looking less sad and does have some obvious advantages: the site of course, overlooking the river, with pleasant gardens in which to sit and picnic, the wonderful 15C Flamboyant church, which Henri IV once described as `the most beautiful chapel in the kingdom', and which survived the fire that devastated most of the town in 1940, and the Saturday market, which fills the Place du Marché with colour, smells and animation. And that's about it There are two hotels in prime positions overlooking the river, which have been here for donkeys' years and are still very popular with the Brits. They are the Normandie - (0)235.96.24.11, rooms, from 46-49€, menus from 15.5€ (not weekends) and the Normotel La Marine, (0)235.96.20.11, rooms from 40-67€ meals from 15.7€. They are both dean and efficient, but a bit impersonal for my taste, and often taken over by groups.

Otherwise

Le Cheval Blanc, ⇆ ☒ S
4. Pl. René Coty.
tel: 02.35.96.21.66
closed: four weeks Jan, Feb.

A simple traditional hotel with 16 good rooms from 32-56€, and classic French cooking in the restaurant on menus from 13.6€.

CÉAUX 50220, Manche

Map 6B
4 km W of Pontaubault by D43

By making a tiny diversion like this from the main road it is often possible to find an unspoiled inexpensive alternative to the parasite hotels and restaurants that prey on tired and hungry tourists in honey pots like Mont St. Michel, just five minutes' drive away.

Au P'tit Quinquin 🛏 ⊠ S
Les Forges
tel: (0)233.70.97.20
closed: 5/1-15/2

There are rooms here but they are pretty basic and not particularly good value at 33€. That said, they do have all mod cons and there is private parking, But really it is the food that is the attraction. The cooking is imaginative and generous and the dining room is always full of French at weekends. Menus from 11.2€.

'We wanted to get off along the quiet D275, wanting to stay close to the Mount but away from the ghastly tourist development. It was lucky we did because we landed up in Céaux at Au P'tit Quinquin. What a discovery! The 12.8€ menus were superb in a restaurant which had a decor and service of an incredibly high standard.' Mike Souter.

CHAMPEAUX 50530, Manche

Map 5A
14 km S of Granville on the D911

'Le plus beau kilomètre de France' is what the sign says. Well that may be pushing it a bit but the coast road is certainly spectacular with its unique view of Mont St. Michel rising out of the watery mists. On the cliff edge is:

Au Marquis de Tombelaine ⊠ M
tel: (0)233.50.40.20
fax: (0)233.61.21.52
closed: Tues. p.m. and Wed. o.o.s. 3/1-31/1; 23/11-30/11

It seems too good to be true to find such an attractive restaurant - low beamed ceilings, flagstones, fresh flowers, romantic setting - that still bothers to give good service and value for money. Menus start at 16€ but I counsel going for the next one up to benefit from dishes like grilled langoustines. There are six bedrooms, but at the time of going to press they are still pretty basic and not particularly good value at 45€. Any news to the contrary would be welcome indeed.

'A very good restaurant. We had the 23€ menu and it took us fully one hour to get through the Assiette de Fruits de Mer, but what a delicious task it was. The waiters were most helpful in coping with our basic French.' Dennis Keen

CHERBOURG 50100, Manche

Map 2A
124 km NW of Caen
Market: Tues. and Thurs.

I'm not sure about Cherbourg these days. The recent changes do not strike me as being advantageous and the trend seems down market. I had high hopes last time I researched the town because of the promising redevelopments around the market and in the Place Général de Gaulle but these seem to have ground to a halt and I could find little new to enthuse about. The little bistros that were blossoming at that time have mostly closed, nearly all my favourite restaurants have moved elsewhere and there is a lacklustre feel to the place. In July the streets were oddly deserted, which I attributed to the Monday blues, (the town is particularly badly affected by the dreaded. 'Mon. p.m.'), except that it was little better on Tuesday. The restaurants that had opened their doors probably wished they hadn't - they were all nearly empty, only the sandwich and pizza bars were doing any trade. Some of the smarter shops have also closed and their replacements are tatty.

A tale of woe indeed, because this used to be one of my favourite ports. All is not lost though. I considered it a challenge and dug one or two gems from the dross.

Hotels: I suppose that Cherbourg is intrinsically a transit town, with most customers staying only for the odd night (can't say I blame 'em as it stands at present), so we are looking for efficiency rather than character here.

Le Louvre 🛏 M
28 r. de la Paix
tel: (0)233.53.02.28
fax: (0)233.53.43.88
closed: 24/12-2/1

As functional as can be but friendly with it. The 42 rooms are spacious and well equipped, and double-glazed against possible noise, but the road outside is semi-pedestrianised these days so a good night's sleep should be assured. Excellent value at 28-57€.

Hotel Mercure 🛏 M
Gare Maritime
tel: (0)233.44.01.11
fax: (0)233.44.51.00

Modern chain hotels are not my all-time favourites, but there's no denying in this case that the Mercure has the best site in town, that is quiet and functional, near the ferry terminal and I would probably rate it as best choice. Avert your eyes from the virulent orange of the bedroom decor and look out of the window at the sailing boats and the sea. 84 rooms cost from 68-79€.

Moderna 🛏 S
28 r. de la Marine
tel: (0)233.43.05.30
fax: (0)233.43.97.37

Just 25 rooms in this friendly hotel, centrally situated, at a very reasonable price of 27-48€. I cannot do better than quote from a recent experience:
'Brand-new bathrooms, excellent beds, linen, breakfasts, and cheerful, efficient English speaking service from the manager, all at British b. and b. prices. Three of us warmly recommend this excellent small hotel.' A. Barker.

La Régence 🛏 ☒ M
42 quai de Caligny
tel: (0)233.43.05.16
fax: (0)233.43.98.37
closed: 23/12-2/1

If you like to eat in your hotel, this recently facelifted Logis de France is probably the best bet. It backs on to a square with good parking and fronts on to the harbour. 17 rooms, recently re-furbed, have all mod cons and range from 45-67€. If you want a view of the port it will be 64€ upwards.The large restaurant is prominent on the main parade and well known for its seafood on menus from 15€.

'*Excellent Sunday lunch, well patronised by locals and tourists.*' John Stock.

Restaurants:

The obvious choice is the string along the quai de Caligny, and indeed you could do far worse than drop in at one of these for a platter of fruits de mer or a bowl of moules. I think I would probably go for the Café de Paris for old times' sake and it is looking quite smart at the moment, all nautically blue and white. My other recommendations, in the back streets, are all new or changed hands since the previous edition. I hope that their future is not so precarious as that of their predecessors.

☆ **Le Petit Marché ⊠ M**
   59 r. au Blé
   tel: (0)233.53.67.64
   fax: (0)233.94.41.43
   closed: Sat. lunch; Sun. (but I have also found it closed on Mon. if there
   is not sufficient trade)

That old Cherbourg character Jacky Pain, whose career I eagerly followed ever since I found him cooking divinely in a three-tabled café in a back street, right up to his Michelin star, is a great loss to the Cherbourg culinary scene (he has decamped to open up a restaurant in Nantes). This was the site of his late lamented 'Le Plouc' restaurant.

His departure was the bad news, the good is that Le Petit Marché is carrying on his good work; the new owners have still to establish a reputation and so are trying extra hard, and their prices are way below those that Le Plouc was able to command at the height of Jacky's success. The two pretty little beamed rooms in the quiet street behind the main market have not been greatly changed. There was a big fire burning in the rear, even in July (a cold and blustery one), in order to cook the charcoal grills which are a speciality. It might not be an ideal choice on a brilliant day when the dark and cosy atmosphere is not what one is looking for, but at any other time the warm and welcoming touch is delightful.

Cloths and napkins are wine coloured, curtains are red gingham, and the odds and ends are eclectic to say the least - antique typewriters and gramophone, old barrels, stuffed animals.

The food is excellent both for its value for money and content. On the 12.6€ menu you could choose home-made terrine and chicken in a cream and tarragon sauce, plus cheese and pud, or on the 19.2€ version perhaps frivolité de saumon fumé (smoked salmon in three guises), fillet of duck with port wine sauce, cheese and a panaché of five desserts. Grills are around 9.3€. In fact I wasn't very hungry on the last visit and could not have been better satisfied than with a dozen oysters for 10.4€ and a generous salad featuring warm wild mushrooms for 4.8€.

Starred for the most interesting food in town.

Le Faitout ☒ M
25 r. de la Tour Carrée
tel: (0)233.04.25.04
closed: Sun; Mon. lunch; Christmas

Another erstwhile Jacky Pain stronghold, in a quiet street near the market one-coloured paint, even tinier than Le Petit Marché, bistro-style, cuisine familiale. That is to say French family style - no burgers n' chips here. A friendly stop with interesting cooking on the 16.5€ menu, or a bargain plat du jour at 8.5€.

CLÉCY 14570, Calvados

Map 5D
37 km S of Caen

Clécy claims to be the 'Capital of the Suisse Normande', and certainly many of that lovely region's activities centre around the village. The whole area is very well organised for tourists; paths and excursions are well advertised and brochures are readily available from shops, tourist offices and cafés. The two most popular outings are south to la Faverie Cross and to le Pain de Sucre, both of which offer spectacular views of the rocks, river and viaduct. Rock-climbing, hiking, canoeing, fishing, bicycling, riding

Moulin du Vey

- if it makes you tired to think of them the day's activity need be no more taxing than to follow the arrows by car. An impressive example is the road to la Houle Rock overlooking the Rouvre gorge. Truth to tell the association with Switzerland is stretching it a bit but certainly it's a particularly attractive area of Normandy with a distinctive landscape of green hills and greener valleys. The river Orne winds peacefully through rich pastureland or dramatically cuts into the rocky escarpment of the Armoricain massif.

1 km east of Clécy on the D1 33a, at Le Vey, an imposing old bridge crosses the wide fast-flowing river and a scattering of restaurants and cafes on the banks makes the most of the setting. Their balconies overhang the river and the inactive can sit and sup watching the fit get fitter in their pedalos or canoes.

Le Moulin du Vey ⊯ ⊠ M

tel: (0)231.69.71.08
fax: (0)231.69.14.14
closed. Dec.; Jan.

I feel that overworked word 'idyllic' coming on again. Here is the hotel with the most perfect setting. Willows droop into diamanté ripples, water lilies beg to be immortalised by Monet, the river bends obligingly to frame the mellow old bridge and the hotel's flower-filled terrace is the perfect vantage point from which to appreciate the chocolate box scene. If you feel like packing a long muslin dress, straw hat and parasol, this is the place to wear them.

The 25 rooms are in the creeper-covered mill or in one of the annexes, the Manoir du Placy nearby and the Relais de Surosne, 2 km away. Attractive these may be but fight for a room in the Moulin - the setting is what you come here for.

The restaurant is in an adjacent building, and usually full at the weekends, so they don't have to try too hard. Menus from 22€, but you would have to go to 35€ for anything interesting. Dover sole, which is my yardstick is a hefty 21€. The rooms on the other hand are very pleasant (but becoming a bit expensive at 85€). I would take a picnic and eat it by the viaduct or slum it a bit in the cafe La Guinguette à Tartine on the other bank. Or you could try the Chalet de Cantepie in the village, which worked well for me but not always for readers.

COLLEVILLE MONTGOMERY 14880, Calvados

Map 3D
5 km W of Ouistreham by the D45A

La Ferme St Hubert ⊠ M
   3 r. de la Mer
   tel: (0)231. 96.35. 41
   closed: Sun. p. m.; Mon. o.o.s. 24/12-16/1

Don't go expecting a farm. Any rustic origins have long since been forgotten. Nowadays it's a modern chalet-like building, set in the middle of nowhere.

Inside is more rustique with plenty of beams and an open fire to help make the atmosphere warm and cosy. Cooking is more sophisticated than you might expect and the restaurant attracts local businessmen and ferry passengers who want to remember their last meal in France as something special but do not fancy the stress of parking in Caen.

Menus from 14.4€ (not weekends) then 23€.

COMMES 14520, Manche

Map C3
2 km SE of Port en Bessin by D514

La Chenevière ⇔ ⊠ L
   tel: (0)231.51.25.25
   fax: (0)231.21.47.98
   closed: Jan

A truly lovely dignified 19C manor house set amongst ancient trees in a spacious parc. Everything about it is elegant and pleasing to the eye - the pastel colours of the bedrooms, the luxurious bathrooms and the light and airy dining room. The only snag is that it has now become well-known and popular with incentive groups and business meetings and the prices will put it in the 'special-occasion' bracket for most of us.

17 rooms from 112-160€, two apartments 144 or 240€.
Menus from 21€ (lunch) then 29-56€.

CONDÉ-SUR-NOIREAU 14110, Calvados

Map 5D
13 km N of Flers
Market: Thurs.

Not a very interesting town, almost completely post-war.

Le Cerf ⊠ M
18 r. de Chêne
tel: (0)231.69.40.55
closed: Sun. p.m.; Mon.; 1 week in Nov. and 3 weeks in Feb.

Tucked away in an unpromising side street, but signed from the main road, flush on the narrow pavement, difficult parking.

That's the bad news, the rest is all very good indeed. Just seven tables were squeezed into the front room on the out-of-season day of our visit. There is another larger, smarter dining room at the rear, but we were very happy where we were, looked after so cheerfully by nice Madame Malgrey. With great daring I had poked my head round the door, announced that we were très pressés (what's new?), and looking for a quick light lunch. And this was the sacred Sunday mid-day! No problem said Madame and no problem it was, even when we ordered just a glass of wine each to go with our snack. Other diners were tucking into the admirable four course 14.4€ Logis de France menu - a duo of homemade terrines, fillet of salmon with cucumber sauce, cheeses and crème brûlée. During the week the price reduces to 10.7€ at lunchtime, with the admirable formula of an entrée du jour, a plat du jour and cheese/pud, but Patrice Malgrey can rise to the heights of homemade foie gras, sautéed lobster and a fondant cappuccino for those prepared to pay 37€ on the special menu for the 10th anniversary of Le Cerf.

Us? I had just the terrines - wonderfully juicy and flavoursome, one boar, one chicken liver-based, while Husband enjoyed panfried fillets of hake.

There are nine rooms here, which I hadn't the heart to ask to see at this busy, under-staffed time, but if they are as clean and wholesome as the rest of Le Cerf, with kind Madame Malgrey officiating, they must be very good news. 32€ or 38€.

*Le moulin de Connelles
Connelles*

CONNELLES 27430, Eure

Map 3G
13 km W of Les Andelys, 37 km SE of Rouen

To follow the D313, which hugs the river from Les Andelys, is a charming way to see the Seine at its most beguiling. As far as Muids the chalk cliffs provide a charming background to the river's contortions. The road then turns inland but the scenery through the valley is no less pretty, peaceful and unspoiled. Ideal picnicking territory.

☆ **Moulin de Connelles** ⇔ ☒ L
   tel: (0)232.59.53.33
   fax: (0)232.59.21.83
   closed: Tues Wed and Thurs luchtimes; Jan.

Auberge du Vieux Logis

When I am very rich, or on my second honeymoon, or both, I shall stay at the Moulin. I shall recline on the island in the river and listen to the gurgle of the water, having bathed in the circular tub, I shall eat a delectable dinner seated at one of the four tables on the verandah overlooking the river, then retire to sleep in the room in the tower. Breakfast will be on the terrace of my beautiful room of course, with another view of the encircling arms of the river. Pure bliss.

All the rooms are attractive, as you might expect: with a price tag of 96-144€, but one with a view of the river is essential here (you can look out over a parking lot elsewhere).

The brochure photo does not do justice to the reality of the mill. What looks like an eccentric gabled Norman folly turns out to betruly lovely with the bonus of a swimming pool. Arrowed for its site and comfort

Some consolation for leaving the Moulin might be to enjoy the drive along the D19, which continues to be extremely attractive, chalk cliffs on one side, river on the other.

CONTEVILLE 27210 Beuzeville, Eure

Map 3F
13 km NW of Pont Audemer
Market: Thurs.

The coast road from Honfleur to the Pont de Tancarville, the D312, is even quieter now that much traffic has been diverted over the new bridge. It's very rural, very green, with glimpses of the river along the way, and a famous restaurant that well merits a diversion.

☆ **Auberge du Vieux Logis** ☒ L
    tel: (0)232.57.60.16
    closed: sun p.m.; Mon.; Tues lunch; 15/2-28/2 12/11-26/11

If you wanted to end a Norman holiday with a meal to remember you should head here before catching the ferry. What very good news it is to know that the family succession is assured and that the good work originated by the renowned M. Louet is continuing in the capable hands of his son Guillaume.

Fresh from stages in some of France's most prestigious restaurants (Robuchon to name but one), he brings with him a freshness and lightness that is a most welcome complement to the richness of the traditional Norman cuisine, but never forgets his origins. Fresh cod is partnered with Vire andouille, sweetbreads are combined with local lobster in a shellfish coulis, delicate millefeuilles are layered with chocolate and served with bitter cherries. The 23€ menu is a bargain - just two choices in each course. For us it was oysters, a palette of salmon with mushrooms and that wonderful feuilleté, this time with apples. Next price up is 39€.

The decor has not changed - call it soigné Norman - and service and welcome are the best - family-orientated but professional.

The star stays, for even better cooking.

COSQUEVILLE 50330, Manche

Map 3B
15 km E of Cherbourg

The stretch of coast between Cap Lévy and Gatteville offers good walks but not a lot else. The beaches are deserted and desolate for ten months of the year, the Plage du Vicq is probably one of the better choices, with fine sand and a handful of fishing boats in a little natural harbour, but the best reason for visiting here lies five minutes walk inland:

☆ Au Bouquet de Cosqueville 🛏 S ⊠ M
tel: (0)233.54.32.81
closed: Tues. p.m.; and Wed. o.o.s.; Jan and 23/6-30/6.

What a transformation since I first discovered this unassuming little restaurant and included it for position and potential rather than for charm and cuisine.

The youthful Pouhiers, Mylène and Eric, have conjured up from very modest beginnings an elegant restaurant, with some of the best cooking, especially seafood, in the region. Their enthusiasm and dedication has not been exhausted and I forecast the rise and rise of Le Bouquet.

Wisely, perhaps, they have concentrated on the restaurant side of their venture and left the rooms pretty much as they were, i.e. extremely simple. At the moment their standard bears no relation to the sophisticated cooking downstairs.

Menus start at 17.3€; on the next one up at 22€ I greatly enjoyed nine oysters, a gigot of lamb, cheeses in perfect nick and a flaky tarts. Langoustines, crab and lobster figure prominently on the carte.

A bouquet and a star for deserved success.

COURTILS 50220, Manche

Map 6B
8 km E of Mont St Michel. On the D75 from Pontaubault to Mont St. Michel

Manoir de la Roche Torin 🛏 ⊠ M-L
tel: (0)233.70.96.55
fax: (0)233.48.35.20

Well-signposted down a lane off the main road, with the Mount well within view across the marshes. It's a 19C gothic-style building covered in creeper and set in well-tended grounds. Its peaceful situation has earned it a place in the Relais de Silence group.

Perhaps the stone walls inside are not strictly original but they give a warm and cosy feeling to the dining room, enhanced by a big log fire, when justified, and polished copper. A new conservatory extension is a welcome addition. The rooms are all different, good-sized, well equipped and tastefully furnished. I believe that anyone wanting a luxurious, relaxing stop near the Mount could do no better but I do have a vague question mark over the food, so all reports particularly welcome.

Rooms from 70-108€ or 126€ for one with spa bath.

Demi-pension obligatory in high season 67-104€ per person.

Menus from 24€.

COUTANCES 50200, Manche

Map 4B
75 km S. of Cherbourg
Market: Thurs.

The largest cathedral in the Cotentin, Notre Dame de Coutances, dominates the town, as it has done for over seven centuries, miraculously surviving the 1944 bombardment The towers of its facade have stood there, in the market place on the hill, for even longer, they were salvaged from the Romanesque original when it was burned in 1218. In complete contrast is the Renaissance St. Pierre, with its striking lantern tower, just a step down the rue Geoffroy de Montbray.

Otherwise the best thing about the town are the public gardens, with Son et Lumière three nights a week in summer.

For a sizeable town, it is bizarre that Coutances has no recommendable hotel nor restaurant. It was not trying very hard to please last time I was there. An unseasonable July drizzle made its inhabitants scuttle in and out of the traffic, and deprived me of the chance to sit outside a bar and sum the place up. The parking lots were all full, the cathedral was closed and sale notices obscured the windows of the shops, but worst of all inescapable pop was blaring out of speakers on every corner. I gulped down my indoor coffee and left, pausing only at the Tourist Information Bureau to make sure I had not missed a winner, all the loyal employee could come up with was The Normandie (pleasant owners but old-fashioned, on a busy corner) and the Cositel (modern cube on the outskirts). She was floundering over restaurants when a local interrupted: 'Forget the town, make for La Voisinière at Savigny' (33.07.60.32). Unfortunately I was heading in the opposite direction, so all reports particularly welcome.

CREULLY 14480, Calvados

Map 3D
19 km NW of Caen, 13 km E of Bayeux. From Arromanches take the D 465, then the D22
Market: Wed.

The little town of Creully, high on its escarpment above the valley of the Seulles, is dominated by the 15C château. This is an area where defence has always mattered. Castles and fortresses abound. At the Château of Creully General Montgomery set up his caravan headquarters in June 1944.

☆ **Hostellerie St Martin** 🛏 ☒ M
   pl. Ed. Paillaud
   tel: (0)231.80.10.11
   fax: (0)231.08.17.65
   closed: Christmas; 29/12-8/1

I was particularly delighted to discover the St. Martin (prompted by a reader) because I fear this kind of small family-run hotel, maintaining exceptionally high standards, is a dying breed. This one scores on all counts.

Standing in the main square, backing on to the château, it was originally part of the market halles, and provided storage space for the victuals destined for the château residents. The restaurant is a delightful room, with vaulted ceilings, rough stone walls and big fire in big chimney. Flagged floor, pink cloths, soft lights, cane chairs and gleaming copper are all just right There are tables too outside on the terrace for summer sipping.

M. and Madame Legrand are the proprietors and he naturally, as in all good family-run affairs, is chef de cuisine. His specialities, naturally again, are regional, and his feuilletés and desserts show what a fine pastry chef he is.

The 12 comfortable rooms (wise perhaps to ask for one away from the square) cost from 35-40€. Menus from 9.6€.

A winner I'm sure and starred accordingly.

Otherwise

CREPON 144880

12 km NE of Bayeux, by D12

Ferme de la Rançonnière ⊨ ⊠ M
   tel: 02.31.22.21.73
   fax: 02.31.22.98.39

Well, not altogether new - the Ferme figured in some of the earlier editions, when it was a humble b.&b. on a working farm. I loved it for several years, until it became too popular and I had a less-than-profitable stay there. Nowadays I sense a new liveliness and willingness to please about the place and I am happy to restore the entry on an 'otherwise' basis until some more up-to-date reports arrive.

It is certainly an attractive place visually - an ancient fortified farm, set in tranquil countryside in the Bessin area, convenient for Caen and Bayeux. The old stone buildings are set round a great courtyard, where meals are served in summer. Otherwise the dining room, like most of the farm, is heavily beamed, heavily atmospheric. Log fires lend cosiness.

With 45 rooms, including some in a recent annexe down the road, the status is definitely hotel rather than b.&b, with appropriate fixtures, fittings and furnishings. Some of the rooms are dark, as to be expected with a building of this age. 48-109€.

Food is nothing special but breakfasts are to be recommended.

CRICQUEBOEUF 14600, Honfleur

Map 3E
6 km SW of Honfleur, well signed off the coast road, the D513

☆ Romantica ⊨ ⊠ M
   Chemin du Petit Paris
   tel: (0)231.81.14.00
   fax: (0)231.81.54.89 R.
   closed: Wed.; Thurs. lunch o.o.s.

At last an exciting but affordable hotel near Honfleur.

In fact the Romantica was built eight years ago, so I am amazed that it has remained such a well kept secret until now. It is built in the Anglo Normand style beloved by architects a generation ago, with full complement of fake beams, turrets and balconies, and although it is set some distance back from the sea, its height enables many of the rooms to enjoy really lovely views over the unspoiled countryside to the water.

The front rooms are super - large and light, some with balconies. I would bag the one on the corner, with an extra large balcony. Rooms range from 57-69€ up to 112€, with breakfast at 7.5€. Menus are priced from 22 to 33€.

With a swimming pool, peace and quiet and proximity to Honfleur this has to be a star.

'*Dinner service was very good and not at all rushed, although they were very busy and there were two sittings. Good selection of pastries. We would return.*' Margaret Lousbrough.

CROIX-MARE 76190, Seine-Mar

Map 2G
8 km SE of Yvetot by N15

Auberge de la Forge ☒ M

On the N15
tel: (0)235.91.25.94
closed: Tues.; Wed.

I am puzzled why there has been absolutely no feedback on this charming little restaurant, conveniently situated on the main road, in an area short of alternatives, and open on the dreaded Sun. p.m and Mon. moreover. I re-assessed it and liked it as much as ever so the recommendation not only stays but could be a star with a few confirmations.

There are several small beamed rooms inside, busy with French families at the weekends. Chef/patron Christian Truttmann is a truly imaginative cook. He likes to experiment with dishes like a terrine of pork trotters, he stuffs raviolis with a purée made from pike and serves it with a chervil cream. The cheapest menu is 16€ but the 25€ version includes good wine so could be a better deal.

DEAUVILLE 148000

74 km SW of Le Havre; 47 km E of Caen.

I left Deauville out of the last Normandy altogether. I had tried and failed to find a restaurant or hotel that I could recommend as good value, there had been no feedback and a notable lack of enthusiasm from readers. I am now coming round to the belief that it should not be entirely glossed over, if only because it makes a good excursion and is quite unlike any other Normandy town. My advice is to home in on Trouville and cross the water to her ritzy neighbour to partake of a coffee, or perhaps more appropriately for the atmosphere, a cocktail. Then hurry back to the real world, but here are a few tentative options.

Deauville has two faces. For a few brief summer weeks it glitters like a courtesan; for the rest of the year it subsides, passé and querulous, into a has-been fantasy, not enticing enough to attract the Beautiful People, not cheap enough for the hoi-polloi.

In high season a stroll along Les Planches, the wooden walkway between the cafes, boutiques, restaurants, and the 'cabines' bizarrely facing inwards towards the sun, not the sea, might well reveal a famous face or two. The glitterati, here for the Grand Prix or the yearling sales and races, still like to be seen at Ciro's, the ultimate in beach cafés, and the least one can do is gawk obligingly.

Out of season, when the only clients for the big anachronistic hotels are conferencees, I find the place depressing. The most exclusive shops are closed, owners migrated with the summer flock, but few chic boutiques sell out-of-season bargains, and the market still functions on Tuesdays. If the weather is fine, at weekends are to be seen those prosperous well-wrapped, stout French couples, arm in arm, walking their well-groomed poodles along the well-groomed prom.

Helios Hotel. 🛏 M-S 1

8 rue Fossorier,
tel: 02.31.14.46.46

If you are hell-bent on staying in the town, here is the exception that proves the rule - a small inexpensive hotel near the casino, that actually makes you feel welcome. It is two-star, modern, with a small swimming pool. Not bad value for 62-78€.

Otherwise:

Yearling ⊠ M
38 av Hocquart de Turtor
tel: 02.31.88.33.37.
closed: Tue and Wed. except August, 13/11-28/11, 14/1-31/1.

Outside the town, and therefore more affordable. 22€ buys three courses on the cheapest menu.

Spinnaker,
52 rue Mirabeau.
tel: 02.31.88.24.40.
closed: Tue. o .o .s. and Mon, 15/11-30/11.

For Deauville, Spinnakers is modest in concept - tiny dining rooms on two levels; its menu at 27€ is good value for a long-established and respected restaurant. Fish and pastries are specialties.

DIEPPE 76200, Seine-Mar

Map 1G
58 km NE of Rouen, 103 km E of Le Havre, 185 km from Paris
Market: Sat.

So many changes. Those who have not visited for a few years will hardly recognise the place without the ferries dominating the old harbour. The new port means less dependence on the state of the tides but a certain loss of bustle and salty character to the town centre.

The newly-liberated quays could have been put to better use, one feels. Sit at one of the restaurants along them now and the view is of a busy car park, not of marine activity. However, it has to be admitted that the parking situation in the town is dire, so perhaps the extra places were essential. So, I suppose, are the exasperating one-way systems. It is usually quicker to walk within the town, so confusing are the limitations.

Walking is best anyway, either along the quays checking out the menus, or for an ozony blow along the seashore, with the backdrop of the great castle, or in the pedestrianised heart of the town, the Grande Rue.

An hour can be passed quite happily here, up one side, down the other, with an obligatory pause at the Cafe des Tribunaux. Perhaps there is less atmosphere than in the days when Oscar Wilde used to linger here and revolutionary young artists - Pissaro, Renoir, Monet, Sickert, Whistler - fascinated by the challenge of portraying the clarity of the coastal light, would sit and argue over a glass of wine or absinthe; the lingering now is by the old ladies sitting on the wall for their evening gossip; les jeunes take over the fussy interior, while tourists like me prefer to put in some serious people-watching on the terrace.

Shopping along the Grande Rue is interesting; no big chain stores apart from a modest Monoprix but individual boutiques, particularly strong on household goods and gifts. The specialist food shops seem to be disappearing but Claude Olivier's establishment in the nearby rue St. Jacques, still sells only the best cheeses, charcuterie, oils, and a selection of good value wines.

But best of all for food shopping is the Saturday market, one of the biggest in Normandy, which spills over from the Place Nationale into the neighbouring streets. Farmers and their families arrive from miles around to display their wares. Cheeses are particularly mouthwatering, especially the unpasteurised varieties that are becoming victims of bureaucracy. Discuss with the vendor the day on which you want to eat the cheese and he will pick out one that will be in the pink of perfection for the show-off dinner back home. For hypermarket devotees (or anyone with a wet hour to kill) the Belvedere Mammouth shopping centre on the Rouen road has 55 shops.

Dieppe's two most famous monuments are her church and her castle. St. Jacques has been built and re-built over many centuries. The 14C central doorway, looking a little shabby alas, is surmounted by a fine rose window, particularly impressive in the evening when the sun spills the colours on to the floor. The nave is 13C, ornamented a century later and there are chapels donated by wealthy ship-builders from the 15C onwards. Look above the sacristy door for the frieze which depicts a file of Brazilian Indians, recalling the travels of Dieppois explorers. It comes from the palace of Dieppe's most revered son, Jean Ango.

You can't stay in Dieppe for long without being reminded, by road and cafe names, of this 16C maritime counsellor to Francis I. He took on the Portuguese fleet off the coast of African with notable success and became Governor of Dieppe. He is buried in the chapel which he donated to St Jacques.

The 15C castle dominates the promenade, with its wide stretches of grass dotted with picnickers and joggers. Inside is a maritime museum displaying not only all things nautical but a fine array of ivory. In the castle's shadow is a plaque commemorating the controversial Operation Jubilee, the costly Anglo-Canadian raid on Dieppe in 1942.

Hotels: It does seem strange that in a town like Dieppe with so many advantages, scenic and practical, there are not better hotels. The obvious ones to choose are those facing the sea, but I cannot get excited about any of them. Readers' first choice is the Plage, + M 20 bd. Verdun tel: (0)235.84.18.28, fax: (0)235.82.36.82, where 40 rooms cost between 40-52€.

There is one good deed in this wicked hotel world, not on the sea front but in a side street near the church:

Au Grand Duquesne 🛏 ☒ M-S

75 r. St. Jacques
tel: (0)232.14.61.10
fax: (0)235.84.29.83

When I called in to see the rooms and asked the jovial patron which were his closing days, he replied 'Never'. They're a hard-working team here, who never like to turn away good custom. Sunday night is a problem in Dieppe. Parisians are homeward bound and the restaurateurs put their feet up after a prolonged lunch session.

Those restaurants that are open seem to attract few customers and the atmosphere is not a cheerful one. On a dark and dirty September night, having had one unfortunate experience (see below) we trudged round the corner to the Duquesne, in a faute de mieux mood, only to find the place buzzing with customers and busy waiters. There was not a table left in the first, more attractive, dining room, but we were happy to grab the last in the rear alternative, rubbing our hands, already convinced that we had found a winner

The food was all that I would wish food to be in an unpretentious family-run hotel, and better. Generous portions, fresh produce, cheerful service. The 11.5€ menu is a real bargain, probably the best in Dieppe, but there are other more ambitious alternatives, up to 35€. On the 18.4€ version the croquante de moules surprised us by its sophisticated presentation: it arrived in a Chinese money-bag of filo pastry containing juicy mussels surrounded by a garlic sauce. Excellent. The terrines are home-made and particularly good, and the presentation is that of a far more expensive restaurant, with attractive china and linen. Just one word of warning - anyone with a sensitive palate should avoid the carafe wine!

This is predominately a restaurant with rooms, but the 12 bedrooms are comfortable, if simple, and cost a modest 30-34€.

La Musardière ☒ M

61 quai Henri IV
tel: (0)235.82.94.14
closed: Sun p.m.; Mon. ;Wed p.m.; and 15/12-15/1

There is a string of tiny restaurants along the main quay, all with tables outside, all strongly fishy. This is one of the newer recruits, long and narrow, pink cloths, trellised walls, mock windows. The service was a bit stretched the night we ate there, with just one girl and a young patronne heavily encumbered by a small baby but the food was o.k. We ate marinated salmon, coquilles St Jacques au jus de l'ail, very tender filet à la Bordelaise, a salad and strawberries - all on the 20€ menu. The cheese board looked a bit tired for Normandy. There is a rather limited 13.6€ menu too.

Les Arcades ⇔ S ☒ M

1 Arcades de la Bourse
tel: (0)235.84.14.12 fax: (0)235.40.22.29
closed: 31/12 p.m.

The tourists all make for the south-facing quai Henri IV, to sit outside the restaurants and snack bars in the sunshine. At right angles are the arcades, which keep the sun off the tables on the pavement there. That doesn't worry the French, who only choose to eat outside if it is very hot, when the arches provide pleasant shade; they otherwise prefer a comforting fug indoors, but the tourists like to snatch every minute of al fresco refreshment and so give the restaurants along here a miss. Their loss because Les Arcades is probably the best of the restaurants overlooking the harbour and the one that the locals recommend first.

Inside is a brasserie-like atmosphere, with benches and bustle, and a very professional approach. One feels that other restaurant upstarts might come and go but Les Arcades is here to stay. Seafood is very good. On the 12.6€ menu we ate mussels à la crème and brill with a langoustine sauce.

Marmite Dieppoise ⊠ M
    8 r. St. Jean
    tel: (0)235.84.24.26
    closed: Sun. p.m.; Mon.; 1 week in June

Another old favourite that soldiers on amongst the flashier newcomers, dishing up reliable traditional fare at prices that please the regulars. Dark and cosy, tucked away in a side street near the arcades, it is perhaps not first choice for a sunny lunch, but it's the food not the view that is important here. Menus from 26€, including lots of fish and the eponymous dish of marmite dieppoise of course.

Méli Mélo ⊠ S
    55 quai Henri IV
    tel: (0)235.06.15.12
    closed: Mon.

'We are greatly appreciated by the British,' said the patronne of this just opened salad bar on the quay. I'm not surprised. It was certainly greatly appreciated by me. I sat outside at one of the pretty white and green tables, enjoying 'La Mistral'- blue cheese, cucumber, nuts, crudités, ham and salad, all for 8€ chosen from a menu of dozens of alternatives, imaginatively combining meat, fish, eggs, cheese, with greenery. There were warm ciabatta sandwiches too for 6.2€ and hot quiches, raclettes and toasted cheeses for chillier days, when the equally attractive interior with yellow flowers on the walls might be more appropriate. The Formule at 12€ offered any of the menu dishes and a dessert like le crumble aux pommes et framboises. Perhaps the rice pudding is a concession for the Brits. All the dishes can be taken away to eat as a picnic. A good choice too at teatime for a cuppa with interesting pastries to accompany. Bienvenu and an arrow for this enterprising newcomer.

Just outside Dieppe in the suburb of Rouxmesnil, on the Arques road, is a little hotel I would never have found without local help:

Otherwise

L'Eolienne 🛏 ⊠ S

20 r. de la Croix de Pierre
tel: (0)232.14.40.00
fax: (0)235.82.19.50
closed: sun p.m.

In a restored stone barn Régine Levasseur, the very pleasant owner, has contrived seventeen bedrooms and a rustic restaurant.

Five of the rooms are equipped with jacuzzis, all are comfortable, with their own bathrooms, and cost 57€ (including breakfast).

The restaurant prides itself on Norman specialities like canards de Rouen, tripes au calvados, and boudin noir grillés aux pommes, plus lots of open fire grills. Friendly atmosphere. Although only 2 km from the town it is surprisingly quiet and peaceful here. I think this would make a very satisfactory base.

Menus from 15.5€.

Bistrot DuPollet ⊠ M

23 rte. Tete-de-Boeuf.
tel: 02.35.84.68.57.
closed: Sun, Mon, 2nd fortnight in March and Aug.

I have few requirements when it comes to cooking fish, but they are absolute:- freshness and simplicity. No brandy flambeeing, no powerful sauces, and definitely no over-cooking. This little marine-flavoured bistro fulfils the requirements admirably.

Carte: from 21€

Les Ecamias, ⊠ S

129 quai Henri 1V
tel: 02.35.84.67.67.
closed: l5/9-15/12

The pick of the quai bunch, evidenced by the number of locals who eat here regularly.

This is the place to sit outside on a fine day and lunch simply on a huge steaming bowl of mussels. Menus from 12€.

DIVES SUR MER 14160, Calvados

Map 3E
2 km SE of Cabourg, 24 km NE of Caen
Market: Sat

If, as many tourists do, you take the coast road, exploring the seaside resorts from Deauville to Cabourg, you will probably miss the heart of Dives altogether and might be forgiven for thinking it is just an undistinguished harbour and marina, facing Cabourg across the mouth of the river from which the town takes its name. The fact is that the most interesting part of Dives is no longer 'sur-mer', since its port, important in the Middle Ages, silted up. Nowadays its heart is several km inland, centring on the magnificent 15C market halls.

Their massive oak frames still look impressively sturdy, easily capable of supporting the old tiled roof. Look inside to find the wrought iron signs that designated the various merchants who used to ply their wares there. On Saturdays this is still the site of the colourful weekly market The halles stand on the Place de la République, on the other side of which is the 16C Manoir de Bois Hibou.

Five centuries before the market halls were built, Dives acquired another distinction. It was here that William the Conqueror assembled 3,000 vessels, the backbone of the fleet that would make the historic attack on England. On the 12th September 1066 they set sail to St Valery-sur-Somme where further reinforcements were waiting and 16 days later began their epic Channel crossing.

The town acknowledges its association with frequent references to Guillaume. Most obvious is the Village Guillaume le Conquerant, an arts and crafts enclave within the precincts of the old inn of the same name. The folksy little boutiques and cafes, though undeniably very pretty (and worth a visit) didn't appear to be prospering when I was last there, but that was in March; I hope that in the holiday season they do better.

Guillaume-le-Conquérant ☒ M

2 r. Hastings
tel: (0)231.91.07.26
closed: Mon. p.m.; Tues. o.o.s.

I am incurably sceptical that anywhere as attractive as this cannot fail to capitalise on its assets and take short cuts. However, readers assure me that it is not so, so I went along to recce. This is the very old inn set in the village; the dining room has massive wormy old beams, a good log fire, striped tapestry chairs, chandeliers and is a very 'serious' restaurant - the absolute opposite of my other Dives entry. Its menus feature expensive delicacies like home prepared foie gras flavoured with morilles, grilled lobster, braised turbot, and if you want sole you must pay 48€ for two people (never come across that one before).

I never actually ate there, so all I can report is that the decor is worth sticking your head inside the door. Readers who know better please write.

Menus start at 16€, but go for the 24€ to get something more interesting.

The rest of the town is nothing special, apart from one enormous bonus that would merit a detour from me whenever I was anywhere near.

☆ Chez le Bougnat ⊠ S
27 r. Gaston Manneville
tel: (0)231.91.06.13
closed: Mon.; Tues. lunch

I had only to push open the door of this mildly insalubrious building in the main street to know I'd hit a winner. The buzz and bustle were the first indication. In no time we were provided with a menu and further evidence that this was going to be good. The problem was that, having eaten well the night before and planning another gourmet exercise later that same day, I knew that I could not do justice to the mouth-watering selection on the carte. Tentatively I explained the situation to the chef, who sorted me out: 'Have just the terrine and a salad.' He added, 'And share it with your husband,' which I thought was a bit odd until I saw the kilo of chicken liver terrine he dumped before me and the family size bowl of salad. But nothing was wasted - that terrine was so juicy and flavoursome (and easily the best I've ever tasted) that I somehow found an appetite.

Everything Chez le Bougnat comes family-sized. Everything but the bill. Here were the cheapest oysters I found in a Normandy restaurant – 8.5€ for a dozen of the best St. Vaast - mussel dishes at 5.6€, six salads at 2.8€ and huge portions of beef, pork lamb and veal at 10.8e€, all served with good fresh veg. and frites. Meat is obviously a speciality but all the fish is prime-fresh; feuilletés are another house favourite.

Most of the locals were taking advantage of the admirable 12.6€ menu, but there was no way we were up to its hefty four courses. Husband compromised with an order for 'just a pork chop'. It came butterfied Barnsley-style, two massive chops complete with crispy crackling, just like pork used to taste before they eliminated all the fat.

If you imagine that by ordering fruit for a dessert here you can accommodate a small appetite, forget it. 'Pineapple' means a pineapple - a whole one, peeled but otherwise au natural. The cheese board would put many a gourmet restaurant to shame, the wine list is fabulous and inexpensive, and you get a complimentary Calva when you ask for the (excellent) coffee.

The food here may be the main reason for a visit, but the decor is something else. While you are digesting, look around. The room is galleried, with some more tables up above. Decor is vaguely art deco, eclectic to say the least, every inch of wall and ceiling space occupied. Helmets, cartoons, an old lift, jugs on ledges, three wooden propellers suspended from on high, a stuffed Charolais head, huge papier maché heads - a chef, a sailor, a clown - a weighing machine. Table cloths are paper, floor is tiled.

I wouldn't choose le Bougnat on a summer's day - it is at its best when a cosy fug is to be preferred to fresh air, I wouldn't choose it for a romantic occasion - too cheek by jowl; I wouldn't choose it if I had a headache - the crescendo of happy eaters, the coffee machine grinding, is prodigious, but in every other circumstance I can't think of anywhere I like more. Long may the establishment thrive and refuse all changes, in spite of recent Michelin recognition. The enthusiastic star stays firmly in place.

N.B. No credit cards accepted.

DOMFRONT 61700, Orne

Map 6C
40 km SE of Vire; 98 km S of Caen
Market: Fri., Sun.

The main road through the town gives no indication of any character whatsoever, being lined with post-war buildings. In order to gain an idea of how it must have been before the destruction it is necessary to park the car and climb the narrow cobbled Grande Rue to its mediaeval heart. Immediately the traffic fret is left behind and all is calm. The ruins of a castle keep are strategically sited to command a view of the surrounding countryside and the ramparts no doubt once helped to keep early invaders at bay.

Unfortunately there are no hotels up here to profit from the noise-free zone, but there are signs of new interest, like the Auberge du Grand Gousier (pl. Liberté). The food is pretty standard on printed-ahead menus (12.2€ menu) but the restaurant is very pretty and comfortable, with check cloths, rough stone walls, and a light and fresh feeling about it that would remedy car fatigue. Alternatives are snack bars and a crêperie.

DOUDEVILLE 76560, Seine-Mar

Map 2F
13 km N. of Yvetot on the D20

Totally unspoiled countryside around here, in the heart of the pays Caux, only 38 km from Dieppe.

Le Relais du Puits St Jean ⍾ ⊠ S
rue de la Nos
tel: (0)235.96.50.99
closed: 15 days in Feb

Here's one that's definitely different, with loads of character and atmosphere. In the unlikely setting of a rather grim large 19C house

M. Lemonnier presides over a kitchen whose speciality, pressed duck, is famous far and wide. If you've never tried it, you don't need to spend a fortune in Paris at the Tour d'Argent; just order it here, where its every bit as good at a fraction of the price. Home produced foie gras is another calorific house speciality. Don't think of eating here without a robust appetite.

The dining room is redolent of leisurely hearty meals enjoyed over the years by leisurely hearty Frenchmen. Nothing distracts from thefood; cloths are white, decor minimal. This is old-fashioned bourgeois tucking-in as it used to be. If you don't fancy the duck there are menus at 9.6€, 13.6€ or 22€ and the carafe wine keeps the bill down even further.

A brief stagger up to bed might be a good idea here and there are four rooms, simple but with bath, at 37€. Half-pension is 45e but you'd need a stay in a health farm afterwards if you stayed here long.

One reader was disappointed to find no pressed duck. Whatever is going on?

DUCEY 50220, Manche

Map 6B
11 km of Avranches

Take the pleasant little D78 rather than the main roads to find the village of Ducey.

☆ Auberge de la Sélune 🛏 ☒ M
rue St Germain
tel: (0)233.48.53.62
fax: (0)233.48.90.30
closed: 15 days over Jan. and Feb.; 20/11-15/12

It was with some misgiving that I re-visited the Auberge. It has had such success since I first found it, now featuring in the brochures of several British tour companies, that I feared the worst: I need not have worried. If anything it is even nicer than I remembered it, and the hardworking owners, Jean-Pierre and Madame Girres, are not at all spoiled by easy custom. On the contrary, they are still looking for ways to improve on what was already delightful.

The entrance hall has been enlarged and smartened up, there is a new dining room, a bigger terrace, the bedrooms have been redecorated, the garden running down to the river from which the

Auberge de la Sélune, Ducey

auberge takes its name is even more flowery and agreeable and the food is said to be better than ever. Bookings may be good (don't go on spec), but prices have not soared. 32e€ for a double with shower and 46€ with bath is excellent value, as is the 12.8€ menu.

Starred for pleasant situation, good food, kind owners, and value.

Le Moulin de Ducey 🛏 M

1 Grande-Rue.
tel: 02.33.60.25.25.
closed: 14/1-25/2

On the banks of the Sélune, an ancient windmill has been converted into a charming hotel, with 28 well-decorated rooms from 48-89€. Ask for one overlooking the river.

ERQUEURDREVILLE-HAINNEVILLE 50100, Manche

4 km W of Cherbourg.

Don't be tempted to follow the signs to 'Le Bourg'. Just stick to the coast road and you will find the little restaurant easily.

La Gourmandine ⊠ M
24 r. Surcouf
tel: (0)233.93.41.26
closed: Sun. p.m.; Mon.; Tues p.m. 15/7-15/8

The entrance is in the main road but there is a garden at the rear, with a view out to sea, something that is not easily found in Cherbourg. It makes a change from the port restaurants that oftenare too tourist-orientated. M. Lebas is a brave man in offering a vegetarian menu in carnivorous France. It looked a good one - three courses for 12€. Otherwise there is the Menu de la Saline for 12€ or (preferably) a 32€ version with some interesting options like hot oysters in Beaumes de Venise.

Give it a try and let me know.

ÉTRETAT 76790, Seine-Maritime

Map 2E
28 km NE of Le Havre
Market: Thurs.

The scene along the beach will be instantly familiar because of the much-painted, much-photographed distinctive arched white rocks. Take a stroll towards them along the prom, fitted with cafes and souvenir shops, fishing boats pulled up on the cobbles providing the colour. For a longer walk continue up the steep hill past the golf course to look down upon the monumental arch of the Porte d'Aval; serious walkers can continue to follow the marked route and make a circuit of three hours. Alternatively at the other end of the beach there is a 180-step ascent cut out of the chalk cliffs to the Falaise d'Amont, where the little seamen's chapel, Notre Dame de la Garde, has a magnificent view of Étretat, its surroundings, the long single beach to the Porte d'Aval and the solitary island-rock, l'Aiguille.

Another church, Notre Dame, is a good reason for a less taxing walk past typically French holiday villas, rose-covered, white-shuttered. It's a wonderfully simple Romanesque church, nine centuries away from the 20C 'amusements' on the prom.

In summer Étretat is a lively little resort, full of happily squealing children, precarious wind surfers and ice cream bars. In winter it gets forgotten and dies. The architecture generally is eccentric Norman, beamed and turreted, and there are reconstructed covered market halls, now used for craft shops.

Not my favourite town, apart from the walks, partly because the hoteliers are almost without exception so unpleasant Their season is short, so that they have to grab every franc while they can. It was high season when I was there last, the hotels were full and their staff weren't wasting any time in being agreeable. The best-known hotels in the main street are the Normandie (17 rooms at 35-56€) and the Falaises (24 rooms at 40-61€), both with adequate rooms and food, but no more.

I did find two exceptions to the general couldn't-care-less attitude:

Hôtel Résidence 🛏 M
4 bvd. René Coty
tel: (0)235.27.02.87

Probably the oldest building in the town, with worm-eaten old beams and impressive staircase. It does not have a standard hotel classification because the rooms and their prices vary so wildly, from 27 to 102€.

The owner broke all the rules - he was young, well-dressed, helpful, polite and ready to show me all the rooms, although he was fully booked for that night The antiquity of the building has not resulted in a gloomy interior. On the contrary, all is bright and cheerful, with contemporary furnishings, fabrics and bathroom fittings. Breakfast is served on a kind of landing lounge. I liked the atmosphere very much here, but as the set-up is so unusual I do need first hand reports.

Le Galion ⊠ M
rue. René Coty
tel: (0)235.29.48.74
closed: Wed. lunch; 15/12-15/1.

An old timbered building in the main street, with lots of character from old beams and pillars; it offers the only serious cooking in the town. The cheapest menu is now 20€, traditional fare, with lots of seafood.

Hötel St Christophe 🛏 M-S

Le Tilleul, 3 km S of Étretat on the D940
tel: (0)235.28.84.19
fax: (0)235.28.84.30

A little modern chalet-like hotel set back from the Le Havre road, with tables outside for repose and drinks.

All is bright, clean, efficient; 21 rooms, including one for the handicapped, with all mod cons. cost from 45€, to 53€. A useful overnight stop on the way to the ferry.

EU 76260, Seine-Mar

Map 1 H
31 km N of Dieppe
Market: Fri.

5 km inland from Le Tréport, a town steeped in history but often ignored by tourists hurrying to catch the ferry or beach-bound. Normandy obligingly bulges its border to the north to accommodate Eu, where its most famous son, William the Conqueror, married Mathilda of Flanders in 1050. The castle where the ceremony took place was destroyed on the orders of Louis XI in 1475. The replacement château, begun in 1578, was one of the favourite residences of Louis Philippe. Queen Victoria liked it too and stayed there on two occasions. It is now used as the Town Hall and houses the Louis-Philippe museum.

The heart of the town is the beautiful collegiate church dedicated to Our Lady and St. Lawrence O'Toole, Primate of Ireland who died in Eu in the 12C. It was erected in the 12th and 13th centuries in the Gothic style. Don't miss the haunting 15C entombment in the St. Sepulchre chapel (second on the right).

The vibrant Friday morning market takes over the area around the church and is the biggest and best in the area. On other days the food shops are particularly good here, in the agreeably pedestrianised area. Mouthwatering charcuteries, chocolateries and patisseries, all of high quality, emphasise that this is a town where the locals shop, not one dedicated merely to tourist fast food. I recommend it not only on this count but for its situation in the valley of the Bresle (lovely walks), surrounded by the forest from which it takes its name, conveniently between the two ferry ports.

☆ **Hötel Maine**
   20 ave de la gare
   tel: 02.35.86.16.64
   fax: 02.35.50.86.25
   closed: Sun p.m.

This is the old Hotel de la Gare, renamed, refurbished, refreshed, but intrinsically old-fashioned in the nicest possible way. The décor remains resolutely Belle Epoque and kindly M. et Mme Maine remain resolutely friendly and helpful to their guests.

The food is so good that the restaurant fills up with locals as well as hotel guests, all enjoying hearty dishes like a terrine of ox tail, duck with wild mushrooms, and strawberry tart. There is a carefully-chosen, reasonably-priced wine list and honest carafe wine.

Rooms have been renovated and some even boast a jacuzzi, but 'simple and comfortable' still describes them best. Their modest prices reflect the fact that this is not a tourist town and here is a hotel where you can safely take demi-pension and rely on the best cooking around.

A star for a real French experience.

15 rooms cost 40-47€, 3 apartments cost 47-66€. Menus from 21-34€.

ÉVREUX 27000, Eure

Map 4G
120km SE of Le Havre
Market: Thurs., Sat.

For a Norman town, a situation near the provincial border has always meant a history of sack and pillage. Évreux from its earliest days has faced hordes of destructive enemies - Romans, Goths, Vandals, Normans, English, French and finally Germans, whose 1940 attack left the town burning for a week. After each devastation the townsfolk have picked themselves up, dusted themselves down and started all over again.

It's truly a miracle that any part of Notre Dame, Évreux's

cathedral, has survived, but there it is, rising up above the rivulets of the river Iton, still the focus of the town, an assembly of every phase of Gothic to Renaissance architecture, with astounding 15C glass, miraculously intact after being removed to safety during the war.

Évreux is a university town and university towns invariably acquire some of the liveliness of their students. This certainly applies to Évreux, with tables on pavements, bars and cafes patronised by an animated clientele.

Hôtel de France ⇔ ☒ M

29 r. St. Thomas.
tel: (0)232.39.09.25
fax: (0)232.38.38.56
closed: Sun. p.m.; Mon, Sat a.m.

I can never work out how the rear rooms and lovely dining room of the France have views over the river Iton, yet I can never find it when I look behind the hotel. It does have a habit of going underground and popping out again at various points around the town. When it does, there are invariably grassy borders and a waters-edge path, which makes for good picnicking, The Hôtel de France has for long been the town's principal hotel, which can sometimes lead to complacency, but this time I sensed an air of renewal, and freshness. The restaurant overlooking the water is one of the prettiest I know, supervised by chef Mario Mathoux and patron Bernard Meyruey.

His clientele, especially at lunchtime, tends to be businessmen and businessmen like substantial meals, so don't chance this one for something light. Menus start at 24€.

The 15 rooms are nothing special but reasonably priced at 41-56€.

Vieille Gabelle ☒ M

3 r. de la Vieille Gabelle
tel: (0)232.39.77.13
closed: Sun. p.m.; Mon.; Sat. lunch; 1/8-21/8

An exceedingly ancient building in central Évreux. Pretty beamed dining room and a 13.6€ menu, Le Retour du Marché, which offers a terrine of quail with grapes, cod steak with leek purée and brie on a salad bed. Next menu up, with more choice, is a four courserat 24€.

Le Bretagne ⊠ S

3 r. St. Louis
tel: (0)232.39.27.38
closed: Mon.; Wed. p.m.; 16/7-30/7

Behind the Mairie, a short step from the Tourist Office.

Very popular with locals at lunchtime. No wonder, with the 11e menu formule including a pichet of wine. Reliable cooking from the chef-patron and generous helpings on the four-course 27€ menu.

I also liked the Brasserie des Arts in the main Mairie square. Fin-de-siècle decor, solid brasserie dishes enjoyed by local businessmen, but no problem about just a sandwich or salad. Excellent frites.

FALAISE 14700, Calvados

Map 5D
34 km S of Caen
Market: Sat.

Mercifully, the 12C keep of the castle survived the 1944 destruction of the rest of the town, and continues to dominate the town as it always has. It was from here that Robert, younger son of Richard II, Duke of Normandy, watched the lovely seventeen-year old Arlette as she washed her clothes in the nearby river, and fell instantly in love. The proud Arlette declined a clandestine affair and rode defiantly over the drawbridge to meet her lover, a liaison that resulted in William the Bastard (the Conqueror). His magnificent statue rears below the castle ruins.

Things to do in Falaise? Take an interesting walk along the riverside path or drive northwards via the N158 to the Devil's Breach, a gorge hollowed out in the typical sandstone crests of the Falaise countryside. The hotels are nondescript, built post-war in the yellow Caen stone but without much character. The Poste in the main street is probably the best, with 21 rooms from 32-65€. The restaurant scene however is distinctly more promising.

☆ La Fine Fourchette ⊠ M

52 r. George Clemerxeau
tel: (0)231. 90.08.59

An old favourite that never lets me down, and actually welcomes customers on the dead Sun. p.m.; Mon. In the main street, decor typical bourgeois French - cane chairs, mock beams, orange drapes - food top quality ingredients lovingly prepared by patron chef Gilbert Costil. His specialities are sophisticated dishes like a gaspatcho (sic) of salmon and tuna with grapes, home-made foie gras in a hazelnut cream, and sweetbreads cooked in dessert wine, but you don't have to spend a fortune on the carte to sample really interesting dishes. On the 13.3€ menu you could dine on a terrine of salmon and pike, then the suggestion du chef (always a good idea), salad and a dessert like a wicked Dôme de chocolat.

Starred for consistent high standards.

☆ **L'Attache** ⊠ **M**
Rt. de Caen - 1 km out of town on the N158, direction Caen, at the l'Attache roundabout
tel: (0)231 90.05.38
closed: Tues pm.; Wed.

Such a pretty little restaurant (just a few tables, so be sure to book) with rough stone walls and a strong feel of Normandy about the decor and the cooking. Chef Alain Hastain believes in using plenty of herbs and spices in his inspired cooking but his basis is Norman ingredients, like using camembert in a kind of quenelle and flavouring it with chives, or roasting langoustines with cardamom. Leave room for desserts, which are particularly good.

Menus from 13.6€ at present but this one is going places, so get there and enjoy a bargain while you can.

A star for encouragement.

FÉCAMP 76400, Seine-Mar

Map 2F
40 km N of Le Havre
Market: Sat.

No doubt that the heart of the town is its harbour; Fécamp is France's most important cod-fishing port and nowadays there is a large marina for pleasure boats too. The biggest tourist attraction however is the Benedictine distillery a few blocks back. In the 16C a monk, Vincelli, found on the chalky cliffs the herbs that gave the liqueur its distinctive flavour. The exact recipe is a closely-guarded secret but visitors are welcome to inspect the 27 plants and spices that are used today in the distillation. A tour round the salle des plantes in the museum is a feast for the nose as well as the eye. The building is a bizarre, Disney-esque piece of fantasy, whose courtyard is heaving with tourists at peak periods. Go early or late in the day.

Above the harbour is Richard I's church, La Trinité, rebuilt in the 12C after being struck by lightning. Subsequent re-building and additions mean that it is now a hotchpotch of architectural styles up to the 18C.

Its well worth arranging a schedule around the Saturday market that takes place in the square and streets around the church. It is one of the best in the area and brings animation and custom to the shops and bars in this area, usually neglected in favour of those along the quays.

Hôtel de la Plage ⇌ S

87 r. de la Plage
tel: (0)235.29.76.51
fax: (0)235.28.66.30

In a quiet street one block back from the port. No sea view, but 22 comfortable, bright and clean rooms costing 5€. Nothing special but the best that the town can offer.

Auberge de la Rouge ⇌ ⌧ M

Rte. du Havre St. Leonard, (2 km S on D925)
tel: (0)235.28.07.59
fax: (0)235.28.70.55
closed: Sun. p.m; Mon.

Now with new owners, Madame Dutch and Monsieur French, the Auberge is renowned locally for its cooking and always fully booked for Sunday lunch.

Unwise to bank on a table on Saturday evening either. There are two biggish rustique dining rooms and a pretty little garden. I thought the cheapest menu (17€, not Sundays) somewhat uninspired and the next one up is 30€, so I'm not quite so excited about the place as when I first found it, but readers have been well pleased with the quality and quantity of the fairly traditional cooking. If you're tired of fish, this is a good place to sample duckling cooked the rouennais way, on the silver press.

The eight rooms cost from 48-59€, are a bit small and dark, but they are really accessories to the highly successful restaurant

La Marée ⊠ M
75 quai Bérigny
tel: (0)235.29.39.15
closed: Sun. p.m.; Mon.; Christmas

On the quayside is a busy fish shop selling fish straight from the boats. Even if you are not thinking of eating you should take a look to learn the names and varieties of the specimens and also to see what pristinely fresh fish looks like. They also sell takeaway delicacies like various fish terrines and pâtés, soupe de poissons, and home-smoked salmon, herrings, cooked lobsters and crabs, etc., so you could cater for a special picnic here.

Upstairs is a large, surprisingly smart restaurant, not aggressively nautical, more sage green and cream than the expected navy and white, with only a few token burgees, knots and boaty pictures hung haphazardly on the walls. Bag a table at the panoramic windows, La Marée's answer to the other restaurants' quayside tables, and you are on to an undoubtedly good thing.

I could not resist a huge simply grilled sole which was worth every franc of 17€, but the 15.8€ menu produced a good creamy crab bisque, a perfectly cooked and herb-crusted cod steak and a dessert.

La Plaisance ⊠ M
quai Vicomte
tel: (0)235.29.38.14
closed: Tues. p.m.; Wed.; Feb.; 1 week in Dec.

The fish and nothing but the fish. Here you can eat it on the quay side terrace if you wish. Fish from the carte is the most popular choice, but there is a menu at 21€, which offers an assiette de fruits de mer, fish of the day, cheese and desserts that are better than in most fish restaurants (i.e. a trilogy of home-made sorbets with a cassis coulis).

Le Grand Banc ⊠ S
63 quai Bérigny
tel: (0)235.28.28.68
closed: Thurs.; 15 days in Dec.

Ask local gourmands about Fécampois restaurants and they will almost certainly quote the Marée first, then the Plaisance, both for irreproachable fresh fish (not so common as you might think in a fishing port) and then Le Grand Banc for qualité-prix. I was pleased to have this confirmation of the unlikely discovery I made a few years ago of a really humble bistro run by an enthusiastic young couple. I recommended it with several reservations (it really was very humble), readers flocked, and reported back that the value was every bit as good as I had found. Now I need have no qualms about the decor. The little restaurant has been smartened up and freshly painted in blue and white, the tables are set further apart, and the menu extended.

Inevitably all this means an increase in prices, but not much. The menu ranges from 11.2€ to 26€, which in this town is still a tremendous bargain, and fresh sole, that yardstick of value, is 16€. There are other items like wild boar terrine, to relieve the fishy diet.

La Ferme de la Chapelle 🛏 M
Côte de la Vierge
tel: (0)235.29.12.19

I write about this one more in sorrow than in anger. I am not recommending it but, because of its marvellous position and the shortage of other hotels in Fécamp, I think readers might like to know exactly what to expect if they do decide to stay here.

First the good news:

Look up at the cliff high above the northern side of the port and you will see a tiny mariners' chapel. Behind it lie the old farm buildings around a courtyard, which someone had the brilliant idea of converting into a hotel. The view from the chapel (though not from the farm) is magnificent: the air is clear and the traffic noise minimal. A large swimming pool is available for the guests' use.

Now for the less-good: Whoever was responsible for the conversion got away with murder. The flintstone wall of the chapel ends abruptly in a hideous concrete and slate erection, used for seminaires. The gilt Madonna on the spire looks down bemused at the folly of man. Her chapel survived the Hundred Years War, the Wars of the Religion, the destruction of 1944, with pillaging and rot in between, only to suffer this desecration.

The conversion of the farm into bedrooms built two-storeys high around the courtyard is very basic. Ground floor rooms have French windows but those upstairs are very dark with tiny Mansard windows. The great courtyard is grassed but entirely bereft of any flowers; the swimming pool is only used in high summer because it is always windy up here and it is unheated.

Furnishings are basic/modern. Blonde wood bed and drawers, white walls, no pictures, apart from a photo of the Fécampois fishing boat after which each room is named (the only nice personal touch)

Breakfast is eaten at tables of six in the barn-like breakfast room. Evening meals have to be reserved ahead on a no-choice, demi-pension basis. Cars have to be left outside the gates and, believe me, with a damaged knee and an upstairs room, it's a long painful hump of the baggage across the courtyard. No help offered.

I found this a great opportunity missed. The situation, the chapel, the courtyard - all could have been turned to such advantage with more sympathetic handling. Rooms 59-85€.

LA FERRIÉRE AUX ÉTANGS 61450, Orne

Map 5D
13 km from Domfront on the D21

A grim little town, dominated by mines and chimneys. All the more surprise then to find:

☆ Auberge de la Mine ⊠ M
Le Gué-Plat
tel: (o)233.66.91. 10
closed: Tues.; Wed.; 15/8-7/9

A very smart little restaurant, run by an enthusiastic young couple, Catherine and Hubert Nobis, who have made up for the greyness outside by furnishing the dining room with bright flowery curtains and dividing it with trellis.

The weekday menu, starting at 18€, is commendably Selon le marché. In other words you get whatever Hubert thinks is the best buy in the market that morning. Otherwise, on the 20€ version you could sample a bavarois of asparagus, a chicken breast roulé studded with fresh herbs, cheese, and a chocolate and almond 'pudding' with an orange coulis.

A real find, good value, highly recommended, and a new star.

LA FERTÉ MACÉ 61600, Orne

Map 6D
6 km N of Bagnoles de l'Orne
Market: Thurs.

If Bagnoles is too ordered, too contrived, head for La Ferté Maché, a pleasant little French town. Except that the parking is a nightmare if you wish to get to the pedestrianised centre.

Le Céleste 🛏 ⊠ S

> 6 r. Victoire
> **tel:** (0)233.37.22.33
> **fax:** (0)222.38.12.25
> **closed:** Sun.; Mon.

Hopeless to achieve by car, except perhaps by ignoring No Entrance signs, which the French are better at than the Brits. Stop near the cathedral, dive into the hotel and ask for guidance.

It's tucked away in a pedestrianised street but easily spottable because of its colour - Barbara Cartland pink. This lapse of taste does not extend inside. And there's a surprising terrace at the back.

Cheapest menu is 14.4€, and the fourteen rooms run from 15-48€, the divergence reflecting their state of refurbishment, the cheapest having only a lavabo.

Auberge du Clouet 🛏 ⊠ M

> at Clouet, on the outskirts of the town.
> **tel:** (0)233.37.18.22
> **closed:**15 days in Nov.

If you do not wish to get involved in the traffic tangle, this is a good bet, well signed from all directions. Peaceful too. It's a long stone building, with a covered terrace. Six rooms cost from 51-64€ and meals start at 14.4€ so it's not exactly a bargain.

FLAMANVILLE 50340, Manche

Map 2A
21 km SW of Cherbourg by D904, to Les Pieux, then D23 and D408

Very peaceful, very rural, near the coast, not too far from the port.

☆ **Hôtel Bel Air** 🛏 M
tel: (0)233.04.48.00
fax: (0)233.04.49.56
closed: 20/12-15/1

A pretty old stone manor house, full of character, once an outbuilding to the Chateau de Flamanville. Dany and Serge Morel have furnished it with flowery curtains and unpretentious furniture and the ten rooms are cosy and comfortable, with every mod con. The 3 beamed rooms in the stables across the courtyard share a salon, good for families at 49-72€. I peeked at the visitors book and found it full of glowing commendations from satisfied customers from all over the world. Delightful garden with pines, palms, lots of tables and chairs. Alas, no restaurant, but the breakfast buffet could carry you through the day, and Dany is happy to recommend local alternatives for the evening. I think this one could well become an FE favourite. New star.

Otherwise

A reader recommendation is the Restaurant de la Paix, 5 Place de lat Poster, des Pléreux – *'a few mniutes down the road, nice atmosphere, good food well presented and prices suit all pockets.'*

Le Sémaphore 🛏 ⊠ S
tel: (0)233.52.18.98
fax: (0)233.52.36.39
closed: Mon; 15/12-31/1

I missed this one, but here is a report from someone who didn't; *'Wonderful isolated position, pleasant dining room and accueil. Excellent lunch at 12.6€ .'* Lesley Goodden.

FLERS 61100, Ome

Map 5D
43 km E of Argentan
Market: Wed., Sat.

Not a particularly attractive town, but one well served with hotels and restaurants, so perhaps a good stopover. Unfortunately both the hotels I was hoping to inspect were closed (contrary to their published times) so all I can report is that the locals recommended Le Galion, 5 r. Victor Hugo (0)233.64.47.47 fax: (0)233.65.10.10. 30 rooms from 32-42€.

I was luckier with restaurants and found two winners:

☆ Auberge Relais Fleuri ⊠ M
115 r. Schnetz
tel: (0)233.65.23.89
closed: Sun. pm.; Mon.; 15 days in Aug.

On an unattractive street corner on the edge of the town, in the quartier St Michel direction, comes a delightful surprise:

A lovely dining room with rough stone wails, elegantly decorated, and nice young Véronique Louvel welcoming and taking orders for the food skilfully prepared by her husband Vincent. His style is modern - light and imaginative - without being showy. Dishes like scallops with a mild curry butter or a lasagne layered with langoustines illustrate his flair. The cheapest 17€ menu (Sundays too N.B.) offers less extravagant ingredients, e.g. mussels, roast rabbit, cheese, dessert, but no less caringly prepared.

A highly recommended place for an enjoyable evening, particularly in winter when the log fire glows so invitingly.

Starred.

Au Bout de la Rue ⊠ M
60 r. de la Gare
tel: (0)233.65.3153
closed: Sat. lunch.; Sun.; 4/8-26/8

A surprise to find in this unsophisticated country town a stylish, fin-de-siècle-themed bistro/brasserie. The paint is dark green outside, dark red within, the atmosphere is cosy and convivial. Find it, as its name suggests, at the end of the road leading to the station.

Patron is Jacky Lebouleux, who cooks variations on old brasserie favourites, like andouille encased in flaky pastry, roast lamb in a rosemary sauce, apricots baked in orange juice. There is a wide choice of dishes à la carte, plus popular plats du jour, for a set price of 24€, and an equally eclectic and reasonable wine list.

A potential star after more reports.

Auberge des Vieilles Pierres ⊠ M

Buisson-Corblin; 2 km S of Flers on the Briouze road, the D924.
tel: (0)233.65.06.96
closed: Mon.; Tues.; 29/7-22/8

A really pretty little restaurant, all trellised, light and airy, with a warm welcome from Madame Cesbron and easy parking for those who do not wish to get involved in town traffic.

The four course Tues, Sat lunch costs 13.6€ otherwise it's two courses for 17€ (terrine of wild boar with pistachios, pork noisette with endives and hazelnuts), or 21€ for three courses.

FORGES-LES-EAUX 76440, Seine-Maritime

Map 2H
42 km NE of Rouen by
A28, D919 and D915

Louis XIII, his Queen and Richelieu used to take the waters in this spa town, whose name derives both from the metalwork that used to be its main occupation unto the 15C and from its waters. You can still drink the ferruginous, clear liquid that gushes from a buvette in the Spa Park - it is said to be very stimulating. Overlooking the park is the lovely facade of a hunting pavilion, formerly belonging to Louis XV and brought here from Versailles. There are several half-timbered 17C buildings in the rue de la République but the central square I find bleak and unattractive in spite of the wealth of flowers lavished upon it It was big excitement in Forges when Club Med decided to open their premises in the grounds of the casino, but in fact the inhabitants keep themselves to themselves, contained in their camp and grounds.

La Paix 🛏 ⊠ S-M

17 r. de Neufchatel
tel: (0)235.90.51.22
fax: (0)235.09.83.62
closed: Mon. Lunch (Jul. and Aug. only); Sun. and Mon. o.o.s.; 23/6-7/7; 3 weeks in Dec.

This is an example of not expecting too much from a simple restaurant. I deviated from the rule and chose the 20€ version, which gave me an unappealing artichoke salad with a few chilly prawns and no dressing on the chopped lettuce, then a small skate wing, dry and disastrously over-cooked in an unsubtle cream sauce. The cheaper menu on the other hand was well within the chef's capabilities and yielded a perfectly good chicken terrine and grilled trout. Madame, described by the next table as formidable, trudged unsmilingly around, and offered no comment on my uneaten fish. A disappointing experience because my first inspection of the hotel and menus had promised a star. I thought it had all the virtues of being unpretentious, family-run and inexpensive. The rooms are new, well-equipped, peacefully sited behind the hotel, well off the main road, and good value at 43-48€, and there is safe private parking.

The hotel is very popular with the British, including many readers. If you stick to the cheap menu and ignore Madame's gloom it could be good news. Perhaps my experience was unfortunate, but no star I'm afraid.

Auberge du Beau-Lieu 🛏 ⊠ M
at Le Fosse, 2 km SE on the D915
closed: Tues.; 15 days over Jan. and Feb.; 1/9-4/9

Local opinion is highly in favour of the Beau-Lieu, the newish restaurant gastronomique just outside Forges. It's a very pretty Norman-style restaurant with smart service and presentation, usefully open on the dread dead Sun. p.m. and Mon. Cooking is based on regional dishes, with a personal touch. Cheapest menu (a very good one) is 16€ (except weekeneds), then 32 and 48€, with an interesting, wide-ranging wine list.

The style of the three bedrooms is simpler than that of the restaurant, but they are comfortable and have excellent bathrooms.

Good value at 37€ for a single and 54€ for a double.

FOURGES 27630, Eure

Map 4H
15 km E of Vernon

The Epte is a particularly appealing river - big enough to be interesting, small enough to be unspoiled. Here it is shallow but fast flowing over rushes and between willow-hung banks. I heartily recommend a picnic, or:

☆ **Le Moulin de Fourges** 🛏 ☒ M
38 r. de Moulin
tel: (0)232.52.12.12
fax: (0)232.52.92.56
closed: Mon.; 1/11-1/4

I discovered the Moulin a while back but had to write 'What a pity that somewhere so utterly charming should be too run-down for a mention'. Not so now. Very good news indeed here. A new enthusiastic team have taken it over, smartened it up and are realising its very considerable potential. It always was ridiculously pretty, so pretty that one thinks Disney-fabricated, but here the wavy roof, huge rustic water wheel, rustic galleries and balconies, faded salmon pink paint, gardens running down to the rivers edge are for read. And now the interior has been re-thought, and tastefully restored. The first floor dining room has high arched beams, tables discreetly wide apart, and sunny yellow decor. The welcome is warm and the service friendly and efficient.

Menus from 16.5€ during the week, which is the time to aim for because with a setting like this its all going to be packed out at weekends, when the menu price goes up to 26€. Cooking is traditional with occasional innovations - tête de veau, turbot with vanilla - interesting wine list. I ration the word 'idyllic', but it is totally justified here, and if you pick a fine day and eat outside on the lawn, I have no doubt you will agree with me.

Starred for setting and accueil.

GACE 61230, Orne

28 km E of Argentan

This is stud country, with the grounds of elegant châteaux put to good use for grazing equally graceful horses. It's all very green and peaceful and far away from any big town, but an easy drive on straight main roads from either port, Caen or Le Havre.

Hostellerie des Champs
route Alencon
tel: 02.33.39.09.05
fax: 02.33.36.81.26
closed: Mon and Tue, 1-Nov- 15-Mar

A 19th century 'gentilhommiere', i.e. a manor-house, in soft weathered stone and grey slate roof. There is a tennis court and swimming pool in the grounds. The fourteen rooms are good value (this is not tourist country) at 48-61€ Menus start at 16€ (mid-week and lunch only) then jump alarmingly to 31€.

This all looks very good news, but so far I have only one reader who has been kind enough to recommend it. Is there a snag, or should it be a star?

GIVERNY 27620, Eure

Map 4H
3km E of Vernon

On the opposite bank of the river from Vernon.

Giverny and Monet are practically synonymous. Here is the housein which he lived from 1883 until 1926, enjoying the proximity of the river Epte and the quality of Norman light He grew to become as passionate a gardener as a painter and his garden is a continuing memorial to his talents as a composer of living pictures. In his old age he was so fascinated by the water lilies that crowded the lake that he painted the scene more than fifty times, working away in the newer of the two studios here. So many visitors want to see the spot that a tunnel had to be built under the busy D5 to the Japanese water garden, where the wisteria-festooned green bridge over the water and the lilies feature in many a souvenir photograph.

The garden in front of the house, Le Clos Normand, is packed with shimmering colour and sensuous scents. The rectangular beds bisected by straight paths are full of cottage flowers - tulips, forget-me-nots, wallflowers and daisies. Nasturtiums scramble freely, as do roses and clematis over formal arches and pyramid frames. In autumn the hectic colours of the season - orange, flame, gold and fuchsia - can seem altogether too much to our sensitive English eye.

The garden has become a victim of its own popularity. It was never intended as a popular showpiece; the scale is domestic and intimate and shuffling round in a line does not add to its attractions. Much of the magic will be lost unless you contrive a visit early or late.

The house itself is surprisingly simple, with painted furniture in the sunshine yellow dining room; the blue-tiled kitchen has gingham curtains and rows of gleaming copper pans.

In 1992 the Musée d'Art Americain Giverny was opened nearby, as the centre of American Impressionism in France. Among the American painters represented are John Singer Sargent's Whistler and Theodore Robinson, who in 1892 painted "The Wedding March" depicting the wedding procession of Monet's stepdaughter Suzanne. There is a 200 seat theatre here for lectures and films, a restaurant and shops and the gardens are beginning to look mature and interesting.

Les Jardins de Giverny ⊠ M

Chemin du Roy
tel: (0)232.21.60.80
closed: Mon.; Jan. and Feb.

An appropriate house for a restaurant devoted to Monet garden visitors. It's Norman, and rambling, and slightly faded, and set in a pleasant garden of its own. Not a place to snatch a quick lunch, but to linger awhile. The menu at 21€ is surprisingly interesting for an establishment that doesn't have to look too far for its clients - a salad of hot Vexin goat's cheese, a fricassée de poulet Normand, more Norman cheese and a good tarte aux pommes. Don't even think of trying to get in for lunch on busy weekends without booking; if you do manage it then the menu starts at 27 up to 39€.

GOUPILLIÈRES Halte de Grimbosq 14210, Calvados

Map 4D
8.5 km N. of Thury Harcourt 50 km S of Caen

All very peaceful, very serene, with the wooded hills of the Forêt de Grimbosq rising from the rivÈer Orne to provide the perfect backcloth to the rural scene. One reader actually witnessed a train on the single track that crosses the D171 at the Halte, but I don't

*Auberge du Pont de Brie
Goupillière*

think the noise from passing traffic, road or rail, would be too serious a problem here.

☆ **Auberge du Pont de Brie** 🛏 ☒ S
tel: (0)231.79.37.84
closed: Mon.; Tues. o.o.s.; 17/12-8/2

The Auberge was one of those happily-remembered spots that one hesitates to re-visit in case all has changed. Here indeed it has. The bad news was that the family who had run this simple little hotel have sold up. The good news is that it has been bought by the young M. and Mme Cottarel and it is better than ever. Tastes change and simplicity is going out of fashion if it means leaky showers and bare boards. The 8 rooms have been upgraded; there are now six with a shower - 43€, one with a bath - 48€ and one family room with mezzanine - 58€ for four.

There have been even bigger changes in the restaurant, now considerably smarter and enhanced by M. Cottarel's cooking. 14.4€ for three courses, or 19.2€ for four courses on the Menu du Terroir. A drink on the terrace overlooking the rural scene or in the little bar would make a wise preamble.

There aren't many recommendable little hotels within easy reach of the port and the coast, and this would make an admirable cheap break, as many Britons seem to have found out. The star stays for the new management

GRANVILLE 50400, Manche

Map 5
26 km SW of Avranches; 104 km S of Cherbourg; 107 km SW of Caen
Market: Sat.

No. 1 choice for me on the Manche coast Granville is a lively town, big enough to maintain interest beyond the overnighter and with something for everyone - a wide sandy beach (when the precipitous tide allows), plenty of rocks to provide shrimping interest, a prom along which to take the ozone, more interesting shopping than anywhere else in the peninsula, excursion options to the Iles de Chausey or Jersey, a sizeable working fishing port and market for piscine connoisseurs, a plethora of bars, crêperies and restaurants, and the interest of the Haute Ville.

The Haute Ville is another world from the bustling commercial town below. Cross over the ancient drawbridge and within the ramparts a sense of serenity is immediately evident Even in high summer the narrow streets seem unnaturally quiet, footsteps echo, the windows of the tall dignified houses remain shuttered and no children play. It's a good spot for a picnic on a bench in the small park at either extremity, both with sensational views of the harbour, the Brittany coast as far as Mont St Michel and the Iles de Chausey. Otherwise there are a couple of crêperies, a bar, a tabac, a church and a restaurant.

Hotels: Not a great choice for such a tourist-worthy town, and nothing in the Haute Ville. The old Hotel des Bains has been considerably smartened up and blessed with a good restaurant, but you're talking 96€ and up if you want a sea view. Fortunately an old favourite at a fraction of the price is back on form:

Granville

☆ Hôtel Michelet 🛏 S
5 r. Michelet
tel: (0)233.50.06.55
fax: (0)233.50.12.25

This erstwhile villa is set sideways on to the road on the hill beside the casino. The recently re-furbished rooms are good-sized, and so are most of the bathrooms, the situation is central but quiet and there is a parking lot. Bag a room with a balcony if you can and then you can have breakfast with a view over the rooftops to the sea and St Malo. 19 rooms from 22-48€, excellent value and starred accordingly.

   Restaurants: Here the scene is much more encouraging. Here are a few of my favourites:

Le Phare ⊠ M
11 r. du Port
tel: (0)233.50.12.94
closed: Tues. lunch; 5/12-beginning of Jan.

The first floor dining room has the best vue panoramique in town, so try and book a table in the window to get your money's worth of fishing boats, private yachts and shabby cargo ships. The owners, Valerie and Philippe Vercella, bank on you looking out of the window rather than at the decor inside, which runs to flashy chandeliers. But it's the fish and nothing but the fish that you come here for. A dozen oysters costs 10.8€, a sole meunière 14.4€ - about par for the course; if you come across 'fresh' fish for much less you should view it with scepticism. Menus from 14.4€ and mammoth platters of f. de m.

Otherwise

The Phare is a long-term favourite and I always head directly there, but amongst the numerous fish restaurants that line the port two others have been specially recommended, Le Cabestan, 70 rue du Port, tel: (0)233.61.61.58, which has more tables outside so if the sun is too good to miss, make for here, and Le Guépratte at 34 rue de Port, tel: (0)233.50.00.85, which has been specially commended by a reader. With these two to choose from you can juggle with opening days.

☆ **La Citadelle** ⊠ **M**
 tel: (0)233.50.34.10
 closed: Feb.; Dec.

Step over the drawbridge of the Haute Ville to find this pretty little restaurant with four tables on the terrace sheltering beneath the dramatically striped blue and white canvas canopies. Inside there are stone walls, and an ambiance elegantly rustic.
 Fish again predominates, especially shellfish from the nearby Iles de Chausey and the menus start at 14€. Indifferent wine list but still a star for charm and good cooking.

La Gentilhommière ⊠ **M**
 952 r. Couraye
 tel: (0)233.50.17.99
 closed: Sun. p.m.; Mon. o.o.s.; 1/3-15/3

No sea view but otherwise Granville's premier restaurant, small but stylish. Recently redecorated, its freshly painted façade catches the eye in this town of granite- Fish is the star turn here, but served with interesting additions, like the turbot on a bed of chicory. Local ingredients like lamb from the surrounding salt marshes and ducks raised in Villedieu-les-Poeles are rightly prominent on the menus and here you can safely go for the cheapest one at 16€. A star for reliably good cooking.

Le Pierrot ⊠ S-M

16 r. Clément-Desmaisons
tel: (0)233.50.09.29
closed: Wed.

Probably the most popular small restaurant in town, thanks to its central position, pleasant owners, M. & Mme Pelissie. Predominately fishy, but with plenty of other options. Menus from 10.4€. All readers reports have been enthusiastic, especially about the generous fruits de mer.

La Poste ⊠ S

8 r. de l'Abreuvoir
tel: (0)233.50.02.25
closed: Sun. p.m.; Mon.

Popular with locals, always crowded, good honest value for both food and wine. Lunch menus from 10.4€, evenings from 11.2€.

☆ l'Echauguette ⊠ S

24 r. St. Jean
tel: (0)233.50.51.87
closed: Tues.; Nov.

An excellent choice for a cheap meal in the Haute Ville, this rustic little crêperie/restaurant offers charcoal grilled meat and fish as well as a range of crêpes and galettes. Everything freshly cooked. The star stays as the best crêperie in the Manche (if you know better please tell me).

GRATOT 50200, Manche

Map 4B
4km NW of Coutances by D244

On the left-hand side of the road (coming from Coutances)

Le Tourne-Bride ☒ M

tel: (0)233.45.11.00
closed: Sun. p.m.; Mon.

An attractive old house standing sideways on to the road, run by Martine and Denis Poisson. Inside the character comes from dark beams, olde-worlde, particularly welcoming if the weather is not kind. The food is easily the best in the Coutances area, and local families and businessmen make up the clientele.

Menus start at 15.8€ (then 22 and 30€) and include interesting house specialities like fricassée de lapin aux girolles à l'ail doux.

HAMBYE 50450, Manche

Map 4B
23 km SE of Coutances; 26 km SW of St. Lô

The village of Hambye is just a wide sloping square of old stone houses and a few shops selling basic necessities. The abbey of Hambye is actually 3.5 km to the south, nearer to Sourdeval in fact, but you won't resent the journey; the road, the D13, runs through delightfully green countryside, following the valley of the river Sienne. You'll know you've arrived when you come to a bridge, with picnic tables thoughtfully provided at the side of the gurgling stream.

The abbey is down a track to the left, backed by a steep escarpment The ruins, approached through a gateway thick with irises, glowing with golden lichen, are open to the public. On weekend summer evenings flaming torches dramatically illuminate the scene and piped Gregorian chant floats up to the Auberge nearby.

☆ l'Auberge de l'Abbaye ⇔ ☒ M

tel: (0)233.61.42.19
fax: (0)233.61.00.85
closed: Sun. p.m.; Mon.

I can't resist a little boast about the Auberge - it is one of the most rewarding stories. I was so impressed with it fifteen years ago that it became the Hotel of the Year in the first Normandy book. Hard to

AUBERGE DE L'ABBAYE   HAMBYE

know exactly why I liked it so much - it's not a particularly attractive building - a post-war slab of grey stone at the side of the road, but certainly its kind owners, Micheline and Jean Allain, had a lot to do with it. Jean was and still is a cook far superior to those in most little country hotels and for Micheline nothing is too much trouble to make her guests feel welcome and cosseted.

The rooms (50€) were very simple then, without much in the way of mod cons, and were really intended as accessories to Jean's cooking. They still are - this is a restaurant-with-rooms rather than a hotel-with-a-restaurant - but recently their space has been reallocated to provide bathrooms with bath or shower, and pastel colours make them bright and light and cheerful.

Pastels again in the large dining room, full at weekends with local gourmets who know how lucky they are to have Jean cook for them. Curtains and walls are pale peachy pink, effective new lighting is by dozens of tiny bulbs, flowers are fresh from the garden.

On the cheapest 18€ menu I enjoyed every mouthful of fruits de mer, brochettes of local lamb charcoal-grilled, Norman cheeses and fresh strawberries, but it hardly matters what you choose here - it is bound to be good. Every night there are two plats du jour, one fish, one meat or poultry, but always plenty of seafood and fresh vegetables. All excellent value.

There have been many changes over the Allains' tenure here, all of them for the better (you can't often say that), with the friendly atmosphere preserved throughout the Auberge's growing popularity. The only snag is that now Michelin has at last cottoned on it is not so easy to get a room or meal. Otherwise a good deed in an increasingly wickedly expensive restaurant/hotel world, and still 101% star-worthy.

LE HAVRE 76600, Seine Mar

Map E2&3
86km W of Rouen
Market: All day every day except Sun. (2 p.m.- 6 p.m.)

They say that Le Havre lost its heart in 1944, when it won the doubtful distinction of being the most bombed port in France, and never replaced it. Architect Auguste Perret tried. He devised two hearts - the Place de l'Hôtel de Ville and the Place Gambetta, amid a grid system of wide roads, among them the avenue Foch, intended to outdo the Champs Elysées. Then he lined the streets with identikit concrete apartment blocks, which give the town its distinctive grey and uniform character. It helps when the sun shines, the waters of the bassin sparkle and the flower beds in the Place de l'Hôtel de Ville provide a vivid contrast to the bleakness, but there is no warmth to any heart any more.

Sadly the only part of the town that tourists generally see is the most boring bit - the triangle between the rue Royale, ave Foch and the bvd. François ler (it was François who ordered the original Le Havre to be built in 1517, to replace the ancient silted-up port of Harfleur.) The scale of the town deters exploration beyond the pl. Gambetta, where the concrete igloos of the cultural centre effectively block off the only interesting view of the town, towards the bassin and swooping white bridge.

The real Le Havre begins behind the Town Hall, where the department stores and small shops begin. I cannot claim that the noisy r. René Coty is Normandy's finest but at least there is animation here, even in winter, when the reconstructed Havre dies.

To paint an even gloomier picture, the town is suffering badly from the competition enduced by the wonderful new Pont de Normandie. Why stay in a characterless port when in no time at all you could be strolling round the colourful Honfleur? A further nail in Havre's coffin was the exit system from the new ferry port, which means that most cars now head directly away from the town. Many of the shops in the rue Royale and the bars along the old ferry quays are shuttered, many restaurants have gone under.

However, needs must. There are times, perhaps with an early ferry departure or late arrival, when a stay here seems strategic. With time to kill, make for the Musée de Beaux Arts, one modern building that is a great success.

Built entirely of metal and glass, it looks out to sea on the point before the road swings back to Ste. Adresse. You proceed up and down ramps in this model of intelligent display to view the collection of Dufy, a native of Havre, Impressionists and Post Impressionists, and of Boudin, born in Honfleur but attracted to Havre. (What would he make of it now?)

Downstairs is a colourful exhibition of marine excitements - beautifully modelled boats, from fishing to steamer, and more paintings.

Shopping? Make for the area around and behind the Hôtel de Ville to find Monoprix, Le Printemps and Les Nouvelles Galeries. Best for food shopping, particularly if the weather is bad, is the Halles Centrales. Find them a street or two behind the pl. Gambetta by walking along the rue Voltaire. Cheap wine here in the Nicolas outlet and easy parking outside.

Two hypermarkets serve the town, Mammouth is at Montivilliers, signposted from the Tancarville road and Auchan in the Haute Ville (take the Cours de la République past the station through the tunnel and follow the signs to the vast Centre Commercial).

Hotels: The uniformity of the blocks makes many of the hotels look alike and I have difficulty in remembering which is which, so dull a bunch are they. However, the following have been endorsed by readers as fulfilling their function of providing a clean, inexpensive night's sleep not too far from ferry and restaurants:

Hotel Vent d'Ouest 🛏 M

4 r. de Caligny
tel: (0)235.42.50.69
fax: (0)235.43.40.17

33 rooms at 74€ with shower, 77€ with bath, and 83€ with living room space.

Otherwise

Celtic 🛏 S

106 r. Voltaire
tel: (0)235.42.39.77
fax: (0)235.21.67.65
closed: 30/12-10/1

14 newly decorated rooms 29-45€

Richelieu 🛏 S

132 r. de Paris
tel: (0)235.42.38.71
fax: (0)235.21.07.28

19 rooms 27-48€.

Restaurants: I asked the chief stewardess of P&O's Pride of Portsmouth which were her favourite restaurants in a town that she must know almost too well. She had no doubt that No. 1 was l'Huitrière (10 quai Michel Féré, tel:02.35.21.24.16), a little restaurant specialising in fish which used to feature in the early French Entrées, but was dropped because of lack of feedback. I am happy to pass on this recommendation from such a discriminating source. She also recommended one new to me, La Taverne Paillette (22 rue Georges Braque 02.35.41.31.50). Let me know if you agree with her.

☆ La Petite Auberge ⊠ M

32 r. de Ste. Adresse
tel: (0)235.46.27.32
closed: Sun. p.m.; Mon.; Sat. lunch; 15 days in Feb.; 5/8-30/8

Well worth making the short journey out of the immediate town centre, via the place de l'Hôtel de Ville, rue Braque, and the rue d'Étretat (which becomes the rue Ste. Adresse) but make sure you have a reservation first - this is a long-term favourite of the Havrais, and of FE readers too. It's small, dark and cosy, serving more or less traditional food of high quality. No fireworks, just the kind of cooking you came to France for.

The prices have risen to 20€ and 22€ weekends for the cheapest menu. Worth every sou and newly starred.

Le Bistro des Halles ⊠ S-M

7 pl. des Halles-Centrales
tel: (0)235.22.50.52
closed: sun.

A welcome newcomer, and first choice for lunch. The marketsquare is always a good place to look for bars and restaurants, andthis is no exception. The 13.1€ formula was obviously popular with theyoungish office workers when I last ate there. Husband volunteeredto guinea-pig and enjoyed his roast duck, three sorbets and glassof Meaux de Lyonnais, compliments of the house. I just had amedley of home-made terrines (6.7€) with a salad, but would have been equally happy with a cheese platter for 5.6€. If you eat à la carte, starters are around 5.6€ and mains 11.2€, with a fillet of sole in sorrel sauce costing 12€.

The Bistro is unusual in that it is also a wine bar, and you can get a decent glass of wine without necessarily eating here. The burgundy coloured paint outside emphasises its vinous connections and wine cases decorate the walls along with the usual bistro baggage of Byrrh, St. Raphael and Suze tin signs, lace curtains, blackboard menus, and iron-based tables.

There is pop music but so subdued that even my over-sensitive ear was not offended.

A Kir costs 2.9€ and I was delighted to see an unusual old favourite of mine, a Lillet. If you're looking for a fresh aperitif, try it here for 3.2€.

The young owners have recently opened up a new restaurant in Ste. Adresse, which might merit a visit. It is Coboco, 6 pl Fréderic Sauvage, with menus at 28€ and open for Sun. p.m. Reports please.

Ste. Adresse, along the coast to the north of Le Havre, is a pleasant residential area and beach resort, with wooden huts on the cobbles, and a bay full of windsurfers and infant sail-training boats following their mother-duck instructor. Some of its fading turreted houses give a faint taste of pre-war character. I used to recommend it for an overnight stop in one of the faded houses, but tastes have changed and it is now too faded, too primitive to be popular.

Le Winch ⌧ S

1 Quai Southampton
tel: (0)235.41.75.18
closed: Sat. lunch; Sun. p.m.; Tues. p.m.

A flourishing little restaurant, with nautical decor and easy parking, is only five minutes from the ferry terminal - ideal for a last meal in France.

The small close-together tables, with pretty tablecloths, are busy from 19:00 onwards. Service is swift, with menus specialising in fruits de mer starting at 15.8€ (not after 8.30 p.m.). Otherwise its 12 or 14.4€. Good-value wines in pichet or bottle (we paid 8.3€ for 50 ml of Beaujolais Villages) and aperitifs from 1.6€.

HÉBÉCREVON 50180, Manche

Map 4B
5 km NW of St. Lô

Take the D972 direction Coutances to St Gilles. In the village centre take the D77 Periers road, direction Pont-Hébert. The château is 3 km further on.

☆ Château de La Roque ⇤ ⌧ M

tel: (0)233.57.33.20
fax: (0)233.57.51.20
closed: 2/1-15/1

There is sometimes a fine line between chambres d'hôtes and small hotels. Because the owners of the Château eat with their guests we decided in favour of the former and included it in Bed and Breakfast in France, but now Mireille Delisle has given me the excuse to enter it here too - she now terms her establishment Auberge de Campagne. In truth it does not come precisely into any category - there are fifteen bedrooms which would tend towards a hotel, as would the fact that it is open year round and meals are available, but then the owners are so involved with their guests that the atmosphere is decidedly more chambre d'. Lets say we have the best of several very pleasant worlds here. However, you have to sleep here in order to eat here.

Its a collection of mellow old stone buildings, 16 and 17C, set round a wide courtyard with well-tended flower beds and a massive pressoir in the centre of the lawn which slopes down to a big lake.

The view is to the verdant valley of the little river Terrette and all is very rural and very peaceful.

The bedrooms are in the two buildings which flank the lawn and are all different, all newly decorated, all very attractive. I liked the one in red plaid with twin beds and a kitchenette, but then that had a shower and I prefer a bath, so perhaps another would be first choice, with a stylish bathroom. It hardly matters, they are all so delightful. 64€ for a double bed or 67€ for twins. Dinner is eaten at a long table in the big dining room - 19.2€ with wine or home-brewed cider, home-made bread and jams feature at breakfast and their own chickens often appear on the dinner menu. I like this one very much indeed - definitely a star for comfortable accomm-odation, in delightful surroundings, good value and friendly owners.

HÉRICOURT-EN-CAUX 76560, Seine-Mar

Map 2F
10 km N of Yvetot by D131

This is one of the prettiest parts of the Caux country, with picturesque villages tucked away in countryside of the deepest green, threaded through by the river Durdent.

Restaurant St. Denis ☒ S
2 rue St. Mellon
tel: (0)235.96.55.23
closed: Wed. and Tues. p.m.

A pretty little restaurant, coral-coloured within, beamed without, where the 14.2€ (not weekend) menu offers good value. We ateavocado mousse, trout from the nearby river, cheese and arefreshing homemade rhubarb sorbet, prepared by chef/patron M. Touze, and considered ourselves extremely well off.

HONFLEUR 14600, Calvados

Map 3A
20 km S of Le Havre. 60 km E of Caen
Market: Sat. a.m.

Once upon a time, not so long ago Honfleur was 57 km from Le Havre, via the Tancarville Bridge; now it is within half an hour of the port, thanks to the Pont de Normandie, which is as beautiful as it is practical. I do not know of a lovelier structure; cobweb-fine, supported by a wishbone either side, it is a pleasure to drive over it, even with the stiff tolls.

Whether or not it is attributable to the new bridge I do not know, but I sense an air of prosperity and enthusiasm in Honfleur, which was previously lacking. The town looks spruced up, freshly painted; there are numerous building projects in progress and lots of new restaurants prepared to claim a stake for the regular tourist trade. Always a fan, I like it better than ever.

Not everyone shares my taste. Those who visit in August or at busy weekends deplore the crowds and the short tempers of overstretched waiters. I have to admit that I have no similar experience because on dozens of visits I have always been lucky enough to see the town out of peak period, when it never ceases to delight Nor do I find the grumbles that it is expensive justified. Sure, there are plenty of restaurants here that cater for rich Parisians who drive out for a Sunday lunch treat expense regardless. I have reluctantly dropped even a mention of the famous Ferme St Siméon because I think any Brit who is prepared to pay 368€ for a room and 88€ for a meal (a) wants his head read and (b) will probably let his secretary do the booking rather than read French Entrée for himself. But there is tremendous competition in the town amongst the smaller less-well-known restaurants and I found no shortage of these to recommend as good value.

The hotel front, I have to admit, is not rosy. It is surprising that in a town with the tourist potential of Honfleur that there are so few. I have been disappointed in even old favourites and two arrows have gone. I am almost (but not quite) driven to say try the chains here; the Mercure group always choose good sites, and Honfleur representative is no exception. No need for further description - seen one, seen them all.

The town is blessed with two centres, both highly photogenic, both ancient, both pullers. The Vieux Bassin (harbour) and the Place Ste. Cathérine, the site of the colourful weekly market The harbour is a gem; years of familiarity have not yet spoiled the impact of the framework of lanky old grey houses, some seven storeys high, reflected in the water, where yachts are bobbing and gulls screech overhead. The historic Lieutenant's house, recognisable from many a postcard, guards the entrance. Hard to think of a more pleasant exercise than to join the strollers round the quays, observing the artists at work, peering down on the boats below, watching it all happen from one of the cafés on the edge. The main fishing harbour, full of brightly painted boats, is on the other side of the lock and part of Honfleur's enduring charm is that it is still a working fishing port, not just a tourist facade. When the summer parasols are folded away it still has its living to earn.

Tearing oneself away from the harbour is made easier by the fact that there is more, much more to see. In Honfleur's alternative heart, the Place Ste. Cathérine, is a most unusual church, which gave the square its name. The Eglise Ste. Cathérine was built by local shipbuilders in the material and style which they knew best - wood and boat hulls, of which the roof of the nave is constructed. This was their thanksgiving that the English had at last departed after the Hundred Years War. Its not the oldest church in the town − St. Etienne on the quayside was built during the English occupation from 1419-50 - but it is undoubtedly the most popular.

Little snippets of historical interest like this keep cropping up in this multi-faceted town. Throughout the eight centuries of its existence it seems to have bred a particularly forceful band of men. Intrepid sons of Honfleur, mariners, explorers, scientists, were forever taking to sea in search of new horizons. One discovered Brazil, one opened up the mouth of the St. Lawrence river, and one, Samuel de Champlain, enlisted local seafarers to sail to Canada and start a colony there.

In the 17C, Colbert ordered the demolition of most of the town's old fortifications designed to thwart the English, and constructed the Vieux Bassin. He bulk three salt warehouses to store the salt necessary for preserving, the fishermen's catch. Two of these still remain behind the Maine (look for the 'greniers de sel' signs). There has been some sensitive restoration of this area recently and it is now a pleasant place to stroll, between the stone and timbered houses, checking the menus of the bistros and crêperies there.

The 19C saw the beginning of a new role for Honfleur - that of an artistic focus. Painters like Boudin and Jongkind, musicians like Erik Saté, writers like Baudelaire, were born or lived there. The town art gallery is named after Boudin; it is in the rue Albert ler, an interesting building, half-modern, half-chapel, though I can't claim that the examples of Boudin's work there do him justice; the museum, which is primarily devoted to the Honfleur school of painting in and around the Seine estuary, has recently been much improved, so it might be worth another look.

Boudin was the centre of the group of young artists fascinated by the effects of the opalescent northern light on the estuary waters, who attempted to capture their impressions on canvas and later became known as the Impressionists and Post-Impressionists.

It is ironic that the meeting place of this group of impoverished Bohemians is the very same Ferme St. Siméon that I now find too expensive to consider. It was once an inn owned by Mère Toutain; Monet, Sisley, Cezanne, Pisarro, all knew it well; Courbet portrayed it on canvas in 'Le Jardin de la Mère Toutain'.

Drive past the old grey stone building now so pristine and manicured, along the steep and winding coast road, the D513, known as the Côte de Grâce, and you will come across the charming 17C chapel of Notre Dame de Grâce, the Mariners' Chapel. The walls and nave inside are crammed with thanksgivings for lives saved at sea - very moving. Whit Monday is dedicated to a special pilgrimage here for all manner of seafarers.

Le Castel Albertine 🛏 M-L

19 cours Albert-Manuel
tel: (0)231.98.85.56
fax: (0)231.98.85.56

Conflict of reports here. I gave it a star for accessibility, comfortable elegant rooms, but one reader was most unhappy:

'There were no rooms available on the garden side so we ended up in a cramped bedroom with a rather ancient bathroom overlooking the main road.'

I don't feel too guilty; the hotel has changed hands, which is a pity because it now lacks the personal warm welcome of the previous owner, but otherwise I think what I wrote still gives a fair picture of what to expect

'A 19C manor-house set back from the main approach road, with the bonus, unusual in Honfleur, of an extensive leafy garden, with a little lake, bridge and rowing boat. As for rooms, you get what you pay for. My favourite, No. 3, all green and cream and Laura Ashley, with long windows opening onto the garden, now costs 112€, (worth every sou) while a comparatively small doubled bedded room overlooking the road (but with little traffic noise at night) costs 72e€ (not such good value). In between is a variety of combinations of double/twin/bath/shower, so state your preference when you book.'

The reception area has been smartened up and a sauna room added but the atmosphere is much the same, and it would remain my first choice in the town.

I still find the rooms overlooking the garden serene and dignified and so did another reader.

' We found Le Castel Albertine fully lived up to your description.'
Ivan McCracken.

l'Ecrin 🛏 L
19 r. Eugène Boudin
tel: (0)231.14.43.45
fax: (0)231.89.24.41

An impressive 18C town house, set back in its courtyard from a quiet street between the town centre and the Côte de Grâce.

Its restoration has been extravagant and the lavishness of its furnishings cannot fail to impress and astonish; sometimes it feels more like a museum than a hotel. Four posters, drapes, swags, gilt, crimson plush, tropical plants, are combined with mod cons: filmstar bathrooms and big colour TVs. There are some new rooms in the Annexe which are somewhat less fussy and still include an excellent bathroom, but these involve climbing a winding narrow staircase. Breakfast is served in an airy conservatory overlooking the garden.

Rooms in the house cost 152€, those in the Annexe 77€.

'We had the most marvellous stay there in one of the bedrooms on the top floor and were beautifully looked after. We simply could not understand how Le Castel Albertine got a thumbs up and l'Ecrin did not. We also felt very secure leaving our car parked in the private forecourt which was locked by 21:00.' Christina Bentley.

☆ Motel Monet 🛏 (S-M)
Cherrière du Puits
tel: (0)231.89.00.90
closed: 15/12-15/2

The best news in Honfleur. To find a base there that is both practical and inexpensive takes some doing, but Motel Monet fills both requirements. It is a pity that it should call itself a motel, because that gives completely the wrong impression. Yes, there is easy access and parking, no, it is not impersonal and concreted.

It's on the hill leading out of the town to the Côte de Grâce, backed by trees, peaceful, an easy five minute walk from the town centre. The ten rooms, not large, but well-equipped, surround a large leafy courtyard, with fine views over the roofs of Honfleur. Each has a bathroom with bath and loo, and an individual terrace where breakfast may be taken.

It was one of the most successful suggestions in previous editions and now it has got even better. New owners, Olivier and Annick Kuentzler, took over in 2000 and have renovated most of the rooms. A new breakfast room has been created and light refreshments and afternoon tea are now available.

Rooms cost from 48-69€, and family rooms are available from 67-86€, with an excellent breakfast at 6.2€.

Safely starred for friendly owners, cleanliness and convenience.

*'Throughout our stay the proprietors and their staff were at all times attentive, polite, friendly,and on one occasion, when we were having difficulty getting a taxi into Honfleur, Monsieur volunteered to drive us into town himself and refused payment. All this, combined with ultra clean accomodation and home-made croissants for breakfast, made our short break a delight.'*Howard Bennett.

l'Ascot ⊠ M,
76 Quai Ste-Catherine
tel: (0)2.31.98.87.91
closed: Wed. p.m. and Thur. Jan.

This is the smartest of the resaurants that line the east side of the bassin. On a balmy October day we sat outside in the sunshine, having prudently booked our table. By 12.30 they were turning wistful customers away and both terrace and the cosy dark interior were full for the day. It is obvious that although Ascot is relatively new, the reaonable prices and quality on offer have already been appreciated.

The accent is on fish but there are plenty of alternatives. No eyebrows would be raised if you asked just for a plateful of *moules*, or a dozen oysters. Allow 22€. for a full meal.

'*Our favourite. A charming small restaurant, friendly service and a very interesting good menu. Opens late also.*' Beryl Brown.

☆ l'Assiette Gourmande ⊠ M-L
2 quai des Passsagers
tel: (0)231.89.24.88
fax: (0)231.89.90.17
closed: Mon.

I can hardly keep pace with the Bonnefoys' shooting-star career. Now that they have moved again, taking Gérard's Michelin star with them to what must be their dream premises in the old Cheval Blanc building along the quay, but retain their previous restaurant premises in the Place Ste. Cathérine as a more modest establishment (see below). May good fortune continue to shower down on their well-deserving heads. Honfleur has many goodish restaurants but anyone interested in seriously talented cooking should not miss this one, especially the 27€ menu, which must be the town's best bargain. I drooled over tartare of salmon with caviare cream, langoustine risotto and the kind of crème brulée that makes me want to give up ever preparing one again. Starred for excellence.

l'Absinthe 🛏 ⊠ L
40 quai de la Quarantaine
tel: (0)231.89.39.00
fax: (0)231.89.53.60
closed: 15/11-15/12

A candidate for Honfleur's most attractive restaurant. In a 16C presbytery on the quay with a plethora of low beams and gleaming copper. The food is classy and pricey, better for an out-of-season dinner than for a sunny carefree lunch. You will eat very well on the 28€ menu. There are now seven luxury bedrooms appended, whose bathrooms boast hydrotherapy jacuzzis. 88-120€. Suites 216€.

La Brasserie du Port ☒ S

4 rue de la Ville
tel: (0)2.31.89.43.44

Honfleur is also short on brasseries, so this new discovery pleased me very much. It is to be found tucked away opposite the old salt warehouses. so you have to forego the sea view, but for a family looking for a well-cooked inexpensive mixed-bag meal, this should be the answer. Menus from 13.6€.

La Fleur de Sel ☒ M

17 rue Haute
tel: (0)2.31.89.01.92
closed: Wed. 2/1-19/1 and 14/3-30/3

The fishing fleet may tie up in the centre of town, but Honfleur has suprisingly few fishy restaurants that I can think of. Here the omission is corrected. La Fleur de Sel (named after the salt marshes of southern Brittany), concentrates on dishing up piscine produce, sometimes tout simple and sometimes with a twist that only comes off in the hands of a competent chef like the youthful Vincent Guyon.

A carpaccio of tunny fish, so red that it was hard to believe that it could be fish, came marinated to perfect tenderness, haddock was combined with baby turnips. There are other specialities, like the pigeon with a honey flavoured sauce, but it seems a shame not to sample the best fish in Honfleur. Desserts he keeps simple, like a bitter chocolate mousse, but uses only best ingredients.

The little bistro-like restaurant is to be found in an old timbered building in that street of old timbered buildings, the atmospheric rue Haute. Menus start at 21.6€.

La Petite Chine ☒ S

14-16 rue du Dauphin.
tel: (0)2.31.89.36.52.

What a treat to sip a cup of tea made with real tea in a real teapot. I do not appreciate the French predilection for a stale teabag in a pot of warm water, with a price tag of around 2.2€.

At La Petite Chine you can name your fancy - from good old English Breakfast to the most exotic *tisane*. Even better, the tea and the delicate *patisserie* come with a view. Although the entrance in the rue du Dauphin is at ground level you find at the rear of the shop that you are way above the harbour, with a fine aspect of masts and rigging. A welcome spot to rest the feet, restore the stamina and enjoy Honfleur.

Au P'tit Mareyeur ⊠ M

4 r. Haute
tel: (o)231.98.84.23
closed: Mon.; Jan.

News of a change of management here had me worried - I likedthe Mareyeur just the way it was - but so far so good. Nothing haschanged decor-wise, the service is even better than erstwhile andthe cooking still some of the best in town at this level, with noconcessions to easy tourist trade. It is minute, so booking advisable.

Menus start at 20€ with extensive à la carte specialising in fish. *'Now being run by a couple who are renting (with option in ayear's time to buy) from the owners. We went twice and enjoyed agood meal on both occasions. The only reservation was that therewas only one 19.2€ menu, with good choice and a very limited platdu jour variation. A choice of different-priced menus would havebeen helpful. Nevertheless Madame was warm and friendly and speaks English, having trained in London.'* David Rasten.

☆ Terrasse de l'Assiette ⊠ M

8 pl. Ste. Catherine
tel: (o)231.89.31.33
closed: Tues.

There is a whole row of restaurants spilling their tables attractively out on to the Place Ste. Catherine. By all means walk up and down and check out the menus, but, if you take my advice, put this one top of the list It is under the skilful direction of Gérard Bonnefoy (he of the Michelin star at 'Assiette Gourmand'), and his expertise and judgment shows. The menus may be more limited than at the parent establishment, the ingredients less exotic, but the standard is still high. Menus from 22.2€.

Auberge du Vieux Clocher ⊠ M

9 r. de l'Homme de Bois
tel: (0)231.89.12.06
closed: Mon.; Tues. lunch; Nov.

Here's another one from way back that has climbed steadily up the ladder from S to M. and a place in the Michelin. I have now run out of really cheap, really fun, really small, really exciting bistros in Honfleur. However, the dining room is less cramped, the plumbing is more reliable and the service smoother. The food is pretty good too, but I preferred paying peanuts to the current 20.5€ cheapest menu.

' *The best meal of our entire stay. On the 24€ menu my husband started with a delicious fish soup served with lot of lovely croutons and crispy things. I had a mousseline of salmon and asparagus with a tomato coulis which was gorgeous. Wonderful home-made bread. Then lamb chops so tender they just melted in our mouths then a selection of local cheeses (goat's cheese just amazing). Husband ordered an apple tart to die for, soaked in calvados. A churn of double cream with ladle was placed on the table for him to help himself. We cannot recommend it more highly.*' Christina Bentley.

Another reader discovered that the cheapest menu is only served till 20:30. Next price is 27€. Black mark, no star.

Château de Prêtreville ⇔ M

Gonneville sur Honfleur
tel: (0)231.89.37.06
fax: (0)231.89.28.39

I'm not sure if this should be included here amongst the hotels, or in Bed and Breakfast in France amongst the chambres d'hôtes, since it is neither, but self-catering accommodation. Since it is so good, I shall bend the rules and put it in both. It's a 19C 'château' set in three hectares, with a variety of self-catering studios and apartments for from two to six people, perfectly equipped, and run by the charming M. and Mme Rémi Bodet, who speak perfect English. The tarif is very complicated, with prices from 124€ for two nights, so do ring and check.

See also Cricqueboeuf and Pennedepie

INGOUVILLE 76460, Seine-Mar

Map 1F
3 km SW of St. Valery-en-Caux

Look for 'le Bourg' of Ingouville and les Hêtres is signed from there

☆ **Les Hêtres** 🛏 ☒ L
24 r. des Fleurs
tel: (0)235.57.09.30
fax: (0)235.57.09.31
closed: Mon.; Tues.; 10/1-10/2

To turn up at lunchtime on a sunny Sunday at one of the smartest restaurants in the département, without a reservation (and without any intention of eating or staying) is asking for trouble. Passing all the expensive cars (French) in the car park I hardly dared to push open the restaurant door but there in a flash was a welcoming Eric Liberge, regretting that they were fully booked but if he could be of service otherwise? Would that there were more Erics around.

After that I admit he had me eating out of his hand but even with a less courteous reception I could not but have helped falling in love with les Hêtres. Set in a tastefully colourful garden, the building is thatched, beamed and very very pretty, both inside and out. The four luxurious bedrooms (and yes, Eric actually took time off to show me these too) are in a separate building, priced (reasonably for the quality on offer) at 93-149€.

Ingouville
des Hêtres

I remember Bertrand Warin, the chef, with the fondest of recollections, at his former eponymous restaurant in Rouen (now les Nymphéas) and missed him, the best cook in the city, when he decamped, so it is good news that he has re-surfaced here and is cooking as divinely as ever. His 37€ menu must be the bargain of the year. Items on the day I visited were Breton langoustines cooked with Chinese-style cabbage, and brochettes of quail served with a beetroot and Parmesan gâteau.

I am going to break a rule here and award a star to an establishment I have not actually sampled personally. The rooms looked so comfortable, I know that Warin cooks like an angel and local opinion was so glowing that it seems a pity not to point readers in this direction. And I hope to make up for my shortcoming very soon.

ISIGNY-SUR-MER 14230, Calvados

Map 3B
11 km E of Carentan. 61 km SE of Cherbourg
Market: Wed.

Not really sur-mer but near the mouth of the Vire, which means oysters and all manner of other shellfish. There is a little quay, with green and red fishing boats tied up and sheds full of baskets of assorted crustaceans. The heart of the dairy industry and pré salé country, where the tastiest sheep graze.

France 🛏 ⊠ S

13 r. Emile Demagny
tel: (0)231.22.00.33
fax: (0)231.22.79.19
closed: 15/11-15/2

An old-fashioned very French hotel in the main road (so could be noisy). The 19 rooms cost from 29-50€, but it is the food that I am recommending.

The 11.5€ menu is a remarkable bargain - three courses of substantial well-cooked fare, with plenty of local seafood. The restaurant is full week-long but at weekends it's bulging and the cheapest menu price goes up to 42€.

Otherwise

Popular with readers for a cheap en-route meal - grills, kebabs, etc. - was the Flambée right on the quay, but I hear that there has been a change of management, so new reports would be welcome.

IVRY-LA-BATAILLE 27540, Eure

Map 5H
17 km S of Pack-sur-Eure
Market: Wed.

Following the little D143 along the meandering course of the Eure makes a soothing alternative to the parallel north-south main roads. It's all very green, very relaxing, passing through flower-strewn villages, like Ivry, with glimpses of water and good picnicking possibilities.

Le Moulin d'Ivry ⊠ M

10 R. Henri IV
tel: (0)232.36.40.51
closed: Mon. p.m.; Tues; 15 days in Oct.; 3 weeks in Feb.

Many changes here in this old watermill straddling two strands of the river. Inside all is much as was - lovely red Toile de Jouy fabrics in the ancient low-beamed dining room, even if perhaps it's all a bit smarter, a bit less rustic, a bit livelier than of yore. But outside there have been unthinkable additions. Tacked on to the side of the mill is a completely new building, pink and green, aggressive and unapologeticalty out of sync with its neighbour. It was not quite finished when I was there and I assumed it was new bedrooms for the restaurant, but, no, I was told it would be apartments. Best avert the eyes and enjoy the lovely setting, with wide terrace running along the river, for summer dégustation. Not surprisingly, one hour from Paris, the mill is very popular on sunny weekends, so be sure to book. The Menu du Marché 26€.

JULLOUVILLE-LES-PINS 50610, Manche

Map 5A
8.5 km S. of Granville

The bay sweeps all the way round from Granville to Carolles, sand all the way and That View (Mont St Michel) dominating the seascape. Jullouville used to be a sleepy little family resort but it's growing all the time and so is the number of souvenir shops and fast food outlets. For bucket n' spaders though it would still be a good choice.

Hotel Equinoxe 🛏 S-M
   28 ave. de la Libération
   tel: (0)233.50.60.82
   closed: 1/10-1/4

A spruced-up villa, one row back from the sea, which means the prices are much more reasonable than these for hotels with sea views. There is a bar, a terrace in the garden for breakfast and drinks, and private parking, which I think makes this really good value at 38-46€. It is on the main road but the traffic noise is minimal. A good twin-bedded room with bathroom would set you back no more than 48€, which in a seaside town in high season is not bad. Good atmosphere too.

JUMIÈGES 76480, Seine-Mar

Map 3G
28 km W of Rouen

The village of Jumièges is dominated by the ruins of the great Benedictine abbey, founded in the 7C, razed by the Vikings, rebuilt in 1067 and consecrated with William, the great Duke of Normandy, in attendance. The monks were forcibly evicted during the Revolution and an auction was held to dispose of the building. A builder and timber merchant made the successful bid and used his new acquisition as a stone quarry. 130 years ago it was rescued and now belongs to the state.

   You get a lot of ruin for your money. The entire nave, roofless, soars 14.4€ high to the sky and some of the chancel and transept

Abbaye de Jumièges

remain. But it is the twin towers either side of the main door that will be familiar from posters. A most rewarding hour could be spent here wondering and wandering through the history-steeped grounds.

From here to Duclair the river makes a spectacular loop; the road, that follows it, the D65, is known as the Route de Fruits, lined with fruit stalls neath umbrellas. Sheltered by chalk escarpments this is perfect picnicking ground and alongside the river numerous families set up their parasols and unpack their copious lunches. There are one or two small restaurants, like La Pommeraie for snacks, and a salon de thé, Le Parc, with a nice terraced garden. Not to be missed.

Auberge des Ruines ⊠ M
   pl. de la Mairie
   tel: (0)235.37.24.05
   closed: Sun p.m.; Tues. p.m.; Wed.; 20/8-4/9; 3 weeks at Christmas.

Big improvements here. An enthusiastic young couple, Agnes and Loïc Henry, have rescued what used to be a dusty and decrepit old inn, only viable because of its superb position opposite the abbey walls, and turned it into an excellent restaurant. I do not know what their plans are for the bedrooms (which were in a disgraceful state when I saw them last), but never mind. For the moment they do well to concentrate on Loïc's cooking.

Given his talent and the site it is not surprising that the auberge is usually full, so plans to eat here should be made in advance. The dining room is not at all plush, but has plenty of atmosphere and bulges with noisy enjoyment at the weekend.

Menus from 14.8€ (weekdays and Sat. lunch only), otherwise 22€ to 30€.

Le Passage ⊨ ⊠ S
   Pont Jumièges
   tel: 02.35.37.04.86
   closed: Mon except fêtes

I cannot imagine a more romantic setting than that of this little restaurant right on the water's edge. You can eat there and watch the little bac crossing from the other side to the tiny 'port' right here.

The older editions featured the café that used to be here, when it had no pretensions to be anything more grand, but then it declined and became a tourist rip-off and I reluctantly had to drop it. So I am delighted to see the new. reincarnation into a restaurant where the food is as good as the view.

Gilles Canal favours 'cuisine campagne', i.e. local meats, home made bread, terrines. His wife Karine smiles and welcomes.

Please write and tell me that this all adds up to a star.

LA RIVIERE-THIBOUVILLE 27550 Nassandres (Eure)

137 km from Le Havre

The river Charantonne, a tributary of the Risle, winds swiftly through its damp grassed valley, its teeming fish providing diligent French anglers ample reward for their patience. Local hostelries are not slow to profit from this abundance and fresh fish features strongly on their menus (which is only right and proper). For non-anglers, the area provides plenty of opportunity for enjoyment in exploring the several Risle tributaries in an area green with beech and studded with Norman castles and churches.

Unfortunately, La Riviere-Thibouville, looking so promising on the map, astraddle the streams, proves disappointing in reality. Sugarbeet mills dominate the little town. However, it would make a good centre from which to spin off in exploration and once again I have good reports of the substantial Logis de France situated there, which was dropped from the last edition.

Le Soleil d'Or 🛏 ☒ M-S

> **tel:** 02.32.45.00.08
> **fax:** 02.32.46.89.68
> **closed:** Sun

Just a perfectly ordinary bourgeois hotel, cheerfully decorated, with a garden for the children to play in and 12 comfortable bedrooms. Dominique Mamaz's cooking is way above the ordinary for this genre of establishment. I admired her original tarte tatin with onions and snails and her salmon garnished with hazelnuts and cauliflower mousse.

Rooms 61-94€, menus from 18€.

LYONS-LA-FORÊT 27480, Eure

Map 3H
35 km E of Rouen
Market: Thurs.

Take the N14 and then the leafy D321 through the forest from which the little town takes its name. In other words a comfortable distance from the city and an attractive drive. No wonder that at the first glimmer of sunshine all the tables (and there are many) in the square are taken and the cafe and restaurant owners have so much custom that they do not have to be pleasant to anyone.

Its a picturebook-pretty town, with some enchanting black and white houses. One of them, on the hill leading off the square was occupied by Maurice Ravel and it was here that he composed Le Tombeau de Couperin. The focal point of the town are the market halls sheltered by a fine 18C timber roof.

I recommend a visit to Lyons but not an overnight stay or even a meal. There are plenty of eating opportunities, but they are becoming more and more of the fast-food persuasion, with the exception of the famous La Licorne hotel and restaurant which occupies prime position overlooking the square. It is a lovely old building, with a delightful shaded courtyard, but since other serious competition has faded away it has become far too expensive and far too arrogant. Readers have not been happy here. The dragon-patronne (I suppose it was she; otherwise she should be sacked instantly) was one of the rudest I have met for a long time. Her hotel was full so why should she bother until it was empty again? The twelve rooms are from 66-94€ and meals start at 30€.

MACÉ 61500 Sées, Orne

Map 6D
4.5 km NW of Sées on the D238

Clearly marked, via various narrow roads in rather dull countryside.

Île de Sées 🛏 ⊠ M
tel: (0)233.27.98.65
fax: (0)233.28.41.22
closed: Sun. p.m.; Mon.; 1/11-1/3

Very imposing gates for such a little hotel. It's modern, but softened by creeper. Nice garden, tables outside, utter quiet. Inside the decor is a bit plush for the countryside, but the lounge is comfy and the dining room pretty in pink and yellow with cane chairs. Menus here are from 13.6€ (lunch) to 30€. Everything well prepared, and good carafe wine. The 16 bedrooms are on the small side, but again comfortable and well equipped at 50-59€.

The Île is featured by several tour companies and very popular with the British, who like its position away (but not too far away) from the town and traffic, and its reliability.

MARTIN-ÉGLISE 76370, Seine-Mar

Map 1G
7 km SE of Dieppe

So near the port yet so far in mood. Take the D1 out of Dieppe and the suburbs stretch almost all the way to Martin-Église, where they suddenly come to an abrupt halt. One minute it's factories and lorries and then, all the more welcome for the surprise, rolling fields and cows. In the centre of the village is:

Auberge du Clos Normand 🛏 ⊠ M
22 r. Henri VI
tel: (0)235.04.40.34
closed: 20/12-15/1

They don't come more rustique than this, a weathered 15C inn with large leafy garden running down to the river Eaulne. Eight simple bedrooms (and more to come) are in a converted stable block, creeper-covered, faded timbers. The only disturbance is an occasional quack.

The chef cooks on an open range at one end of a dining room almost too pretty to be true. His theme is Normandy – roast duck, fresh brill, tarte aux pommes. Dark beams, shining copper, red ceiling, white napery, high-backed cane chairs and lots of flowers

Auberge du Clos Normand.

contribute to a warm and cosy atmosphere that is textbook Norman.

Because of its ideal position and attractiveness, the auberge has a core of faithful customers and it is not easy to get a room. I think perhaps this might be the reason that the prices are on the high side for the amenities - 67€ for a double with bath, 56€ with shower, and menus from 29€ - but if you want a guaranteed peaceful night near Dieppe, with only a step across the garden towards a good dinner, this one takes some beating. Dinner is obligatory, which loses the star.

MAUPERTUS-SUR MER 50840, Manche

Map 2B
10 km E of Cherbourg

The Route Touristique du Val de Saire east of Cherbourg, starts off badly through shabby suburbs. Persevere and reward is at hand. Surprisingly soon the road begins to climb, buildings fade away and the view is of rolling countryside to the right and the Channel far below to the left. At Anse de Brick is a good sandy beach set in a sheltered bay, with a cluster of snack bars. High above is:

La Maison Rouge ⊨ ☒ M
tel: (0)233.54.33.50
closed: Mon.; In Jan. only open at weekends

Readers have been delighted to discover this comfortable restaurant, with panoramique view so near to the port. It's a bar and salon de thé as well, so a drive out in this direction might well be enhanced by a drink with a view, but don't think of arriving straight from the beach with damp cozzies – it's not that kind of situation at all. Catherine and Philippe Delsaut have smartened the place up and the decor is blue and yellow rather than the old red that gave the restaurant its name. Lots of seafood of course (16.5€ upwards); the French clientele were busy demolishing expensive lobsters purported to have been trapped in the rocks below. Menus start at 14.4€. There are three new bedrooms, but you have to crane a little for a sea view. 32€ without a loo, 53€ with bath.

MENESQUEVILLE 27850, Eure

Map 3H
28 km SE of Rouen by N14

Relais de la Lieure ⊨ ☒ S-M
tel: (0)232.49.06.21
fax: (0)232.49.58.87
closed: 20/12 - 15/01.

M. Trapagny caught me snooping round the back of his roadside hotel, having looked in at the bar and thinking perhaps it was not worth wasting too much time here. I was very glad he did, because the Relais is much better inside than out.

The 16 rooms in the annexe at the rear, well away from traffic noise, are surprisingly large and well-equipped - good value at 41€ - 51€. Meals are served in the rusticated dining room next to the bar and menus start at 14.4€.

MÉRY CORBON 14370, Calvados

Map 4E
26 km SE of Caen
Market: Wed.

Actually in the hamlet of Lion d'Or, on the main Caen-Lisieux road the N13, in the commune of Méry-Corbon.

Le Relais du Lion d'Or ⊠ M-S
Tel/Fax: (0)231.23.65.30
closed: Sun. p.m.; Mon.

An old favourite and a star under the previous management. I was sorry to hear that it had been sold but all reports of the new regime are favourable. Virginia and Christophe Dabout are said to be carrying on the good work and changing very little the winning formula of imaginative but simple food served in the charming wayside restaurant

It is much prettier inside than out, with two small stone-walled dining rooms. Floors are flagged, chairs are cane, fires are log and the death-defying spiral staircase still has to be navigated in order to get to the loo. I look forward to more reports to reinstate the star.

Menus are 16€ for lunch, others 25€.

MESNIÈRES-EN-BRAY Seine-Mar

Map 2H
5.5 km NW of Neufchâtel via the D1

A sleepy flowery village dominated by the great Renaissance chateau, now housing a private institution.

Auberge du Bec Fin ⊠ M
1 r. de la Gare
tel: (0)235.94.15.15
closed: Mon.; Nov.

Extremely pretty, black and white, on the corner next to the château, with a nice garden and tables outside on a terrace hung with (plastic) wisteria.

Inside is equally delightful, all dark beams, copper, lots of flowers, smart covers, smart service, lots more room than one might imagine from the cottagey exterior.

This is the only gastronomique restaurant in the region and understandably popular, but they have not loaded the prices accordingly. There were really interesting items on the cheapest menu, at 12.8€, and the 30€ would be a feast.

A few more reports please for a star.

MESNIL-VAL 76910, Seine-Mar

Map 1 H
5 km SW of Le Tréport

A peaceful village, nestling in a gap in the characteristic chalk cliffs, that only stirs and comes to life in the season. Nearby Le Tréport provides the buzz.

Hostellerie de la Vieille Ferme 🛏 ☒ M

23 r. de la Mer
tel: (0)235.86.72.18
fax: (0)235.86.12.67
closed: Sun. p.m. and Mon o.o.s.; 4/12-5/1

A very popular, long-established hotel, distinctively black and white in the style designated Anglo-Norman. Very pretty garden to sit in and geraniummed window boxes at every aperture. An old grape press lends further character. The tiny beach is 200 metres away.

The 34 rooms, for the most part in two detached houses in the grounds of the hotel, are calm and agreeable, though not large and not luxurious. Some of them involve climbing steep steps, so the infirm should check before booking.

And book you will have to, well in advance, since the biggest disappointment expressed by readers has been failing to get in.

The best deal is demi-pension (obligatory in high season), since the food is said to be good, 70€ per person. Otherwise it's 45-72€ for the room.

Royal Albion Hotel, Mesnil-Val-Plage

Royal Albion Hotel 🛏 M-L
1 r. de la Mer
tel: (0)235.86.21.42
fax: (0)235.86.78.51

One of the few establishments approaching L grade along the coast and particularly welcome because although the ambiance is de luxe the prices are not. Still new and trying hard.

The building is said to be an old manor-house, but the conversion has been total and stylish and now it is more reminiscent of New England than Normandy. Very attractive are the white clapboard porches and rocking chairs on the balconies.

The rooms are set around a wide courtyard at the rear; although there is admirable architectural cohesion, they are all different in size, decoration, facilities and outlook. Choose any combination of four poster, double-twin, modern and bright/pretty-pastel, courtyard/garden/seawards.

It's all very peaceful and away from the traffic fret, with extensive parc at the rear, dotted with recliners. No restaurant but the Vieille Ferme is nearby and all the fishy options of Le Tréport are a ten minute drive. The gentlemanly, English-speaking owner will be pleased to advise.

Prices range from 64€ for a standard double with bath overlooking the patio to a king-size room with four-poster overlooking the sea at 109e and buffet breakfast is 6.4€.

A promising new find. Reports please for a star.

MONTIGNY 76380, Seine-Mar

Map 3G
4 km W of Rouen by D982

Most of Rouen is contained in a huge loop of the Seine. Cross the river into the forest of Roumare and immediately you are in deep greenery, far away from the stress of the city. Nearby at St. Martin-de-Boscherville is the glorious 12C abbey of St. Georges, which I urge you not to miss. It has recently been cleaned and the white stone is now gleamingly pristine. It was the last abbey to be built in the Norman style and has survived through the centuries intact, with only one addition - the vaulted nave butts on intersecting ribs, which itself is no parvenu - it was built in the 13C.

Le Relais de Montigny 🛏 ☒ M
tel: (0)235.36.05.97
fax: (0)235.36.19.60 R
closed: Sat. lunch

My heart sank when we pulled up outside the Relais. I had imagined that a relais in the forest would have some character and here was a great ugly modern building of the kind I usually avoid. Thank goodness I had a reservation and it was getting too late to move on. As I ought to know by now, outward appearances in France are not always to be trusted and I nearly missed a gem.

First the location - to be this near to Rouen, in a quiet village, is a huge bonus. Second the staff, and management are most friendly, helpful, and professional.

There was a wedding party in the large and leafy rear garden at the time we arrived and all the staff were fully occupied, but they made absolutely sure that we were welcomed and shown to our rooms with attendant baggage-carrier (increasingly rare). The 22 rooms are large and exceptionally well-equipped, as are the bathrooms.

Most of them have balconies overlooking the garden. Ours was huge - ideal for breakfast, as an alternative to the general terrace.

The price was a bargain at 66€. We ate in Rouen so I cannot vouch for the food served in the pleasant dining room (menus from 22€ and good carafe wine). All reports welcome.

MONTREUIL L'ARGILLÉ 27390, Eure

Map 4F
22 km SW of Bernay on the N138
Market: Tues.

In the verdant valley of the Charentonne.

☆ L'Auberge de la Truite (Chez Jacky) (R)S
R. Grande
tel: (0)232.44.50.47
closed: Tues. p.m.; Wed. 15/1-beginning of Feb.

The star is not a suggestion, it's a command. No-one passing through this area should fail at least to drop in at Jacky's, even, as in our case, it was far too early for lunch. I really wanted to snoop and a café crème at the bar and a visit to the loo provided the opportunity to view two of the remarkable collection of fairground organs for which Jacky's is famous. I needn't have been tentative.

Madame left her ironing and set the huge 1930 Orgue Mortier into action. The volume was overwhelming, with drums, accordions, cymbals, bells, all taking their turn, sometimes solo, sometimes all together. Entrancing. In the room upstairs reserved for functions there are others, all highly colourful, and in deafening working order. Parked outside the restaurant is a green vintage car, so that brides can ride back from the church to the function all in the same time-scale.

The restaurant is pretty enough in its own right, even without its unique decoration. Rustic-simple, with blue checked cloths, brass implements on the walls and friendly service. Menus from 15.5€, as yet untested by me but obviously approved of locally judging by the numbers starting to arrive by mid-day when we left. Reports welcome for food - the star is for the decor!

P.S. An item for a pieces of useless information collection. The organs are known as Orgues de Barbarie. But why? After much questioning I elicited eventually that they were originally built by a M. Barbarie.

MONT ST. MICHEL 50116, Manche

Map 6B
22 km SW of Avranches

I have admired the Mount in winter, grey like the sea and the sky, remote, eerie; in the spring, when its colours change like those of nature from sullenness to sparkle; in autumn, when it swims in early mists and catches fire from late sun - but never before has there been an occasion to visit in summer. This was part-deliberate - I am naturally crowd-allergic and this miraculous place has particular claim to be experienced in peace - and part-accident; I simply hadn't been in the vicinity in high season and was happy to glory in the prospect dominating the bay from afar across the glittering water.

Until this year. July was the time allocated and July it had to be, and I am in a way glad that it was because now I can urge with every possible emphasis that no French Entrée reader should ever contemplate a visit then. They say this is the most-visited monument in Europe and it qualified for the title on that one afternoon alone.

Husband took one look at the thousands of cars parked as far as the eye could see and flatly refused to be involved. I, dear readers, am made of sterner stuff and trudged the half-mile queue to the entrance, muttering about sheep. I meant the tourist variety, but the other kind were out there too, munching away at the salty vegetation that would lend them such fatal flavour. I really needed to check up on all the foodie options on that one steep drag, but on this occasion duty called in vain. The procession of pilgrims was solid and hardly moving. Even my well-campaigned elbows would have made little impression. So all I can reliably report is that there are dozens of possibilities for everything from a pizza to a Mère Poularde omelette, currently selling at an iniquitous 15.5€ (and the main secret ingredient is air!). In fact there are so many eager outlets that the customer does get the benefit of the competition: the prices looked very reasonable and you can hardly go wrong on

Mont Saint-Michel.

a plateful of mussels for 7.5€, particularly if you choose one of the restaurants on the right-hand side and bag a table near the window for that fantastic view.

Enough of summer - just don't do it. For the rest of the year the Mount lives up to its appellation Le Merveille. From a northern approach particularly it dominates every landscape, glimpsed from little seaside resorts around the bay, to Avranche's heights, to surrounding marshlands, and the magnetism is undeniable. The Archangel Michael, whom it honours, is said to have become irritated with the tardiness of Hubert Bishop of Avranches, who failed to build the customary hilltop shrine in his honour on Mont St. Tombe, as the mount rising from the forest was then called. A few preliminary dream visitations failed to spur Aubert into action, so Michael tapped him so forcibly on the forehead that he dented his skull - there for all sceptics to see for themselves in St. Gervais in Avranches.

Left in no doubt about his boss's wishes, Aubert built the first oratory in 907, replaced by a Carolingian abbey on which successive generations piled more and more elaborate edifices in Romanesque and Gothic styles. Each one demanded formidable dedication of skill and industry, with granite blocks having to be imported from the Chausey Islands and Brittany and hauled up to the crest of the Mount. The many sections are too complex to describe here but those of the 14C Merveille to the north of the Mount are certainly not to be missed. Allow more time than you might think necessary. Ideally a circumference on foot (tides permitting!) is the way to assess the scale. You may have to paddle.

The combination of this man-made miracle, set in the natural miracle of the racing water, which leaves only a causeway for the pilgrims across the water meadows and at new and full moons surrounds the Mount completely, has always drawn admirers, so perhaps one should not carp that it still does. Just make sure you have space, time and peace to make your pilgrimage a blessing not a penance.

St. Pierre ⇔ ☒ M

Grande Rue
tel: (0)233.60.14.03
fax: (0)233.48.5)9.82

Rather like Disneyworld, the way to get this big tourist attraction to yourself, before or after the hordes have left, is to stay on site. This little hotel built into the ramparts, is a surprisingly good bet. The 15C building, classed as a Monument historique, has attractive well equipped rooms and probably the best restaurant on the Mount.

Food is admirably simple - gigots, grilled lobster, good fruits de mer - menus starting at 29€.

21 rooms from 88€ for a double.

Otherwise

New hotels are springing up on the digue - the approach road to the Mount. Personally I wouldn't choose them because they lack character and are purely functional for Mount tourists. If all you care about is somewhere to put your aching feet up you could look at the Relais du Roy and the Digue. Otherwise consider Beauvoir, 4km south on the D976, where the Hotel Beauvoir has 18 rooms.

MORTAGNE-AU-PERCHE 61400, Orne

Map 6F
38 km NE of Alençon
Market: Sat

My favourite town in the area. Perhaps I would not go along with the proudly proclaimed "Le plus beau bourg de France", but I'm pleased that someone thinks so, because it is not a town appreciated enough by the Brits. It deserves better - here is an unusually animated town centre, several squares, several bars, with a wealth of old houses and monuments in intriguing narrow mediaeval lanes, having survived many a war and hostility. Affluent townhouses like the Hôtel du Receveur des Tailles (the tax collector's house), which was built by a Parisian banker in the time of Louis XV, are pleasures to behold, as is the Hôtel Ste. Croix with a pleasing 18C curved facade. Behind the Town Hall is a small public garden with a vue panoramique, a gentle panorama of venerable trees and the softly rolling countryside of the Perche.

Good for picnicking (or take an excursion to the La Trappe and Perche forests, divided by the river Avre to the north-east of the town, where you can snack by one of the many lakes).

Amongst all its many attributes, there is one of which the Mortagnais are particularly proud. Their town is the home of the boudin noir. Every year at the Black Sausage Fair no less than five kilometres of sausage are consumed! The competition to produce the No. 1. black sausage is predictably keen and every year the heat is on to name the proud butcher who is judged to have succeeded. What used to be a local contest has spread and our North Country entrants have several times had the temerity to win.

You might like to consider becoming a new member of the Knights of the Black Sausage. You would be welcomed at the spring meeting so long as you are prepared to swear to eat black sausage once a week, to vaunt its qualities and to promote its consumption.

A super little town deserves a super little hotel and, belatedly, there is one such:

☆ Hotel du Tribunal 🛏 ☒ S

4 pl. du Palms
tel: (o)233.25.04.77
fax: (o)233.83.60.83
Open: every day except 25/12

A charming old stone building, both 13C and 18C, set in a strikingly quiet leafy square just behind Notre Dame. It always had great potential and now, praise be, that has been realised by M. and Mme Le Boucher, who took over the faded hotel in 1993 and have completed their refurbishment. The interior courtyard, flowery and quiet, is a joy, particularly for summer breakfasts, and in winter the dining room looks out onto the greenery. Make sure you ask for a room with this aspect.

The bedrooms are good value at 45-51€, with choice of bath or shower; one has a large terrace overlooking the courtyard, and a family room comes complete with a jacuzzi. The menus won't break the bank either ranging from 15-30€. The Menu Terroir, featuring a Salade Percheronne (with meltingly hot local cheese), the famous boudin noir and a tarte aux pommes flamed in brandy, costs 16€, but there is a cheaper Menu Formula, good for a quickie lunch, at 14.4€, for one main dish and one dessert.

I really like the atmosphere here, with friendly Madame Le Boucher officiating. A star for good position, good value.

Genty Home 🛏 ☒ M

4 r. Notre Dame
tel: (o)233.25.11.53
fax: (o)233.25.1.38 R
closed: Sun. p.m.; Mon; 28/7-13/8

Very compact, an ancient stone house squeezed into a side street leading into the main square. The eight bedrooms are compact too, but furnished in the same style as the restaurant below, i.e. in the elaborate mock Louis XV decor so beloved by French restaurateurs. Each has a shower, loo and basin and costs a modest 37-47€.

The dining room is intimate and best by candle-light, when the chandeliers and boudoir atmosphere seem more appropriate than for a summer's lunch. The French would not agree with me - there is no shortage of businessmen tucking into substantial tucker,

Hotel du Tribunal
Montagne-au-Perche

especially on a Monday when Madame de Gournay obligingly stays open. Trust them to cotton on to a good thing - the 14.4€ menu is very good value, and the carafe wine too, served in such elegant surroundings.

The enterprising Madame de Gournay never lets grass grow under feet. Her second venture was the Château des Carreaux, a lovely 18C château five minutes drive from the town, set back from the RN 12. This, described as an annexe to the Genty Home, would suit those who prefer to stay in the country (the nationale does not intrude) in somewhat grand style at a not very grand price. The rooms are furnished in the same Louis XV style but here it looks exactly right in the dignified and high-ceilinged salon and four spacious and gracious bedrooms. They cost a very reasonable 56€. Throw in tranquil grounds in which to stroll and it all looks a very good deal, but you would have to drive into Mortagne for dinner.

The enterprise does not stop here. Next door to the Genty Home is a cheaper establishment known as La Grillade; that too is now under Madame's auspices. It's all very light and cheerful, with plenty of tables outside commanding the best view of the square. Just the kind of place to know about if you're looking for a quick inexpensive meal or a coffee stop. 24€ menus, and an omelette costs 5.6€.

NÈGREVILLE 50260 Bricquebec, Manche

Map 3A
22 km SE of Cherbourg; 8 km W of Valognes

We are talking seriously deep countryside here. If you look up Nègreville on the maps (always supposing you succeed in finding it) you are in the wrong place. Rocheville would be nearer and if you asked there, someone might just know. Far easier though to give up and turn off the RN 13 at the St. Joseph exit to follow the spasmodic signs that James Boekees has been allowed to erect to guide his would-be guests. Five were the maximum allocated to him and he has decided to use them all in this direction.

☆ **Le Mesnil Grand** 🛏 ⊠ M
   tel: (0)233.95.09.54
   closed: Sun. p.m.; Mon.

It's worth persevering. The almost tangible peace and quiet that awaits you makes even the most tortuous journey worthwhile. I came across it when it had only been opened a few months, but even then I sensed a winner and winner it has proved to be. James is English, married to Pascale, who is French. He used to teach in a hotel school, so is now able to pick the most promising graduates and prevail upon them to come and cook here. At heart he considers this a restaurant-with-rooms, rather than a hotel-with-a-restaurant, and as the rooms are very nice indeed that's fine by me. He and Pascale and the bank dedicated much time, thought and money in restoring a derelict old farm (ask to see the photos to see what they have achieved). Money may have been tight but he was determined not to take short cuts and the result is tasteful and efficient. A bar was top priority - a rare hotel accessory in France. A carpenter relation carved the one behind which James presides. Drinks can spill out into the pleasant garden whenever the weather is kind. Pascale chose all the Laura Ashley fabrics and wallpapers in the bedrooms. and are still among the best in the region, with good bathrooms apiece. Highly significant is the fact that the dining room is always full at weekends (and often midweek too) with French, who dearly consider it worthwhile to drive into the country to eat as well as this. The cooking is imaginative and uses prime ingredients. Demi-pension at 120€ is the answer to anywhere as remote as this, and in this case it is no hardship. 99€ for two people covers a double room, breakfast and a four-course dinner. There is no choice unless you particularly don't fancy any item on the menu, but personally I rather like being forced to try something that someone else has chosen for me. Certainly I would not have picked fillet of pork from the menu but was very happy with the tenderness and creamy sauce of the version that was offered. Equally good was starter of warm spinach and mushroom salad and the raspberry tartlet. Only the cheeses were less than first-rate. Menus are 22€ and 32€. The friendly relaxed atmosphere is what wins most praise of all. James has proved a friend in need several times during his tenancy, in cases of illness and loss. At the Mesnil Grand you will feel secure, comfortable, cosseted and well-fed. I think that adds up to another star. Readers have unanimously agreed. 'Superb! The Boekees are a delightful welcoming couple and the converted farmhouse is just my cup of tea - solid and rustic but luxurious too. The food was excellent. Could not be faulted.' Sue Robinson

Le Mesnil Grand
Négreville

'This place really is a treasure. We certainly would not have discovered the Mesnil Grand without your book but now we shall certainly return.' Diana Holmes

Note from James: 'The French Minister for Tourism awarded the Mesnil Grand with a bronze medal for its contribution to tourism within the area. I bet they had to bite hard giving that to a Brit!'

NEUFCHÂTEL EN BRAY 76270, Seine-Mar

Map 2H
36 km SE of Dieppe
Market: Wed. and Sat.

A prosperous farming town, whose wide central street is the scene of an important market, where you will be able to buy in various shapes and sizes the Neufchâtel cheese which has own appellation d'origine, insisting that it can only be produced locally.

To the south-west of the town is the forest of Eawy (pronounced Eehvee), the most extensive beech forest (16,500 acres) in Normandy. Cut through by an arrow-straight divide, the Allée des Limousins, it covers a jagged crest, bordered by the Varenne and Bethune valleys, and makes a delightful change from the surrounding predominantly flat country.

Les Airelles ⇔ ⊠ M
2 Passage Michu
tel: (0)235.93.14.60
fax: (0)235.93.89.03

A dignified creeper-clad white house, grey-roofed, set well back from themain road behind a lawn, and surprisingly peaceful. It is well-knownand appreciated locally and banking on a table at weekends wouldbe bound to lead to disappointment.

The 15.5€ menu is particularly good value - copious and traditionalfood of high quality.

There are 14 simple but comfortable rooms, from 37€.

NOCÉ 61340, Orne

Map 6F
8 km E of Bellême on the D203

Deep in the heart of the lush Perche countryside, near the forest of Bellême.

☆ L'Auberge des Trois J. ⊠ M
1 pl. du Docteur-Gireaux
tel: (0)233.73.41.03
closed: Sun. p.m, Mon.

Everyone who knew I was compiling a restaurant guide recommended the Auberge as being No. 1. in the département, let alone the Perche region. It is surprising to find such a renowned restaurant in a small sleepy village, not very near anywhere. It's in an old Percheronne farmhouse in the main village street, with an unpretentious bar for the locals. Once inside the dining room the story changes - rustic elegance is the theme, with blue predominating.

The three Js. are M. Joly, père, and his two sons. The younger, Stéphan, is a chef of outstanding talent. Catch him while he's young and you can afford his prices.

The 30e Menu du Perche suggested a salad of shrimps, salmon and avocado in a spicy sauce, then an old farmhouse dish, poule au pot, enriched with local farm sausages, then cheeses and a pudding that might well be a version of English crumble with apples and pears, served with honey ice cream and poached figs. For imaginatively cooked freshest fish it is necessary to go up one to the 41€ version, presenting roast scallops with a confit of endive and lime, or bass in a pastry case.

One caveat - the wines can push up what looks like a bargain alarmingly. You can, however, rely on the carafe here.

A real treat and starred for good food.

OMONVILLE-LA-PETITE 50440, Manche

Map 2A
24 km NW of Cherbourg, 6.5 km NE of Nez de Jobourg

So near to the port in miles, so far in character. This part of the Cotentin is quite different from anywhere else, more Cornwall than France, with deep green valleys and time-warped hamlets inland, and magnificent cliffs at the western extremity You are almost certain to lose your way and then you have a problem because there is never anyone about to consult. The sleepiness is so evident that not a cat stirs let alone a human being. It's all very delightful and well worth the effort even if you do not intend to stay here. Even better if you do, so I tried hard to find somewhere congenial. Not easy.

La Fossardière 🛏 S-M
> **tel:** (0)233.52.19.83
> **closed:** 15/11-15/3

In the hamlet of La Fosse. Look for Digulleville and you're not far away.

It will have to be that word again. Idyllic is the only one that will do for the setting of this little stone cottage, set in a garden blazing with old-fashioned flowers, stream trickling through towards the old bakery, a tiny stone building where breakfasts are now served. Giles Fossard has contrived ten rooms out of this building, and two other modern purpose-built constructions just across the road. All is very tasteful, pretty, efficient and not expensive at 42-59€ for a well equipped room with bathroom. No restaurant could be a bore in bad weather, but there is a bar and the splendid Moulin à Vent nearby at St. Germain des Vaux.

ORBEC 14290, Calvados

Map 4F
20 km SE of Lisieux
Market: Wed.

Orbec how can I ever forgive you? You used to be one of my favourite little towns, peaceful, historic, full of interest, to be gently savoured. And now you lose all affection by introducing my bête noire - compulsory pop music. Yes, those unspeakable loudspeakers have been rivetted to every corner, to assault every eardrum.

We had ear-marked a table outside in the main street for a people-watching elevenses break, but soon realised our mistake and fled. What can the authorities hope to gain by such an incongruous introduction? I can only hope that we were unlucky and that the punishment is not continuous, but those instruments of torture looked pretty permanent

Assuming that either (a) the din is not perpetuated or (b) that you are hard of hearing and therefore immune, I can still recommend Orbec. It lies in one of the most attractive of the valleys of the Auge, and would make a good base from which to explore the region, rich with châteaux and manor-houses. Some are open to the public, some offer only tempting glimpses down long avenues, some are well-maintained, many are shabby by our houseproud standards. Bellou, Grandchamp, St. Germain-de-Livet and the moated Coupesarte are within an easy drive. A pleasing diversion is the source of the Orbiquet; take the Vimoutiers road, then turn left onto the D130 and D130A to La Follètiere-Abenon on the right bank of the river. Park just before the bridge and follow the path to the spring. Take a picnic.

The town is steeped in picturesque antiquity. The rue Grande has ancient wooden gabled houses and glimpses of courtyards and gardens. Debussy wrote "Jardins sous la Pluie" in one of them. Typical is:

☆ **Au Caneton** ⌧ **M**
  32 r. Grande
  tel: (0)231.32.73.32
  fax: (0)231.62.48.91
  closed: Sun p.m.; Mon.; 5/8-1/9

I am assured that this is a favourite restaurant of our royal family, but failed to discover which members. Enlightenment please. Certainly the Queen has a penchant for small typically Norman country establishments (see Breuil-en-Auge), which serve exceptionally good food. Au Caneton fits the bill – 17C, heavily beamed, warm and cosy, with Didier Tricot performing superbly in the kitchen, and Chantal offers an encouraging welcome. The eponymous duck does not feature as prominently as of yore but you can sample sauvageon grillé at 42€ for two people, or an escalope de canard au vin de cidre for 14.4€. It doesn't show at all on the cheapest 15.5€ Menu d'Affaires but on the 22€ Normand (and this is the one I would recommend) you can kick off with pâté de canard, followed by aiguillette de canard. Lots of other options of course, including grills on open fire.

All very agreeable. Starred for good food in an exceptionally attractive town, muffled from the blast outside.

Menus from 16€. (not Sat p.m.) from 26€ at weekends.

L'Orbecquois ⌧ **M-S**
  60 r. Grande
  tel: (0)231.62.44.99
  closed: Wed. p.m.; Thurs.; 17/6-29/6

Lacking the seal of royal approval perhaps but still a worthy contender for Orbecquoise culinary honours. What's more, it is usefully open on the two dead days, Sun. p.m.; Mon.

It's smaller and much less imposing than its rival, with almost a bistro feeling about it, but pleasantly furnished and with a good atmosphere, generated by its young owners, Hervé Doual and Karine. There is a no-choice three-course lunch time menu at 12.5€, which looked perfectly adequate, but you get an extra course for

16€, with some interesting dishes - leek soup with cockles, cheese, tarte Tatin, alongside the old traditionals like boeuf bourgignon.

I liked it very much and I already have one reader's approval. One more for Orbec's second star.

Menus at 12.5€, 16€, 24€, 27€ and 33€.

OUILLY-DU-HOULEY 14590, Calvados

Map 4E
11 km NE of Lisieux by N13 and D137

A picture-postcard rustic Norman inn, set in picture-postcard rustic Norman countryside, complete with river Paquine flowing by. Don't even try and pronounce the name of the village - we settled for Ooly du Hooly

Auberge de la Paquine ⊠ M
tel: (0)231.63.63.80
closed: Tues. p.m.: Wed. 11/1-1/1

In summer you can eat in the flowery garden which must be very pleasant indeed. For us it was a chilly March night and the log fire was most welcome. The auberge at first sight appears to be as simple as can be - just six tables, tiled floor, red roof between the beams, and the necessity to brave the dark and dirty night in order to visit the loo, with a mad dog going frantic behind his wire. But the cooking is something more than simple Norman fare. The 29€ menu yielded a terrine of skate and scallops, breast of duck with cherry sauce, cheese and a tarte aux pommes that indicated a skilled pastry chef. This would certainly be a star, since readers have approved, were it not for lack of welcome. I wondered if we had been unlucky, but local opinion agreed that it was the one thing lacking. Pity.

OUISTREHAM RIVA BELLA 14150, Calvados

Map 3D
14 km N of Caen
Market: Tues. at Ouistreham, daily at Riva from 156-31/8, then Fri.

Ouistreham nowadays is associated for the most part with

Brittany Ferries, and no longer as merely a little fishing port at the mouth of the Caen canal. However it still manages to retain a good deal of character and to avoid the concrete and commerce of a big port. If we arrive early for the ferry (after a long drive), a walk over the lock and along the canal or out towards the sea over the sand dunes is something to look forward to, as is the busy Friday market when local seafood stalls offer the possibility of taking home some caught-today fish.

Riva Bella to the west is totally different in character, more geared to the French bucket and spade customers than to the Brits in transit. The sands are splendid but the gaudy funfair and casino perhaps less so. One street back and it all becomes sedately residential with rows of maisons secondaires shuttered out of season. The hub is the bvd. de la Mer, on which are concentrated all the shops. Recently pedestrianised, this has become a lively, cheerful space to while away an hour or so. Better, certainly, than sitting in the car in the ferry car park.

Yet another aspect, which few tourists bother to explore, is the bourg of Ouistreham, a few km inland, where the locals shop and worship in the interesting 12C fortress church, a survivor of the wartime destruction that removed so much of interest in the surrounding countryside. Well worth a visit to observe its ancient buttressed belfry and Gothic chancel.

Around the main square in Ouistreham are grouped a variety of cafés, restaurants and hotels, almost entirely devoted to ferry passengers. I would choose from this bunch:

Normandie 🛏 ⊠ M

71 ave. M. Cabieu
tel: (0)231.97.19.57
fax: (0)231.97.20.07
closed:15 days in Dec.

A little Norman-styled building set back a little from the main square. Ouistreham's prosperity has been reflected here in the glossy increasingly ambitious menus, upgrading of the dining room and the prices. Menus (not weekends) start at 15.5-64€. The 22 smallish rooms cost 57€, without bathrooms.

At Riva Bella an old budget entry has got new management:

Le Chalet 🛏 S

74 ave. de la Mer
tel: (0)231.97.13.06
fax: (0)231.96.31.47
closed: Dec.; Jan.

This central hotel established a loyal following under the previous ownership and the current incumbents seem likely to build on that. The 18 rooms are simple but clean, modern and efficient. The best one, with new bathroom, costs 41€, so you can see that this would make a very reasonable overnight stop (or longer for a seaside holiday base). There is a useful bar which serves snacks as well as drinks. Plenty of restaurants nearby. Lots of reader approval.

Le Métropolitain ⊠ M

1 Rte. de Lion
tel: (0)231.97.18.61
closed: 1 week in Oct./Nov.

The theme is that of the art deco entrances to the Paris metro. Tables are in carriage-like compartments, lamps are low and swinging. The seafood is particularly recommended on menus from 11.5-32€.

PENNEDEPIE 14600 Honfleur, Calvados

Map 3E
1 km W of Honfleur

Take the winding dipping coast road, the D513, along the surprisingly unspoiled Côte de Grâce.

Moulin St Georges ⊠ S

tel: (0)231.81.48.48
closed: Tues. p.m.; Wed.; 15/2-15/3

There are two beamed rooms in this unsophisticated bar/restaurant at the road side. It has remained resolutely unsmartened up over many years, and the bar is still popular with the locals - both unusual attributes in this area. 13.1€ buys moules, poulet Vallée d'Auge and dessert. 23€ produces an assiette de fruits de mer, hare cooked in cider, salad and cheese and a tarte maison. Carafe wine helps to keep the bill down.

Readers have approved of the no-frills value for money here.

LA PERNELLE 50630, Manche

Map 2B
32 km E of Cherbourg; 10 km S of Barfleur

One of those surprising mounds that rear up unexpectedly through the flat Norman landscape, as though some divine landscape designer has thought, 'This view is too good to miss - better give 'em a vantage point' On the St. Vaast to Barfleur road it is signed on the left. Drive up past the weird grotto carved out of the rock to the ancient church, inspiringly simple inside; take a photograph of what must be the smallest Mairie in the land and get your bearings from the table d'orientation. Straight ahead is the point at Réville, that island is Tatihou, to the right on the promontory is the fort of La Hougue and the bay curves round the landing beaches all the way to Le Havre at its extremity.

Le Panoramique ☒ S

   tel: (0)233.54.13.79
   closed: Sun. p.m.; Mon.

An up-market crêperie, surprisingly large inside; so many tables suggest it might get very busy at peak periods. I use it for elevenses or at teatime, when you get the view thrown in with the cuppa. They do seafood and a variety of snacks, but don't invest a lot of money here. The brasserie meals start at 8€, the 'restaurant gastronomique' at 16€

PIERREFITTE-EN-AUGE 14130 Pont l'Evêque, Calvados

Map 3E
5 km S of Pont l'Evêque

Turn west off the D48 south of Pont l'Evêque, on the D280A, following the sign La Route des Douets.

Douets are the streams that flow into the river Touques and add even more character to this picture-postcard region of Normandy, to be found, amazingly enough, only a few km either side of the autoroute. They tumble into mini-cascades, as at Clarbec, or fill the mediaeval lavoirs, as at St. Hymer, adding their sparkling, gurgling contribution to the intensely rural scene.

Les Deux Tonneaux ⊠ S

tel: (0)231.64.09.31
closed: Sun p.m.; Mon. o.o.s.; 15/11-1/3

My, how things have changed here! It used to describe itself as café-collation, tabac-épicerie, in other words the centre of the village and provider of all its necessities, but on my most recent visit my request for a café crème at 11a.m. was turned down - they were too busy setting up the dozen or so tables that now furnish the ancient beamed room for the party they were expecting for lunch.

The bad news is that I can no longer write that les Deux Tonneaux is 'undiscovered', nor 'totally unspoiled' judging from the cool reception. But I suppose this is inevitable. I heard that it had featured on a BBC cookery programme, and I even saw a glowing report on its rustic charms in a glossy Italian magazine. Tourist offices recommend it as typique, so I suppose its going to be less typique every year. The good news is that the basic character of the restaurant, as I suppose I must now call, it hasn't changed. Admittedly whereas you used to sit round the edge of the room on upturned barrels, there are now chairs and tables, but the red and white gingham cloths are in keeping and apart from adding a larger bar and service area, they haven't tarted up the place. The two barrels from which the name is derived are still there, dispensing good farm cider.

As for the food - well, the menu hasn't changed much (22€). The farm chicken still figures prominently (book ahead), with bright yellow omelettes, home-made terrine and local cheese. And when the lady of the house, Jacqueline Rayer, is around, the welcome is more evident. Reports differ widely: *'Having sampled their basic menus, we booked ahead to enjoy the 'farm chicken'. We were served with what can only be described as two legs of supermarket chicken in plenty of fat. Chips were extra! The chicken cost 11€.'* Alternatively: *'It was marvellous to find this real gem, so friendly and the pre-ordered roast chicken came freshly cooked all crackly hot. We loved it.'*

Ann Soames, and: *'We enjoyed our "collation" a glass of Pommeau, pâté and cornichons, omelette and locally made cheese - as much as our chat with the lady of the house.'* H. J. Brooks.

Hmm - I leave you to make up your own minds on this one, but with such conflicting evidence the star will have to go.

PONT AUDEMER 27500, Eure

v41 km SE of Le Havre via the Pont de Normandie, 24 km SE of Honfleur
Market: Mon. and Fri.

The heart of Pont Audemer is like a sweet kernel encased in the hard-to-crack shell of dusty concrete, railway sidings and traffic jams. Persist, and you will be rewarded. Old bridges cross rivulets of the river Risle, overhung by ancient beamy houses. The main street, the attractive rue République, is closed to traffic on market days. Monday is for general household goods and clothes and Friday for the Marché maraîcher, probably the best in the whole area for food. The stall holders seem to take particular pride in Pont Audemer in laying out their wares, and the whole street glows with neat displays of whatever is in season at the time.

In springtime on the stems of the nice old church, St Ouen, overlooking all this activity, are flower sellers selling posies of wild daffodils for a few francs. Just the thing to brighten up the gîte. Look inside for some magnificent Renaissance stained glass (and some by Max Ingrand too).

Alas there is neither outstanding hotel nor outstanding restaurant to make a stay in the centre feasible, but in an unlikely situation just outside is a star.

Auberge du Vieux Puits 🛏 ☒ M

6 r. Notre Dame du Pré.
tel: (0)232.41.01.48
fax: (0)232.37.28
closed: Mon.; Tues. o.o.s.; in season Mon. and Tues lunch; 17/12-7/1

I know several Brits who consider any visit to Normandy that omits a visit to the Vieux Puits unthinkable. It has been there as long as they can remember, dispensing good food and hospitality to

Auberge du Vieux Puits

generations of francophiles. I hope they might be interested in learning a little of its history, partly gleaned from recent conversations with Hélène and Jacques Foltz, the present proprietors.

The original building in fact dates from 1630, a maison de maître, with three wings. In the 18C it was enlarged and used as one of the 80 tanneries which were the main commercial activity at the time of Pont Audemer, whose numerous streams were utilised to wash the skins. One of these runs, partly subterranean, around the property today.

In 1920 a former master-tanner, M. Harlay, took on the task of restoration. His respect for the original Norman character was so passionate that he spent two years searching the region for suitable materials.

In Rouen he discovered an ancient relais de poste due for demolition. This in fact was the Hôtel du Cygne described by Flaubert as the trysting place of Emma and Léon in "Madame Bovary". With infinite care he carted away the old 17C well and

195

installed it in the courtyard of his home, where it gave its name - Le vieux puits - to the budding.

In 1934 the father of the present proprietor, Albert Foltz, fell in love with the place and opened it up as a hotel. Ten years later the bombardments of 1944 destroyed twenty bedrooms but miraculously spared the rest of the ancient ensemble, over which Albert presided lovingly until his death, decorating the rooms with a unique collection of Norman furniture, utensils and antique faience, still intact today.

Jacques and Hélène succeeded him in 1964 and in 1985 constructed a new wing, totally in harmony with the old section, and installed six new bedrooms. They too have fallen under the spell that the old house exerts and recognise that it is not simply an Auberge, it's an institution and a valuable part of the region's patrimony.

So much for the past, what about the present? The old well still takes pride of place in the willow-hung courtyard that is such an agreeable contrast to the dusty road outside. The blackened beams, low ceilings, copper utensils, fresh flowers, log fires and bonhomie continue to charm the faithful British clientele, (and those of many another nation). Jacques Foltz has resisted the temptation to 'smarten up' his restaurant, gilding the lily with tapestry chairs and velvet drapes or cocktail lounges. The floors are still bare stone, the table linen minimal, and if you want a drink you sit on hard chairs in a little side room. Ask to see the stunning room upstairs, which is used for functions.

Jacques knows better than to omit from his menu those dishes that have been bestsellers since his father's day - the duck with bitter cherries for which the restaurant is famous, roast pigeon and Trout Bovary, a local trout cooked in champagne. Menus are 38€ (not dinner, not weekends). Most people eat à la carte, for which you should allow at least 54€.

Bear in mind that this is a restaurant with rooms. It is very pleasant to cross the courtyard after dinner and fall into bed, but the 12 rooms are tiny. They cost from 43-69€. An additional six more are now available in the 'new wing', open year round, and have private baths.

You are experiencing much more than dinner-bed-and-breakfast here - a slice of Norman history, which justifies the star.

PONT D'OUILLY 14690, Calvados

Map 5D
19 km W of Falaise by the D511
Market: Sun.

Nature was kind to this little town, surrounding it by the lovely craggy countryside of the Suisse Normande, but history was not - it placed it in the path of the Falaise Gap devastation, so that almost the entire town was wiped out Mercifully the old market halles survived and lend a modicum of character.

Le Commerce 🛏 ☒ M-S
> **tel:** (0)231.69.80.16
> **fax:** (0)231.69.78.08
> **closed:** Sun. p.m. and Mon; 15/1-15/2 1/10-7/10

A solid Logis situated in the market square, with an excellent local reputation and much approved of by FE readers too. The food is predictably traditional Norman, on menus at 12, 13 and 15.5€, and the 16 rooms, though small, are not expensive at 40€. It is quieter at the rear, with space for repose.

Auberge St Christophe 🛏 ☒ M-S
> **tel:** (0)231.69.81.23
> **fax:** (0)231.69.26.58
> **closed:** Sun. p.m, Mon.; 20/8-5/9

2 km out of town on the D23, with lovely views over the surrounding countryside from most of the bedrooms. The clientele for the hotel can sometimes be exclusively British, but the restaurant is valued by locals too and is often packed out The seven rooms decorated in simple country style are on the small side (or cramped as one reader described them), 45€. It is certainly very agreeable to eat on the terrace in summer. Menus from 16.6€.

PONT ERAMBOURG 61790, Calvados

Map 5D
3 km E of Condé sur Noireau on D511

A pretty village in the heart of the lovely Suisse Normande. The D511 follows the river.

Au Poisson Vivant ⊠ S
   tel: (0)231.69.01.58
   closed: Tues. lunch

A modern restaurant in an old building, managing to be tasteful in spite of lots of bright orange. Packed with local fans.

   Menus in English are not usually good news, but here that does not apply. The 15.4€ version offers interesting possibilities: sea trout with ginger-flavoured butter, cheese and dessert - an unusual formula. For slightly more you could choose a terrine of wild boar, followed by red mullet on a bed of cabbage. Dover sole aux agrumes (i.e. with citrus fruits) is 35€, and the sauté of venison comes with fresh pasta.

PONT L'EVÊQUE 14130, Calvados

Map 3E
48 km NE of Caen, 11 km S of Trouville
Market: Mon.

The town was almost completely destroyed in the 1944 bombing and has never regained much character since, allowing the few fine 16C buildings that survived to deteriorate. Traffic thunders through its narrow main street, adding dust and confusion to the scene and further threatening the fabric of ancient timbers. So the best news for a long time was to find that one of the most impressive structures, the old staging post hotel, L'Aigle d'Or, which looked disgracefully shabby for years, has been granted a new lease to what I hope will now be a very long life:

☆ Auberge de l'Aigle d'Or ⊠ M
   68 r. de Vaucelles
   tel: (0)231. E5. 05. 25
   closed: Wed. in Aug.; Tues. p.m.; 15 days in Feb.

That busy road might still cause concern but penetrate round the back into the well-preserved Norman courtyard and the scene changes. No dust but fresh white paint and black beams, no noise but bird song, no grime but many flowers. Inside the transformation continues, with everything spic and span and freshly polished, while the attractive old beams and flagstones have been judiciously retained. It's a delightful halt now, and the management, M and Mme Aimé Stephan, are still obviously trying hard. Their 34€ menu includes wine or cider, and lists well-presented old favourites like pâté de canard pistaché, farm chicken in cider and fresh pasta. An arrow to encourage to catch the excellent value while it's still going.

Menus 34 to 46€.

Auberge de la Touques ☒ M
pl. de l'Eglise
tel: (0)231.64.01.69
closed: Mon. p.m.; Tues.; Dec.; Jan.

Perhaps the auberge suffers from being tucked away behind the old church, beside the river from which it takes its name. Although it is long-established, although the dining room is pretty enough with its pink cloths and beams, although the 18.4-28€ menu appears good value (moules, trout, dessert), the place is rarely full. I detect a certain lack-lustre. Am I right?

PONT ST. PIERRE 27360, Eure

Map 3G
21 km SE of Rouen by N14 and D126

In very pretty country, green with the Andelle valley and green with the forest of Longboel. A loop of the Seine curves to within four km of the village, and this would be a good touring base.

Hostellerie La Bonne Marmite ⇔ ☒ M-L
10 R. Réné Raban
tel: (0)232.49.70.24
fax: (0)232.48.12.41
closed: Sun. p.m.; Mon.; 22/7-11/8

Once a coaching inn, and still looking exactly like one. If it has not been used for a film set by now it should have been. Beams wherever feasible, both inside and out, and a pleasant rear courtyard. The hostellerie is well-known and so is its chef Maurice Amiot, who goes in for gastronomic competitions and often wins them. His cellar is his particular pride. The atmosphere is warm, cosy, pampered; it's the kind of place from which you see prosperous red-faced French families emerging around four o'clock of a Sunday afternoon, blinking at the sunlight and heading for a kip. The nine comfortable rooms cost 59-89€ and menus start at 16€ during the week, 24€ weekends.

l'Auberge de l'Andelle ⊠ M

27 Grande Rue
tel: (0)232.49.70.18
closed: Tues. p.m.

From the exterior the auberge looks attractive because of the window boxes, its position between the little river from which it takes its name and an imposing chateau, but inside is pretty too. Two small rooms are heavily beamed. Cooking is less fussy than at the Bonne Marmite, but well-prepared and presented, based on fresh seasonal products. Menus start at 12.5€ except at weekends, when it's 18.4€, you would be wise to book.

PORT BAIL 50580, Manche

Map 3A
10 km S of Carteret

Such a pretty village, full of character, with wide chestnutted square, lovely old abbey church dating from the 8th and 12th centuries and an incomparable beach. If you feel the urge to be secluded you can always find a stretch of sand to meet that requirement; just lie down and watch the wind surfers doing all the work.

All the more pity then that there is now not a single hotel or restaurant that I can recommend. La Fringale is getting decidedly scruffy, though if you firmly resolve not to spend much money on a more expensive meal, their moules marinières are not a bad deal. You eat upstairs, with a view from the window seats or drink with the locals in the bar below. Les Pêcheurs across the road, though potentially attractive inside, is even worse gastro-wise.

Far far better to take a picnic. Turn left before the old bridge for a glorious walk along the estuary, animated with wild life and a better spot to set up a table and spread out the pâté and wine I cannot imagine.

That was my view, but a reader alerted to me to a new possibility across the causeway...

La Ferme des Mielles ⊠ S-M

   tel: 02.33.04.85.96.
   closed: Mon and Tue. except high season

A young local couple, Valérie and Frédéric Roulland opened here four years ago in a converted Norman farmhouse. The restaurant is in the old stone main building and at the surrounding farm buildings have been adapted to be used as a relais equestre. Children are in heaven here, either riding the ponies or just feeding them.

They try to make the most of local dishes - galettes, crêpes, smoked ham cooked in cider, on menus from 9.6-25€.

Valérie tells me that her parents have also recently opened a restaurant in Port Bail, Le Cabestan, right on the port, with seafood specialities. I look forward to trying them both and am delighted that such an attractive location can now offer a choice of eating possibilities.

PORT-EN-BESSIN 14520, Calvados

Map 3C
9 km N of Bayeux, via the D60
Market: Sat.

If the cultural attractions of Bayeux have been covered, it makes a head-clearing change to head for the salty invigoration of a little fishing port like Port-en-Bessin. Its little harbour is always lively and colourful, with plenty of non-tourist activity from the fishing fleet based there. Take a walk to the end of the jetties for a good gulp of ozone or climb up the cliff path to the old blockhouse for a photo opportunity of the harbour.

This is a popular Sunday excursion and there are plenty of cafés, souvenir shops and restaurants to cater for all tastes. M. Criquet, the butcher, is recommended for a picnic stock-up of terrines and saucissons.

☆ Bistrot d'á Côté ⊠ M
12 r. Lefournier
tel: (0)231.51.79.12
closed:. Tues. p.m.; Wed. o.o.s.; 15/1-15/2

You come to Port en Bessin to eat fish; by association you assume that the fish comes straight from the quay to your plate. Dream on!

In most of the fishy-orientated restaurants here and elsewhere along the coast it has travelled much further than that, via the deep freeze. It's all in the price and anyone who believes that fresh fish ever comes cheap nowadays is kidding himself. Here, one street back from the promenade, in this stylish little nautical-themed bistro, it is fresh and priced accordingly.

However, you are not committing yourself to big spending. If you are content with a plate of marvelous moules and frites, the bill will be 15.5€ - far better than an illusory bargain menu for the same price elsewhere. A weekday menu here is 20€. Another option is twelve oysters and a glass of Muscadet for 15.5€. A sole, which is my yardstick for fish restaurants, is admittedly on the steep side at 20€, but 24€ for the platter de fruits de mer is very fair. So are the wine prices and there is good house carafe wine available. Thoroughly approved by readers, so a star.

PORT MORT 27940, Eure

Map 4H
10 km S of Les Andefys on D313

Another pretty stretch of river, well worth trying.

Auberge des Pêcheurs ⊠ M
Grande Rue
tel: (0)232.52.60.43
closed: Sun. p.m. Mon. p.m.;Tues.; 12/8-1/9

I would never have looked twice at this rather dull-seeming

restaurant on the main road had it not been for a reader's fervent recommendation. I'm glad I did. Ignore the undistinguished decor and the fake beams and concentrate on the 18.4€ menu. It offers mousse de canard, fillet of ling with leek purée, and a dessert. If you want one of the house specialities, like the stuffed boned pigeon or the home-made foie gras you will have to go to 24€. Service in the pretty rear garden in summer.

PUTANGES-PONT-ÉCREPIN 61210, Orne

Map 5D
17 km SW of Falaise
Market: Thurs.

The nice little twin towns of Putanges and Pont-Écrepin are connected by a modern bridge, which replaces the mediaeval one blown up in 1944, over the willow-fringed river Orne. The market on its banks has taken place there for over 400 years.

The Lac de Rabodanges is just a few kilometres away, and here you can bathe, picnic, take refreshment at a water's-edge café and mock the amateur wind surfers and water skiers.

Hotel Lion Verd ⇆ ⊠ S
Pl. de l'Hôtel de Ville
tel: (0)233.35.01.86
fax: (0)233.39.53.32
closed: 23/12-1/2

A very popular and well-documented Logis, so book well in advance. It's not surprising that it is so well-esteemed, being one of the most agreeable hotels in the area, with wide gravelled terrace overlooking the river, and the big pink dining room likewise. Cooking is good and getting better all the time, the rooms, if not stylish, are undoubtedly comfortable (bag one overlooking the river) and the prices extremely reasonable.

19 rooms cost from 40-51€, with variations of bath or shower, double or twin beds.

I particularly recommend the cheapest menu at 12e which offered terrine, poulet de Vallée d'Auge, salad or cheese, and dessert. The plat du jour is a mere 5.6€, which suits the locals just fine. The size of the dining room reflects its deserved popularity.

QUETTEHOU 50630, Manche

Map 2B
28 km E of Cherbourg, 10 km S of Barfleur
Market: Tues.

The Tuesday market takes place in Quettehou's wide central street and is a meeting place for the owners and tenants of the many gîtes and British-owned holiday homes in the area. Its the place to take care of the everyday nuts and bolts shopping too, with several restaurants and bars. Readers agree with me that the best is:

La Chaumière 🛏 ☒ S-M

> Pl. Gén de Gaulle
> **tel:** (0)233.54.14.94
> **fax:** (0)233.44.09.87
> **closed:** 3 weeks in Feb.; 3 weeks from the end of Oct.

The obvious lure of the seaside towns ensures that their hotels are often full and more expensive than bed and board inland. La Chaumière's five bedrooms, all with bathrooms, would make a good alternative at 33-48€. But it is the restaurant that is the star turn here. M. Orange takes good care of the cooking, leaving wife and daughter to deal with front-of-house. The whole enterprise is spic, span and spotless, and the food way above average. Fish is fresh from the nearest port. Unlike many holiday hotels, la Chaumière knows that it has to rely on locals to come back and back and so the menus are varied and enticing.

Menus from 9.3€ midweek, then 13.6, 18.4, 20.8 and 33€ and good carafe wine. Breakfast is 4.5€.

QUETTREVILLE-SUR-SIENNE 50660, Manche

Map 4B
10 km S of Coutances

The river Sienne is little-known, little-appreciated. That's a shame because it is a delightful river, flowing through some of the prettiest country in the peninsula. With an idle hour to spare, it would be well worthwhile following its course. Here it flows wide and free; my idea of heaven would be to buy a picnic and eat it on the banks, where the river flows through the village, but a happy alternative would be:

Au Chateau de la Tournée 🛏 ☒

1 r. de la Libération; On the D971 at a crossroads.
tel: (0)233.07.82.07
closed: Sun. p.m.; Mon.; Wed. p.m.; 17/9-17/10; 15 days in Feb.

A puzzle this one. Why is it not listed in any guidebook except this one? Thought I had over-estimated it and there might be hidden snags, but no, it's looking better than ever. You step inside from the buzz of the main road into a lovely old room with ancient beams and a decoration of dried hops. The patron collects antiques and objets d'art, his eclectic tastes run to an amazing illuminated crêche in the giant fireplace and a suit of armour in the overflow dining room, but the impression is more of appreciation of fine craftsmanship than of eccentricity. Lucien Quémener and his family have been here for five years and built up a considerable local clientele as well as the passing trade for which his position is ideal. His cooking is both traditional and experimental - coming he claims from 'tous les pays du monde'. For example on the 22€ menu an original Tatin d'Endives, a Papillote d'Agneau à l'Orientale and interesting desserts. The cheapest menu is 14.2€ for lunch (not Suns).

The ten rooms are gradually being redecorated. When I visited they cost 32€ for one with shower, there is one with a bath and two double beds and two have their own w.c.s.

I should very much like to have some first-hand reports on what looks like a potential winner and see if we can solve the mystery as to why this place is not better-known.

RÂNES 61150, Orne

Map 6D
20 km SW of Argentan by D916
Market: Sat.

A nothing-special little town on the main road, where it might be useful to know of a halt that stays open on Sun. and Mon.

Le St Jean ⊠ S

> **tel:** (0)233.39.75.16
> **closed:** Fri. pm

A solid stone building on the comer of the market square, with a friendly bar and friendly patronne.

Excellent value on the 12.5€ lunch menu, good carafe wine. House specialities are sweetbreads with asparagus, duck with cider and bass with sorrel. At weekends the menu starts at 14.2€.

There are twelve uninspected rooms available here at 42-55€.

REGNÉVILLE-SUR-MER 50590, Manche

Map 4A
11 km SW of Coutances

It was a reader's prompting that led me to explore for the first time the bay of the Sienne; it's a region of vast skies, vast open spaces of sea, endless marshes; little boats lie for most of the day high and dry, tossed on to dry land like a child's abandoned toys. The sands stretch for ever and when the wind howls across the estuary any exposed skin gets prickled with the flying grit. On a sunny day, however, the palette of colours is unlimited, and walking is a delight.

l'Hostellerie de la Baie, Le Port 🛏 ⊠ M

> **tel:** (0)233.07.43.94

It is hardly surprising that any restaurant/hotel here should take advantage of the panorama, and sure enough the Hostellerie's plate-glass windows make the most of the view of sea and sand. It's a popular destination in summer, when the terrace comes into service, but the large dining room is cosier than most seaside establishments, with beamed ceiling, copper pans and exposed stone, and if you did hit bad weather a meal inside, sheltered from the ferocity outdoors, could be very comforting. The food would certainly help. Predictably it is seafood and fresh fish that is the speciality here, with prices reasonable for the quality offered. I would always counsel eating one beautiful dish à la carte when it comes to fish but the menus, starting at 15.5€, are a viable alternative. The biggest surprise was the standard of the bedrooms.

They are very well equipped, with bath, telephone etc. and freshly decorated. The sea views from their windows might well be expected to push the prices up, but No; I think 48€ is well justified here. Breakfast is 4.8€.

Didier Lecureur is a hands-on patron, usually behind the bar, always with a welcome. With a few more reports this could well be a star.

RÉVILLE 50760, Manche

Map 2B
32 km E of Cherbourg, 3 km N of St Vaast

Take a drive along the flat coast from St. Vaast to the Pointe de Saire for good views of the rock-strewn bay. There are lovely sands at the point but too many bungalows and caravans in recent years. On the way, on a sharp corner, you will pass:

☆ Au Moyne de Saire 🛏 ☒ S
Village de l'Eglise
tel: (0)233.54.46.06
fax: (0)233.54.14.99
closed: Wed. o.o.s.; Feb; 15 days end of Oct.

I had been briefed by readers to expect changes here but the reality far exceeded expectations. What had once been a cheap stopover, typical of many undemanding undistinguished Logis all over France, is now exceptionally agreeable. The youthful Marguérys have transformed drabness into lightness and brightness. The extended dining room is particularly pretty in its apricot reincarnation, and the bedrooms, though simple, are country-style fresh. The garden is new, and offers a welcome opportunity to relax for drinks or tea, and there is a private parking lot at the rear. M. Marguéry is a member of the Jeunes Cuisiniers Restaurateurs of the Manche and lists as specialities some far-from-simple dishes like home-prepared foie bras, gravad lax, fillet of beef in port and kidneys in a mustard sauce. Menus range from 13.3-38€.

The eleven rooms cost from 26-47€ and demi pension is 41-43€ (or breakfast 5.4€). I wish there were more simple but good accommodation like this, allied to good food and a smile. A star for encouragement

ROUEN 76000, Seine-Mar

Map 3G
87 km E of Le Havre
Market: Every day

Number one choice in my book for an off-season break. There is so much to see and do - so many museums, the wonderful cathedral, the ancient churches, the Joan of Arc associations, the river traffic - that one could never be bored. And if the sun should shine, do as the Rouennais do - make for one of the multitude of chairs set out on the pavements outside a restaurant or bar, and enjoy the parade.

Most important, it is a city with a clearly-defined heart. You can hardly get lost in Rouen, you can hardly fail to find its centre, which is compact and easily walkable. Big big problem is parking. You can either cruise around and try to spot someone leaving a slot by the road (which fill up quite early in the morning) or take the easy way out (as I do) which is to follow the signs to the Parking in the Place du Vieux Marché, grab any gap you find on the way or accept the inevitable and pay up for the Parking. Its probably better anyway because your car is less likely to get bumped there and you don't have to worry about feeding the meter.

The Place du Vieux Marché marks one limit of the most interesting and popular section of the city centre; the church of St. Maclou is at the other end, with the pedestrianised rue du Gros-Horloge leading up to the cathedral in between. Cover this part at all costs and then, if time allows, explore some of the side streets, especially those to the north of the cathedral, the oldest part of Rouen. The area between cathedral and river was heavily bombed and almost totally destroyed in 1944, so there is little of interest to detain you there. Stop off at the Tourist Office, in one of the sty's most beautiful buildings just opposite the cathedral, to pick up maps and current programmes.

In the Middle Ages it was in the Place du Vieux Marché that public executions took place. A mosaic stone marks the place where, on May 30th, 1431, Joan of Arc was burned alive.

Nowadays the centre of the Place is occupied by a modern architectural complex of church and small covered market, open every day for high quality produce. The steps leading down to the market provide seating for students and backpackers and there is always a lively and colourful atmosphere here. It is fitting that the centre of the square should be food-orientated because the surrounds have of recent years become almost exclusively a guzzler's paradise. I never actually remembered to count the restaurants and bars round the perimeter but there must be dozens. And then there are the speciality shops selling foie gras, sophisticated charcuterie, wine, beer. It would be a difficult palate or an empty purse that could not find gastronomic satisfaction here.

Many of the charismatic old-fashioned shops that lined the rue du Gros-Horloge have closed recently, making way for more young-fashion outlets and innumerable shoe shops. The standards get higher the further away from the marketplace you stroll. Even the shopping-allergic will find plenty of interest in this, the city's most famous thoroughfare. Old cobblestones and attractive 15-17C half-timbered houses lend plenty of character and of course there is the most popular monument in Rouen, surveying the scene from its prominent position above the archway spanning the road - le Gros-Horloge. The gilded single-handed clock was removed from its belfry in 1525 by the people of Rouen, and re-positioned in the specially-designed arch so that they could get a better look at its magnificent face.

The vista down the rue is blocked at the far end (about ten minutes stroll from the Place) by the bulk of the cathedral, set in a great square. Monet took a room in what is now the tourist office in order to paint it in some of its many guises, early or late in the day or year, and then in the following year stayed in another building, now alas replaced by a particularly repellant post-war erection, so that not all the twenty different versions of the scene are angled from the same viewpoint. Sit quietly in the square for a while to take in some of the details of the exterior, but avoid buying a drink or snack here - you could do better and cheaper elsewhere.

Developed over eight centuries, the building might serve as a catalogue of ecclesiastical architectural styles. From the 11C onwards each generation contributed its finest work to the ensemble. The differences between the two main towers flanking the 16C west door are immediately striking. On the left the Tour St. Romain is a relic of the 12C church, early Gothic on a Romanesque base; the right-hand Butter Tower is pure Flamboyant Gothic. The story goes that it got its name in the 17C, when the wealthy burghers who did not want to be deprived of their butter during Lent were prepared to finance the building of the tower in exchange for official forgiveness, but as a scholarly guide pointed out to me, butter was not around at that time and fat would have been more like lard. Pity, it's a nice story. One thing I can say with confidence - the spire is the tallest in France.

Of course it is a miracle that the cathedral survived the wartime devastation and there are plenty of tales of unexploded bombs that might have wrecked it. What an appalling thought. This is not the place for an inventory of the interior, just take my word for it that it's worth investing in a detailed brochure, and go early or late to avoid those dreadful people - tourists.

Continue the walk by following the north side of the cathedral, the rue St. Romain, past the Archbishop's palace, which is not open to the public. The outline of the cathedral spire is framed by a window, a lonely relic of the chapel where Joan of Arc's trial was held and where her rehabilitation was proclaimed in 1456.

Cross over the busy rue de la République to find another must see, the jewel of French Gothic architecture, the abbey church of St. Ouen, now restored and open for concerts, where the magnificent organ, one of the largest in the country, sometimes comes into its own. Stunningly beautiful choir, double clerestory, and some 14C glass.

Many people miss another treasure hidden away in the picturesque rue Martainville, the Aître St Maclou. There is no indication from outside that this unique curiosity is worth a visit - just a shabby doorway and an inconclusive courtyard, with art students wandering about. Proceed to the far doorway on the right however and you enter another world. Here is one of the last examples of a mediaeval plague cemetery. It takes the form of a square of grass surrounded by half-timbered galleried buildings, built in the early 16C. Look at the carvings on the pillars to discern the purpose of the grisly enclosure. They depict the Dance of Death, with stylised macabre motifs - skulls galore, crossbones, and sundry tools whose use it may be best not to ask. The bodies were piled up in the gallery, while the lower storey, now closed in, was an arcaded walkway. To see the happily chattering, blissfully unaware young students of the École des Beaux Arts occupying the gruesome old charnel house seems bizarrely inappropriate.

Cathedrale Notre Dame

Restoration of war-time devastation has been highly successful and imaginative. It is well worthwhile exploring some of the older areas, where treasures are continually being cleaned and repaired. Walk down the rue Damiette, lined with half-timbered houses, and offering a pleasing vista of the tower of St. Ouen, awaiting restoration; note the picturesque cul-de-sac of the rue des Hauts Mariages. Look at the Palais de Justice, formerly the site of the Normandy Parliament. Shell holes from the 1944 damage are much in evidence but the restoration of the elegant building is impressive. At every visit I find another small area to admire, like the rue Eau de Robec, just south of St. Ouen. Canalised streams of water flow through this little street, lined with restored old houses, making it particularly pleasant on a hot summer's day. Few tourists seem to discover the way here. The delightful little restaurant listed below would be a good excuse for a visit Do not fail to look up on your tours of discovery. For example in the enchanting rue Martainville, with its marvellous 15th-17C houses, there is a gold canopy with swaying tassels above some carved angels, set high in the wall of number 210.

Other high spots include (and you should certainly buy a specialist guide because there are so many to enjoy) the Renaissance Hotel de Bourgtheroulde, which has famous basreliefs of the Field of Cloth of Gold, La Tour Jeanne d'Arc, which is the keep of the 13C castle where she faced torture, and the Musée des Beaux Arts is one of the most important art galleries in France, particularly strong on post-Revolution artists, like Géricault and David, as well as Impressionists and Post-Impressionists.

Hotels: Rouen does have one serious deficiency - it lacks a good range of hotels. There are several in the modern re-built area that are practical, clean, inexpensive and fill the bill if a central bed is all that is required, forget the character, but you hardly need me to describe them, so I shall save the space for the more unusual and just list three that readers have confirmed are exemplary.

Hôtel Viking 🛏 M

21 quai du Havre
tel: (0)235.70.34.95
fax: (0)235.89.97.72

38 rooms from 40€. Locked garage 7,2€.

Hôtel Québec 🛏 S
18 r. Québec
tel: (0)235.70.09.38
fax: (0)235.15.80.15

38 rooms from 27-52€.

Hôtel Notre-Dame 🛏 S
4 r. Savonnerie
tel: (0)235.71.87.73
fax: (0)235.89.31.52

30 rooms 47-54€

Here are two that I can personally recommend:

☆ Hôtel Frantour Vieux Marché 🛏 M
15 r. de la Pie
tel: (0)235.71.00.88
fax: (0)235.70.75.94

This is my old favourite Colin's Hôtel, taken over by a chain. Disaster was my original reaction but no, nothing has changed except the management and that appears to be very friendly at the time of going to press. Conveniently situated in the SW corner of the Place du Vieux Marché, and therefore ideally placed for restaurant visits. The exterior is uncompromisingly modern - a sheet glass profile on the rue de la Pie and another behind a quiet and ancient courtyard in the rue du Vieux Palais. A different story inside where the starkness gives way to soft pastels and deep armchairs in the reception area. The bedrooms are furnished with expensive chintz drapes and bed covers to offset their simplicity. Nothing over the top, but comfortable, quiet and with parking facilities, which is a huge bonus in this situation.
45 rooms, double rooms at 81€.
Starred for practical comfort, but I need constant updating please.

☆ Hôtel de la Cathédrale 🛏 M
12 r. St. Romain
tel: (0)235. 71.57.95
fax: (0)235.70.15.54

The best possible news is that this charming little hotel, right in the heart of the mediaeval city, has been taken over by new enthusiastic owners., who are systematically improving the shabby rooms. Previously the superb location had been a justification for lackadaisical management and no effort to provide parking. It's still not easy but there are several lock-up garages available and the family-owners will do all they can to help.

At the rear is an unexpected flowery garden, in which to sit amid the greenery and recover after a day's foot-slogging.

Several rooms have been entirely renovated in the style of the 18th century, among them the reception and the room where a good buffet breakfast is served. As to be expected in a very old building, the bedrooms vary wildly - those with shower cost 48€-53€, with bath 62 to 80€

No hardship that there is no restaurant - they abound nearby. Quite the nicest place to stay in Rouen and not extravagant. A star of course.

☆ **Les Nymphéas** ⊠ L
7 r. de la Pie
tel: (0)235.89.26.69
fax: (0)236. 70.98.81
closed: Sun. p.m.; Mon.; 1/7-7/7; 24/8-31/8

The prettiest restaurant in Rouen, now owned by Patrice and Thérèse Kukurudz, late of le St Pierre in La Bouille, where Patrice once had a Michelin star. To his intense delight this has been restored to him here.

Glass doors open on to a very pretty and colourful courtyard, perfect for summer dining. Inside is pretty too, thanks to peach curtains and walls, which lighten the effect of the dark beams. Immaculate tableware and service, especially from Thérèse, whose keen eye never misses a trick.

There is a midweek 26€ menu, which is excellent value; otherwise it's a 43€ "gastronomique" - surely enough for most stomachs to handle, especially as the preliminary amuse bouches and the mignardises served with the coffee are too good to skip. I had a perfect terrine of fresh duck foie gras, then a sublime mixture of scallops and langoustines in ravioli, served with a beurre blanc flavoured with Noilly Prat. With the irresistible cheese board and pancakes imaginatively accompanied by grapefruit and a grapefruit

Le Gros Horloge

sorbet, this more than filled the bill. As did the wine - not cheap.

The only proud possessor of two Michelin stars in Rouen is Gill on the embankment, but as his restaurant is severely stark and a touch serious, I am going to award the star for the restaurant I would most like to visit for a special occasion to Les Nymphéas.

☆ l'Ecaille ⊠ M
26 Rampe Cauchoise
tel: (0)235.70.95.52
fax: (0)235.70.83.49
closed: Sun. p.m.; Mon.; 8 days in August

This is my number one for fish. You will find it not far from the Vieux Marché by following the rue Cauchoise in the NW corner. The decor is an appropriate navy blue and green.

There is fish and then there is messed-about fish and I generally prefer the former. The exception is when there is an inspired chef in the kitchen who respects his natural ingredients and does not allow any fancy additions to mask their intrinsic fishiness. Such a paragon is Marc Tellier. After I had sampled his combination of red peppers and anchovy butter with red mullet fillets, and clams and parsley purée with John Dory I doffed my cap in respect.

The prices are good too for a fish restaurant, where cheapness usually equates with frozen-ness. And the wine list will not break the bank either.

The recommended menu is 29€ (not Sat. p.m.; or Sun.). There are others at ranging up to 42€ and even 72€ if you insist on lobster.

Hotel Dandy ⇔ M
93 rue Cauchoise
tel: 02.35.07.32.00
fax: 02.35.15.48.83
closed: 26-Dec to 2-Jan

Location, location, location - the Dandy is ideally sited in a pedestrianised mall just off the Place du Vieux Marche, Just 18 bedrooms ensure that there is a personal involvement and the price of 69-76€ is reasonable for the comfort on offer. Furnishings are repro Belle Epoch, not plastic.

☆ Hotel des Carmes 🛏 M
33 pl. des Carmes
tel: 02.35.71.92.31
fax: 02.35.71.76.96

A new hotel to recommend in the centre of Rouen is cause, for celebration. Les Carmes in fact is a very old building, managing to conceal its very modern facilities, regularly updated. Bright colours for walls and fabrics, patchwork quilts on the beds, banish the gloominess that can affect old timbers. Prices are modest for the value on offer - the twelve rooms cost between 38€ and 43€. More reports please to confirm my view that this is a real find.

Le Beffroy ⊠ M
15 r. du Beffroy
tel: (0)235.71.55.27
fax: (0)235.89.66.12
closed: Sun. p.m.; Tues.

Chosen as the representative of the incredibly-picturesque-oldeworlde-typically- Norman group. (Others in this category are Dufour at 67 rue St Nicolas and La Couronne, the oldest restaurant of them all, in the Vieux Marché.)

Taken for granted are dark beams, big fireplace, glowing copper. It is all very cosy and comforting, as is the traditional cooking. This is the place to try canard à la rouennaise and tarte Tatin. Wine's a bit pricey.

I picked it originally because it is central, open on Mondays, and has a good value starter menu, even more appreciated since it has a Michelin star.

Menus 16€, 32€, 44€.

Le Bistro du Chef en Gare ⊠ M
1er etage, SNCF.
tel: 21.35.71.41.15
closed: Sun; Mon dinner; Sat lunch; Aug

The Michelin-starred Gilles Tournadre (proprietor of Restaurant Gil) has opened a bistro/brasserie above the station buffet. At the signature restaurant the bill would be around 70€ if you ate à la carte; expect to pay less than half that here, where the ambiance is a good deal more lively and the décor more amusing. International touches like bruschetta grace the menu, which for France is really something,

Les P'tits Parapluies ⊠ M

46 r. du Bourg l'Abbé
tel: (0)235.88.55.26
fax: (0)235.70.24.31
closed: Sat. lunch; Sun p.m.; Mon.; 10/8-20/8

An old favourite, to be found near the Hotel de Ville, which has gone from strength to strength since I first wrote about it. It has now risen to the dizzy heights of a Michelin star (and inevitably its prices have risen too). Readers still rave about it though, describing their meal there as `the best of the whole holiday. It's name comes from the old umbrella shop that used to occupy the site, and the decor is stiff nostalgically `retro'.

The cooking, although obviously of a sustained high standard, remains unpretentious. Familiar bistrot-type dishes recur, but stylishly presented. A favourite with the young, chic, and hungry.

'On the 9.4€ menu, I started off with six oysters, then skate with delish sauces, then crème caramel.' J.T. Deprez.

It is hard to select favourites from the Place du Vieux Marché range, nearly all with tempting tables outside. I hear that the Toque d'Or, which used to be my number one choice then fell from grace, is back on form. I like Le Rouennais very much, one of the prettiest, looking very classy, but keeping its prices down, but if I had to plump for one it would probably be:

Bistrot d'Adrien ⊠ M

37 pl. du Vieux Marché
tel: (0)235.7).57.73

A very old restaurant in a very old building, but with newish management, who have wisely not changed the character.

'You can still have nine oysters on the 15.8€. menu and they were excellent, as was the fish soup. We thought more of the desserts than you did. Three sorbets were excellent and the cornucopia of fresh fruit was splendid. A wonderful atmosphere. '

Menus from 24€ (lunch only, wine included), then 32, 41€.

A brasserie, recommended by a reader, is La Walsheim in the rue

Martainville. Also usefully open every day, all hours, and with the advantage of a terrace overlooking St. Maclou.

Le Petit Bec ⊠ S

182 r. Eau de Robec
tel: 02-35.07.63.33.
open: lunch only, except Fri and Sat
closed: Sun

An excellent tip-off because both the restaurant and the area are delightful. Streams of water give the street its name and antique shops predominate.

The restaurant is indeed petit, and is full to bursting every lunchtime with local office workers. It's pretty, painted yellow, light and airy, good for tasty light meals, like quiches, gratins, salads and pastries, all home-made. Menus: lunchtime 11€, 14€. Evenings à la carte.

Le Petit Zinc

20 pl. du vieux Marche
tel: 02.35.89.39.69
closed: Sat p.m. and Sun

Getting less petit all the time, This useful bistro/bar/whatever in the square has taken over the tearoom next door, open during the daytime under the jurisdiction of Madame Simon, while her husband, Alain, presides over the restaurant which spills out on to the terrace whenever feasible. His is un-fussy bourgeois cooking, in a cheerful animated atmosphere. A good choice of wines by the glass makes this a useful and agreeable rendezvous. 26-30€ à la carte.

Au Temps des Cerises ⊠ S

4 r. des Basnage
tel: (0)235.89.98.00
closed: Mon. lunch; Sat. lunch; Sun.; 1/8-15/8

The rue des Basnage runs parallel with the rue Jeanne d'Arc, between the rue Ganterie and the rue Lecanuet.

You wouldn't think it possible to devise a menu where every item had cheese as an ingredient and still make it interesting, would you?

Wrong, 'Cherrytime' does just that. You don't of course have to have three courses, but if you did you might find dishes like oeufs cocotte au Reblochon, or salade de chèvre au miel chaud, faux- filet au Boursin, fondues, etc. all featuring fromage blanc flavoured with honey accompanying ice creams for dessert. I like it for the times when I feel just like a plateful of assorted cheeses - you can get one here with six different prime specimens for 10.4€ or three for 5.6€, served with lovely crusty bread. The decor is suitably cheesy - huge plaster cows and old cheese boxes, and there is a very pleasant large terrace. Lunch menu 10.4€ otherwise à la carte from 15.5€.

SAHURS 76113, Seine-Mar

Map 3G
80 km from Le Havre, 65 km from Dieppe, 16 km from Rouen.

Access either by A 13 to Maison Brûlée, then ferry from La Bouille, or from D982 via D367 from Canteleu. From Rouen follow the river on D37.

The Seine snakes into a great boucle here, almost making an island of the Forest of Roumare. Its very pleasant unspoiled countryside, with plenty of opportunities to view the mighty river.

Le Clos des Roses ⇔ ☒ S

    tel: (0)235.32.46.09
    fax: (0)235.32.69.17
    Restaurant closed: Sun. p.m.; Mon.

A modest Logis chosen for its easy proximity to Rouen and peaceful setting. (Not overlooking the Seine alas, but in the village)..

Josette Danger welcomes and her husband Gilbert produces traditional Norman fare. They have 19 rooms, of which 15 have en suite facilities.

Rooms 24€ simple, 42€ with bath.

Menus from 12.5€, but you'd probably want to pay a bit more to get something really interesting.

ST. ANDRÉ D'HÉBERTOT 14130, Calvados

Map 3E
9 km E of Pont l'Evêque by N175 and D17 south

Hard to credit that by turning just a km off the nationals one could arrive at such intensely rural, utterly unspoiled countryside as that which surrounds St André d'Hébertot, a picture-postcard hamlet if ever there were one. As you mount the hill you come across a lovely old grey château, privately owned, set in sweeping parkland; its lichened walls line the village street, hard by an ancient Village church. Opposite is the old priory.

Auberge du Prieuré 🛏 ☒ M-L
tel: (0)231.64.03.03
fax: (0)231.64.16.66
closed: Wed.

The building is as stunning as ever, set in green lawns sheltered by gracious trees, so quiet that you can hear yourself think, and the reception area and dining room are exactly as I remembered them - huge beams, lots of flowers, flagged floors, stone walls, old doors opening out on to the gardens. Lovely. But there have been many changes since I last wrote about Le Prieuré. It has sprouted a hideous annexe, whose rooms totally lack charm. O.K. for them to be modern but do they have to be so dark? Windows are perversely let into the roof, so there is no chance to see the beauty around - surely the whole point of coming here. And the prices have increased dramatically. That's the bad news.

The good news is that the rooms in the old building are said to be unchanged. They were all full (with a seminar which does not bode well) when I visited, so I cannot confirm this and should very much like to hear from someone who can. I wrote: 'There are seven lovely bedrooms, decorated in appropriate country style, all with bathrooms and windows looking out on the garden.' I hope very much that this is still true and if it is I strongly advise a request for these rooms only.

The other good news is that there has been a swimming pool installed and that the food is vastly improved. That too has rocketed in price and so have the wines, so this is never going to be a bargain break, but the setting is so special that I think le Prieuré squeaks in. But no star.

Rooms 83€. Menus from 32€ (lunch only).

Auberge DU PRIEURÉ

ST. AUBIN LE VERTUEUX 27300, Eure

Map 4F
4 km S of Bernay

I found nowhere to stay in Bernay, so looked around the surrounding countryside drove down the D833, followed the sign on the left and discovered:

Hostellerie du Moulin Fouret 🛏 ☒ M
    tel: (0)232.43.19.95
    fax: (0)232.45.55.50
    closed: Sun. p.m. and Mon. o.o.s.

An ancient water-mill, but not a particularly attractive building from the outside, covered in creeper and a bit gloomy. Investigate round the back however and the picture changes. Here streams from the river Charentonne trickle appealingly through the garden and a pleasant terrace set with many umbrellas and recliners makes the best of the outstandingly attractive aspect

Once inside the mill and the 16C origins become obvious - heavy beams and low ceilings add plenty of character, as do soft table lights, fresh flowers and pretty china.

François Déduit cooks traditional and regional food, with more lavish use of Norman cream than is today fashionable. Take dinner here and you will be happy to stagger upstairs.

The eight rooms are somewhat disappointing in this setting in that they are more functional than charming, with showers not baths, but the view over the river makes up for a lot and they are not unduly expensive.

Menus from 28€.; rooms from 47€.

ST. DENIS-LE-GAST 50450, Manche

Map 4B
5 km W of Hambye on the D13, 15 km N of Villedieu.

In the heart of the pretty valley of the Sienne.

Hôtel St Evremond 🛏 ⊠ S
    4 r. de Clos d'Égypte
    tel: (0)233.61.44.42
    fax: (0)233.61.33.77
    closed: Mon.; 20/9-20/10

A recommendation from Madame Allain (of l'Auberge de l'Abbaye at Hambye) was good enough for me. I checked out this extremely simple little hotel/restaurant and found it to be clean, bright and cheap. Rooms cost 32€ with shower, 35€ with bath, and the 12.5€ menu is said to be more than adequate. Owners M. and Mme Cassis aim to please.

ST. GERMAIN-DU-CRIOULT 14110, Calvados

Map 5C
4.5 km W of Condé-sur-Noireau on the rte. Vire, D512

Auberge St Germain 🛏 ⊠ S
tel: (0)231.69.08.10
closed:; Sun. 1 week in Aug.

An old-fashioned Logis, simple rooms, simple food, simple good value. Heaving on Sunday lunchtimes, with the flushed Mme. Baude endeavouring to serve, chat to regulars and cope with nosy-Parkers like me.

Her husband cooks local specialities like Haddock in sauce Normande, sauté of beef in cider, and of course tripe with calvados, on a modestly-priced 11.5€ menu.

The rooms are basic but clean and functional – 38€.

ST. GERMAIN-DES-VAUX 50440, Manche

Map 2A
29 km NW of Cherbourg, 8 km Nez-de-Joburg

Right at the tip of the Cotentin's north-western finger, near the impressive viewpoints of the Cap de la Hague and the Nez-de-Jobourg and 'the smallest port in France', Port Racine. A drive in this direction adds a new dimension to a knowledge of the area's witty diverse attractions.

☆ Le Moulin à Vent ⊠ M
tel: (0)233.52.75.20
closed: Sun. p.m.; Mon.; evenings in winter

Turn right in Joburg and the Moulin is well signed off the D203. The lanes are long and narrow, the high hedges with occasional glimpses of the sea remind me of south Devon. The tower of the old windmill stands silhouetted against the rocks in a wild windswept landscape. Comfort is at hand in the shape of an excellent little restaurant, which deserves to be better known and assured of more custom, but before investigating and in order to work up an appetite, a walk along the cliff path would bring rewards in the shape of fabulous views of rollers far below. Next stop America. In winter it is untamed nature at its fiercest but when sunshine mellows the harshness of the rocks it is a truly lovely spot, perfect for picnics if a restaurant meal is not envisaged.

An ideal introduction to a guaranteed first-class meal is to sip an aperitif in the garden, admiring the view, and choosing from the menu. The fresh bass is to be recommended, so is the smoked ham from Vire, or the tunny tartare with a spinach garnish. it hardly matters - everything is fresh and cooked à point. The decor is pink and deep red, the patronne friendly and helpful. Full marks all round.

Menus are 16€ and 27€.

A star for exceptional cooking in an unspoiled beauty spot

ST. JAMES 50240, Manche

Map 6B
19 km S of Avranches by D998

Already on the hub of five roads, this little town is a useful stop-off now that the new Caen-Rennes autoroute is completed, passing a few km west. Its a pleasant enough typically French small town, with plenty of stocking up shops and easy parking in the big square.

Normandie 🛏 ⊠ S
pl. Bagot
tel: (0)233.48.31.45
fax: (0)233.48.59.45 R
closed: 27/12-17/1

A change in management here means that the place has been smartened up but the welcome is not as friendly as it used to be. However the 14 rooms are clean and cheap at 43€, all with showers, and the food simple but good on menus 19.2, 24 and 31€ with house wine helping to keep the bill manageable.

ST. JEAN-LE-THOMAS 50530, Manche

Map 5B
17 km S of Granville
Market: Sat.

Just one long main street makes up this pleasantly sleepy village.

It trickles down through flowery cottage gardens to a vast sandy beach, where the ride recedes for miles. Mont St. Michel swims on the horizon, and you can hire a guide, with or without a pony, to ride across the treacherous shifting sandbanks towards the vision.

With time to spare, follow the coast road towards Avranches for more unique views of La Merveille. From Bec d'Andaine stick to the minor road along the flat salt marshes, in a world of old stone barns and primitive farms, past Le Grand Port (not very grand) and Le Grouin du Sud. For refreshment there are somewhat grotty snack bars at the end of sandy lanes and several possibilities to hire a horse for a promenade equestre along the immense beaches.

Hotel Des Bains 🛏 ☒ S

8 Allée Clemenceau
tel: (0)233.48.84.20
fax: (0)233.48.66.42
closed: Tues. lunch; Thurs lunch; 2/11-5/3

The daughter and son-in-law of Madame Gautier have now joined the family team; I'm not surprised that reinforcements were necessary, since the Gautier web now covers half of the village. There is the original building, with very pleasant garden and popular heated swimming pool, a large new bar and snack restaurant presided over by s.-in-l. Latish for lunch, we arrived, not hungry enough for a big tuck-in. 'Could we have just a salad or a sandwich perhaps?' 'No problem.' Pushing our luck: 'In the garden maybe, now that the rain has stopped?' 'Certainly. I'll just wipe down the tables.' With just a glass of wine, not a whole bottle?' Why not?' It was a very good salad and served with a smile.

Just across the road are two more houses annexed for additional beds and, best of all, down on the beach is the Villa Les Dunes with four more rooms and a big terrace overlooking the sea. At 48€ a room, I imagine you have to be pretty quick off the mark to book this one and it was certainly occupied on my visit so I cannot report on the standard. The rooms in the hotel are pretty basic but adequately fitted with a variety of showers, baths, single, twin or double beds at 48-54€. Those with a balcony are 59€. Meals are from 13.6€ and the quality is said to be high.

'Exactly as you describe, excellent value, charming family, delicious

food. Carpeted walls and dodgy plumbing, but the beds were superbly comfortable.' Sally Barlow.

ST. MARCOUF-DES-ILES 50310, Manche

Map 3B
7 km S of Quinéville, 15 km SE of Valognes

I was reproached by a reader for commenting that the coast south of St. Vaast was dreary and hardly worth a detour apart from the historical interest of the landing beach, Utah. Always a martyr to duty, always ready to be corrected, I re-inspected, hoping to be proved wrong. I wasn't. Dreary it still is, in my view. However, for those with more tolerant tastes and an appetite, sustenance is at hand:

Le Relais des Îles 🛏 S ⊠ M
tel: (0)233.21.00.98

Panoramic view from the dining room, where, predictably, seafood stars. Humble rooms, nice terrace. Menus from 12.5€.

ST. MARTIN-DE-MIEUX 14700, Calvados

Map 5D
5 km S of Falaise on the D511, signed Putanges

☆ Chateau du Tertre 🛏 L
tel: (0)231.90.01.04
fax: (0)231.90.33.16
closed: Mid Oct.-Apr.

A stunning 18C château, where the world if not his wife seemed to have slept: Marcel Proust, Gustave Flaubert, Guy de Maupassant, to name but few, have lingered here in the park of 40 acres, and loaned their names to the bedrooms.

The rooms are charmingly furnished and equipped, each one individually styled. Worth the price tag of around 115€ for a special occasion (or even 176€ for an apartment for a very special occasion).

The gardens are lovely. There is a large vegetable plot to supply the chef with nothing but the freshest, a duck pond, lots of roses

and a croquet court
   Sadly, there is no longer a restaurant.

ST. PIERRE-LANGAIS 50530, Manche

Map 5B
8 km SE of Granville on the D973

Just a hamlet on a crossroads, at which you turn left (if heading south), following the signs to the ruined abbey of la Lucerne d'Outremer (a pleasant peaceful spot if you're in picnicking mood).

ST. QUENTIN-SUR-LE-HOMME 50220, Manche

Map 58
5 km SE of Avranches by D103 and D78

Just a pleasant tiny village, in whose centre is:

☆ **Le Gué du Holme** 🛏 ⊠ M
   Le Bourg
   tel: (0)233.60.63.76
   fax: (0)233.60.06.77
   Restaurant closed: Sat. lunch; 1/10-Easter Sat. lunch and Fri; Jan.

A chunky stone building with orange blinds and geraniummed window boxes with a pleasant garden behind for summer snacking. Annie and Michel LeRoux have worked hard to upgrade their ten bedrooms, which are now very comfortable and well equipped at 64€, and the menus, from 25€, feature plenty of local seafood. Father and son, Michel and Guillaume share the cooking. Much favoured by Avranchin businessmen for lunch. It would certainly make a peaceful and agreeable base for a visit to Mont St. Michel or en route to Brittany. Readers report enthusiastically so a new star.

ST. VAAST-LA-HOUGUE 50550, Manche

Map 28
30 km E of Cherbourg

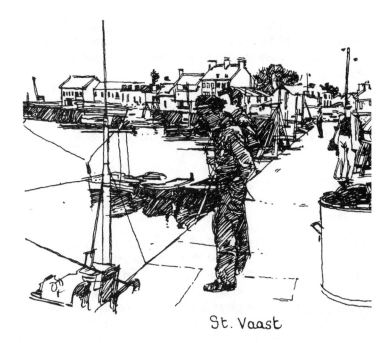

St. Vaast

Market: Sat.

Gets bigger and busier. Some hold that the marina and its inhabitants have swamped the character of the little town and its residents, but there's still enough fishy activity in evidence to lend loads of atmosphere. The red-faced weather-beaten fishermen still mend their nets on the quay side and gossip with their copains before wobbling home on antique bicycles, fortified by a stiffener or three at one of the many local bars on the quayside. There is still a very sizeable fishing fleet competing for attention with all the glossy yachts of many nations; the quiet backstreets are still lined with modest grey stone cottages that have no truck with the tourists.

The surroundings are just as lovely, just as unspoiled. Offshore island Tatihou with its marine museum can be reached on foot at low water and another not-to-be-missed walk leads along the stone sea wall, battered by waves in rough weather, along the little isthmus that links the former island of La Hougue, with its landmark fort, to St. Vaast. From here you can view the whole coastal panorama around the vast bay, past the landing beaches to Grandcamp-Maisy, and the islands of St. Marcouf. Do not fail to call in at the bijou Mariners' Chapel, with its heart-rending wall plaques in memory of beloved husbands, fathers and sons "Péris à mer".

Parking can be a problem, especially on Saturdays. Its a great market but not for the car-encumbered.

Hôtel de France, Restaurant des Fuchsias ⊨ ⊠ M

20 r. Mal-Foch
tel: (0)233.54.42.26
fax: (0)233.43.46.79
Restaurant closed: Mon. and Tues o.o.s.; 1/1-15/2.
Hotel closed: Mon o.o.s.; 1/1-15/2

An enduring favourite with the Brits because of its comfiness, sheer prettiness and the cornflakes on the breakfast buffet, and with the French for the good value and excellent food.

The eponymous fuchsias have recovered their vigour after the frost blight and rampage as brilliantly as ever up the facade of the little hotel in the main street They are the theme that runs throughout the public rooms. The curtains are fuschia-ed, the china too, the table linen is pink and the trompe-l'oeil mural in the large new conservatory features the flowers prominently. Charming.

Their use as a house emblem was the idea of the young Madame Brix, daughter-in-law of the original owners who now leave most of the day-to-day concerns of the hotel in the capable hands of the charming Isabelle.

The conservatory dining option, light, bright and cheerful, is in complete contrast to the older, more traditional restaurant, all dark beams and cosiness. On the weekly menu 14-52€ I ate soupe de poisson, six creamy St Vaast oysters and a divine croustillade de truite de mer- a crispy golden parcel of filo pastry encasing sea trout cooked à point. In the surrounding sauce were infantile vegetables, broad beans and carrots, fresh from the family farm. Normandy cheeses and a crème brulée flavoured with chicory (as in coffee not salad). Husband's choice was langoustines in raspberry vinegar, fillet beef and a feathery tarte aux pommes. There is a perfectly good weekend menu from 22-52€. Demi-pension here would make good sense.

In a separate building at the end of the pretty garden are some extra rooms, furnished with flowery chintzes, cane furniture and modern bathrooms. Those overlooking the garden are particularly agreeable, especially in summer when a magnificent Kiftsgate rose garlands the maple tree in airy white swathes. These are the most expensive; we had a smaller one overlooking the road last time and there was little traffic noise, but on market days there is considerable early morning activity. This cost 55€. In the main building there are decisions to be made - bath or shower, twin or double, overlooking garden or courtyard? They range from 77€.

I like almost everything about the F. et F. - the food, the good value and the charm of the management, but readers have been less happy, so the star must go.

La Granitiére 🛏 M

74 r. Mal-Foch
tel: (0)233.54.58.99
fax: (0)233.20.31.49
Hotel closed: 10/12-1/3

As the name implies, a granite house. Substantial, immaculately presented, on the main approach road to the port - but set well back. There are now seven spacious well-equipped rooms, furnished with repro antiques, all with luxurious bathrooms of the maroon/dark blue persuasion. Most readers have been pleased with the comfort on offer, but one found the owners 'tight-lipped'. There's certainly not the atmosphere of the Fuchsias here but the mod-cons might be considered just as important. Rooms 64-93€ including breakfast. Sadly, there is no longer a restaurant here.

Restaurants there are aplenty, mostly along the quayside, predictably specialising in fish. Readers have recommended most of them and its just a question of walking along, viewing the menus and the clientele and deciding which one appeals. You will get what you pay for. I have a new favourite:

La Chasse Marée ⊠ M

8 pl. du Gén. de Gaulle
tel: (0)233.23.14.08
closed: Sun. p.m. o.o.s.; Mon. lunch; Jan

A smart little bistrot, distinctive with its navy blue and white striped awnings. Inside all is nautical chic - simple but not designed for fisher folk. The fish here comes sophisticated - fricassée de Saint Jacques et crevettes, choucroute de poissons - or straightforward - a perfect sole meunière - on menus at 16 and 22€ or, of course, as is often preferable in fish restaurants, on the carte.

ST. VALÉRY-EN-CAUX 76460, Seine-Mar

Map 1F
32 km W of Dieppe, 32 km E of Fécamp
Market: from June to September, Fri.

The steep chalk cliffs slope down to enclose the harbour of this little fishing town. its centre was razed in 1940 and the re-building is dull, apart from an eccentric church in the market place, whose windows pitch down to the ground. Worth looking inside - far better than you might think. A forest of masts rises from the yachts tied up in the mouth of the river and fish is sold straight from the fishing boats along the quays. The beach is stony and seemingly forever windswept, but St Valery still attracts its share of holiday-makers and there are plenty of cafés in the flowery main square to cater for them.

The other side of the harbour suffered less damage and dignified old houses still look down upon the water. I had never thought to look for a hotel up here before, but discovered:

Hotel Henri IV ⇔ S
16 rte. du Havre
tel: (0)235.97.19.62

On the main road but with an unexpected courtyard at the rear, most rooms look out over the harbour (make sure you ask for one of these). The friendly owners serve breakfast in the courtyard and encourage their guests to use it for relaxing and for picnic lunches. The rooms, some with baths and some with showers, are bargains at 38-47€, with real furniture not all plastic.

Les Terrasses ⇔ ⊠ M-S
Front de Mer
tel: (0)235.97.11.22
fax: (0)235.97.06.83

closed: Sun. p.m., Mon. and Tues. lunch o.o.s.

Better than its bleak modern facade facing north on the windy sea front might suggest. Readers have leapt to its defence when I described it as austere. The twelve rooms have been re-furbed and now have cheerful fabrics and bathrooms apiece. Try and get one facing the sea of course at 56€. The dining room makes the most of the marine view and is heavily booked at the weekends. Seafood figures prominently and menus start at 21€.

ST. WANDRILLE-RANÇON 76490, Seine-Mar

Map 2F
4 km NE of Caudebec by the D37

A pretty village, embalmed in the peace that seems to emanate from the abbey in its centre, to which I strongly recommend a visit.

The abbey is named after the 7C Count Wandrille, who, on the day of his marriage to a young and lovely bride, gave up his life at the court of King Dagobert to consecrate his life to God. His wife entered a convent and Wandrille joined a group of hermits and was subsequently ordained at St. Ouen in Rouen. His saintliness and magnificent physique earned him the nickname of God's Athlete.

Even on a busy Sunday afternoon the silence in the abbey grounds was striking. The ruins of the soaring slim columns which used to support the 14C nave are still impressive, as are the wonderful Renaissance stone carvings, in total contrast to the simplicity of the tiny chapel, built by the monks after the 1944 bombing. Inside are bare hard benches, flowers and white walls, hung with some amazing modem paintings, which I like very much indeed. There is a pleasant walk to St. Saturnin chapel built at the edge of the abbey park.

Auberge Deux Couronnes ⊠ M

Pl. de l'Église
tel: (0)235.96.11.44
closed: Sun. p.m. and Mon. 5/1-1/2

A charming typically Norman old building opposite the abbey gate.

Two small and cosy beamed dining rooms are always packed at weekends, and the Complet sign goes up regularly (so book).

The food is traditional Norman, as you might expect, well-cooked and presented, on good menus, from 22€ and there is carafe wine.

STE. CÉCILE 50800 Villedieu-les-Poêles, Manche

Map 5B
2 km E of Villedieu.

The Manoir is well signed on the D554, off the Caen road

Le Manoir de l'Acherie 🛏 ⊠ M-S
   tel: (0)233.51.13.87
   fax: (0)233.61.89.07
   closed: Mon. o.o.s.; Mon. lunch; 2 weeks in Feb; 2 weeks in Nov.

An old stone house, peacefully set in a pleasant garden. There are two cosy dining rooms with log fires and dark beams and the bedrooms look out on to lots of greenery. The food is said to be very good but I thought the 15.5€ menu looked a bit boring and it would be necessary to pay more for an interesting meal. Demi-pension is from 49-54€ per person.

Rooms range from 35€ to 56€ for one with bath, or 53€ for twin beds.

Readers have been well satisfied with the quiet relaxation on offer and this is a reliable and friendly stop.

STE. MARGUERITE-SUR-MER 76119, Seine-Mar

Map 1 G
12 km W of Dieppe signed from the D75

Take the road signed to the Phare d'Ailly, a pleasantly wooded route towards the sea, with good walks towards the beach at Vasterival.

☆ La Buissonnière ⊠ M
   rte. du Phare d'Ailly
   tel: (0)235.83.17.13

closed: Sun. p.m.; Mon.; Jan.; Feb.

Utterly charming, utterly unexpected. La Buissoniére looks like a private home, a kind of chalet bungalow, white, brown-shuttered, flowery garden, parasols and deckchairs on the lawns. And indeed that is what it was until its nice owner decided to share her cooking skills with the public. Now you can sit in her light and airy dining room or on the terrace overlooking the rhododendrons at the rear and sample the fare of someone who is dearly in love with her craft.

The menus are innovative and always changing according to the season and the market. The cheapest is 28€, which represents excellent value.

SÉES 61500, Orne

Map 6E
23 km SE of Argentan; 22 km N of Alençon
Market: Sat.

Quite a sizeable town, once a busing Gallo-Roman provincial centre, now a sleepy backwater, with narrow quiet streets of old houses and several squares. It centres on the gorgeous 13th century cathedral 'one of the finest examples of Norman Gothic' enthuses Michelin, and the Bishops' Palace on the other side of the place. Son et Lumière floods the cathedral, and the whole town, on summer evenings.

Le Dauphin ⍾ ☒ M
31 pl. des Halles
tel: (0)233.80.80.70
fax: (0)233.80.80.79
closed: Sun. p.m. and Mon. o.o.s.; 1/11-7/11; 15 days in Feb./Mar.

An ancient relais de la poste next to the market halles. The building, picturesquely beamed, has been wisely restored. The 7 rooms are not large, but attractively furnished and equipped, some with four poster beds - 54-70€, the latter price for an apartment. Cooking is good - Norman specialities on menus that start at 22€ (12€ for lunch) - a langoustine soup, shoulder of lamb stuffed with mushrooms, cheeses and desserts, served in a pretty dining room -

Sées.

tapestry chairs, pink and black curtains.

It's all better than I've made it sound, probably because it was closed last time I visited and I was unable to add anything to previous impressions. Readers confirm that it is a comfortable and reliable stop.

SERVON 50170, Manche

Map 6B
16 km S. of Avranches just north of the N175

Auberge du Terroir 🛏 ☒ S
Le Bourg.
tel: 02.33.60.17.92
fax: 02.33.60.3.26
closed: Sat lunch, Wed o.o.s. and 17/11-6/12

Rather than stay in the crowded, expensive, artificial atmosphere of Mont St.Michel, choose this little country inn, tucked away in a nearby village. There are six cheerful rooms, (48-60€), but the real strength is the cooking. The 15€ menu leaves little to be desired, but there are others up to 39€.

More reports would be particularly welcome.

SILLY-EN-GOUFFERN 61200, Orne

Map 5E
10 km from Argentan, well indicated off N26

In deepest countryside, down lengthy green rides through the forest. Utterly peaceful.

Pavilion de Gouffern 🛏 ☒ M
tel: (0)233.36.64.26
fax: (0)233.36.53.81
closed: Sun. p.m. and Mon. lunch o.o.s.; 15/11-15/3

Included for its position and lovely leafy grounds, this old hunting lodge could have been restored with more taste and less obvious commercial consideration. The flags of many nations that flutter at its gate seem totally out of harmony with the surroundings. However, although the 19 bedrooms are disappointingly characterless, they are undeniably comfortable, with every mod con and gloriously rustic views. Over-priced at 44€ for a single and doubles 64-80€. The trellised, light and airy dining room overlooks the garden; on its 15.5-20€ menu were a hare terrine, brochettes of pork and a dessert.

SOTTEVILLE-SUR-MER 76740, Seine-Mar

Map 1 F
25 km W of Dieppe

Not a lot to recommend Sotteville as a beach resort. Not a lot of fun sunbathing on those cobbles. Press on to Veules, or halt for refreshment at:

Les Embruns ☒ M
tel: (0)235.97.77.99
closed: Sun. p.m. and Mon.; 5/9-1/10; 2 weeks end of Jan./beginning of Feb.

A tiny beamed restaurant, where the cost of your main dish determines the price of the whole meal. There is a commendably short menu, with menus from 12€ during the week, 22€ weekends. Good value, good choice.

SULLY Calvados

Map 3C
3 km NW of Bayeux by D6

On the little road that leads to Port-en-Bessin.

☆ Château de Sully ⇔ ☒ L
Rte. de Port-en-Bessin
tel: (0)231.22.29.48
fax: (0)231.22.64.77
closed: R. Mon. lunch; Tues. lunch; Sat. lunch; R. and H. closed 25/11-10/3

Bayeux is surrounded by luxury château hotels, but this is the one I like best At L prices one expects near-perfection and I think Sully is the château that comes nearest to meeting that demand. It's a stunning 18C mansion set in 15 acres of grounds, with the huge advantage of a large covered swimming pool. It's fortunes, since it was converted into a hotel, have been muted; British investment was involved at one time, but there were problems. The new management, headed by Inka and Antoine Brauti, both graduates of the prestigious hotel management school of Lausanne, have now got the mixture right, profiting from the previous expenditure, adding professionalism, and retaining a friendly atmosphere. There are only 23 rooms, which helps to keep the personal touch, and they are exquisitely furnished and equipped. The prices I was given personally were cheaper than those on the tariff, so it might be worth checking. They ranged from 77€ for a really luxurious double to 56€ for the cheapest on offer, tucked away in the roof with mansard windows. At this price I could put up with a bit less light considering that all the other amenities of the hotel would be at my disposal, but of course it is always a good idea to go for the best you can afford for a special occasion (Bridal suite 118€). It would definitely be a special occasion here, with so many attractions nearby - the coast, Bayeux, and the lovely local countryside.

The dignified amber-coloured dining room is a fitting setting for the excellent cooking, which has won the Château de Sully a Michelin star. Again the prices are fair. Menus start at 27€ and rise to 59€ for the lobster brigade.

A star for the very best in the whole region.

THURY-HARCOURT 14220, Calvados

Map 4D
26 km S of Caen
Market: Tues.

A sad shadow of its pre-war self, but a useful first or last night stop, in the heart of the enchanting Suisse Normande.

Relais de la Poste 🛏 ⌧ M
7 r. de Caen
tel: (0)231.79.72.12

fax: (0)231.39.53.55
closed: Sun. p.m. and Mon. o.o.s.; 22/12-5/1

A long-established solid hotel in the centre of town. The 12 rooms are comfortable and have not increased vastly in price so that they are now affordable at 48-67€.

Good Norman cooking on menus from 15.5€ lunch to 25€ evenings, in a delightful vaulted dining room.

TOUQUES 14800, Calvados

Map 3E
3 km SE of Deauville by N834
Market: Sat.

Do not make the mistake of supposing that Touques is just a suburb of Deauville. T'other way round if anything, since Touques has been around since mediaeval times. In the 11C it was an important port on the mouth of the river from which its name derived. Thomas à Becket built a church here, the Dukes of Normandy were regular visitors. The few ruins that remain of William the Conqueror's castle at Bonneville-sur-Touques are witness to the town's early eminence. A bigger contrast to its more popular parvenu neighbour cannot be imagined.

The town, alas, without direct access to the beach, was allowed to fade somewhat until recently, when a clever pedestrianisation and planting policy makes it distinctly more attractive. Deauville it can never ape, but I have a feeling that Touques is up and coming and would provide a reasonable alternative to staying on the coast

Le Village ⊨ ⊠ M

64 r. Louvelet Briers
tel: (0)231.88.01.77
fax: (0)231.88.99.24
closed: Sun. pm, Mon, and Tues. o.o.s.; Jan.

A pleasant little hotel in the town centre, opposite the Mairie. It is fo its restaurant that it is particularly well-known. Chef pleases locals and Deauville visitors alike with his cooking which he describes as soigné. You should book if you want to eat at popular times. The dining room is certainly more soigné than one would imagine from the exterior, with attractive stone walls and elegant place settings.

There are 8 comfortable rooms above. It might be wise to ask for one au calme.

Rooms 40€.

Menus from 23€.

Verte Campagne , Trelly

TRACY-SUR-MER 14117, Calvados

Map 3C
2.5 km SW of Arromanches, 7 km N of Bayeux, signed off the D156

Just a hamlet in peaceful green fields.

Hotel Victoria 🛏 M
24 Chemin de l'Eglise
tel: (0)231.22.35.37
fax: (0)231.21.4t.6fi
closed: 1/10-31/3

A nice old grey stone manor-house, covered with roses, dating probably from the last century and now a useful haven from the tourist activities from which it derives its customers. There is a flower-filled courtyard, a large garden and enclosed car park. The fourteen rooms, built for a more stately age, are spacious and gracious and cost 87€ with breakfast. The lack of a restaurant is hardly a deterrent, with so many enticing alternatives nearby. Pity the prices have rocketed.

TRELLY 50660, Manche

Map 4B
12 km S of Coutances

The hotel is actually in the hamlet of Le Chevalier, well-signed from both the D7 and the D971, in the green heart of Normandy. Set in a maze of narrow leafy lanes is the aptly named

☆ **La Verte Campagne** 🛏 ☒ M
   tel: (0)233.47.65.33
   fax: (0)233.47.38.03
   closed: Mon.; 15 days in Jan.; 1 week in Dec.

Anywhere as pretty as this usually has a snag - often the price or the attitude of the owners. Not so here. I re-visited with great trepidation because although I was terrified of the previous owner, the doughty Madame Meredith, I always loved staying in her charming home.

It's an 18C erstwhile farmhouse, smothered with climbing roses, as picturesque as can be, utterly peaceful. Inside is cool, dim, stone-walls, big fireplaces, fresh flowers, copper - you know the kind of thing - all immaculately presented. The new young owners have wisely changed nothing here.

Upstairs is pretty well as I remembered it too, except that some of the rooms have been redecorated. Madame Meredith was always full so I could never look at rooms other than mine, the only single and of course the smallest. This time I was able to see the other six, all lovely. I particularly liked the one decorated in red Toile de Jouy, twin beds, with bath opposite (only two have en suite bathrooms). What has changed is the food. The youthful Pascal Bernou has been a chef for 20 years, working in Michelin-starred restaurants, but this is the first time he has been chef-patron. A Michelin star in 1996 was his reward for innovative and skilled cooking, served in the charming dining room. Rooms from 35-61€, menus from 22e. Demi-pension would be a wise choice here, at 45-56€ per person.

A truly lovely place to stay - one of my favourites in all Normandy. Starred for delightful situation, owners and food.

LE TRÉPORT 76470, Seine-Mar

Map 1H
30 km N of Dieppe

Lively, cheerful, good-humoured. The fish and little but the fish. Terrible beach but plenty of ozone. It's pleasant enough to stroll out along the wooden pier to the lighthouse, or along the prom and up to the viewpoint on the impressively sheer cliffs.

It's also pleasant to acquire an appetite by strolling along the quayside inspecting the menus of the almost exclusively fishy restaurants. Well they may throw in a token bifsteak or lamb chop but it would take a real pisciphobe to choose meat here. The limited closing dates are a good indication that the customers are not just summer tourists.

Don't necessarily go for the cheapest; with so much competition for customers there's going to be corners cut to get the prices down. With fish you get what you pay for, sometimes less but never more. There are usually special promotions - lobster at so much a gram, which always leaves me choosing something else because I can't work it out.

Spoiled for choice but my favourites are:

Le St Louis ☒ M

43 quai François ler
tel: (0)235.86.20.70
closed: 20/11-15/12

Quite smart inside, with well-set tables. Absolutely classic fish dishes like a wing of skate with beurre noisette, a steak from a wonderful turbot hoiked out of the Tréport waters very recently or a pristinely fresh sole. What more could one ask? Menus from 15.5€ (lunch).

La Matelote ☒ M

30 quai Francois ler
tel: (0)235. 86.01.13.
closed: Tues. p.m. o.o.s.

More adventurous perhaps, in a decor that is modern, navy-blue, fishing-net bestrewn. Scallops are combined with sweetbreads, the fillets of sole are served in a sauce thick with seafood. Pleasant service. Menus at 12.5€. (Lunch mid-week), then 15€. (except dinner at weekends), 20€.

Otherwise

Le St Yves 🛏 ⊠ S-M
Quai Albert Cauet, Place de la Clare
tel: 02.35.86.34.66
fax: 02.35.86.53.73
closed: 15-Dec to 2-Jan, Sun p.m. and Mon.

A reader's suggestion, not yet inspected. sounds promising. Madame Boucher is a friendly and hospitable hostess in this family-run Logis de France where the price of the 14 rooms is very reasonable at 42-55€. There are also three suites at 64-106€, which would make good family accommodation. The cooking is very good and there is plenty of fresh seafood, but unfortunately the restaurant is only open in season, i.e. June, July, August and September.

BENY-BOCAGE 14350 Calvados

13 km NE of Vire on the D577

Castel Normand 🛏 SRM
Place du Marche
closed: Sun p.m. and Mon, 1-Aug to 8-Aug

If your priorities are food first and hotel second, the Castel Normand fills the bill nicely. This dignified granite building, covered in Virginia creeper, in the centre of the village, is a restaurant with rooms. Just seven of them, cost: 43-52€. The food is much more important. Interesting menus run from 27€.

TROUVILLE 14360, Calvados

Map 3E
3 km E of Deauville, 41 km S of Le Havre, 47km NE of Caen
Market: Wed. and daily in July and August

The beautiful new Pont de Normandie has brought Trouville within easy reach of Le Havre, making it equidistant between the two main ferry ports.

No distance at all across the other bridge to its more elegant sister, Deauville, but there is little family resemblance. When Deauville dies out of season or when the weather is too inclement for the delicate Parisians to venture out and brave the sea breezes, Trouville gets on with its workaday existence as a busy and colourful fishing port. The catch, enviably fresh, ends up on the fish market stands and it makes a diverting little exercise to walk along and speculate what you would buy if you had the excuse.

While Deauville is jet-set, Trouville is family-set The kids get the beach and Dad gets the casino, at the mouth of the river, the smarter end of town, where dignified Edwardian villas, some reincarnated as hotels, line quiet streets. I get the distinct impression that the town is smartening itself up. There is a whole new area of pleasant pedestrianisation and interesting little shop and cafés just behind the main drag.

Hotel Carmen 🛏 ☒ S-M

24 r. Carnot
tel: (0)231.88.35.43
fax: (0)231.88.08.03
closed: Wed o.o.s.

Readers have been well satisfied with this little hotel in a side street near the casino, run by M. and Madame Bude. Demi pension is obligatory in high season, but this is no great hardship since the standard of cooking is way higher than you might expect from a two-star hotel.

17 rooms are modestly comfortable, at 73€.

Menus 12.5 (week) and 15.5€ (weekend). Half pension 57€.

Along the boulevard facing the fish market is a string of fishy restaurants, serving similar food at similar prices. If you wish to eat at a table outside one of these on a sunny Sunday, you should have booked. Otherwise it's musical chairs, strolling casually up and down, observing who is at the coffee stage and making a strategic dive at the right moment. Our favourite has always been Les Vapeurs, a veteran of some 70 years, run like a Parisian brasserie, with impatient waiters in black-and-white uniform. We were thwarted at our last attempt and knew better than to believe the frantic maître d' when he promised us a table in half an hour. We got lucky a few doors away at La Marine and squeezed in gratefully, ready to accept second-best. But in fact the food was every bit as good and the waiters less cocky. I pigged out on oysters and Husband was very happy with his 13.6€ worth of moules, fried plaice and crème caramel. All irreproachable and generous. A visit to the loo gave me the chance to notice a nice stone-walled room inside, complete with vivier, and another upstairs, so good news for cloudy days too.

As we left, around 3 o'clock, our table was eagerly appropriated yet again, making me wonder why our British fishing ports don't offer the same formula - fresh fish, simply cooked, eaten in the sunshine (and don't plead the weather - this was March).

Menus from 13.6€.

La Petite Auberge ☒ M

7 r. Carnot
tel: (0)231.88.11.07
closed: Wed.

A change from the noisy row of restaurants on the front, this one is quieter, more rustique, serving regional food and of course good fish. Readers have approved this long-standing recommendation and it is very popular with the locals.

Menus from 22.7€.

Chez Nicolas ☒ S

32 r. des Bains
tel: (0)231.88.56.10
closed: Wed. o.o.s.; 10 days at the end of Jan.; 10 days in Nov.

Just a few blocks back from the river, in the newly smartened up area. A change from the salty scene, this is a new bistrot, tiny, usually full, cooking traditional Norman food, not necessarily fishy (though they do specialise in oysters and six best St. Vaast will cost you 8€). If you take the 24€ menu, you get six for the first course anyway, plus skate/boeuf bourguinon and dessert. Nice atmosphere.

Bistrot les 4 Chats ⊠ S
8 r. d'Orléans
tel: (0)231.88.94.94
closed: Fri. lunch; Sat. lunch and Sun. lunch

Another innovation, in the same area. This is a menu-on blackboard, scrubbed tables, arty kind of bistrot, specialising in tapas. It does have a carte too, listing inexpensive dishes and snacks. Different, young at heart, and fun.

VALMONT 76540, Seine-Mar

Map 2F
10.5 km SE of Fécamp via the D150

In a green and fertile valley dominated by a castle on a rocky spur, the Romanesque keep and a Louis XI wing are open to the public and certain other rooms house temporary exhibitions. The Benedictine Abbey of Valmont, founded in the 12C, became the private residence of cousins of Delacroix in the 19C and the artist used to stay here. The graceful Lady Chapel (or the 'Six o'clock chapel' because the monks celebrated mass here at that time) has remained intact among the ruins.

l'Agriculture ⊠ S-M
9 r. d'Estouteville
tel: (0)235.29.84.25
Fax(0)235.29.45.59
Restaurant closed: Sun. p.m.; Mon.; 10/9-17/9; 15/1-15/2

Several readers' reports first alerted me to the value to be found here in this solid stone building on the main road. The restaurant is a few hundred yards away on the other side of the road, a more modern, glass-sided building, looking out onto the garden. It is a surprisingly large room, which I'm told gets very busy at weekends and, when I visited, stiflingly hot (but it was an unusually sunny day).

Apart from that quibble, the news was good. Michel Guérin is a friendly and helpful patron, as well as being a fine cook, and his menus, starting at 9.4€ for mid-week lunch, are good value. Others are at 15-31€. Behind the hotel is a pleasant terrace on which to relax, and there is safe parking and a room for the handicapped. All the eighteen rooms are pleasantly furnished with real furniture and good value, at 37€. Its the kind of place where demi-pension would be a good idea, at 35-45€ per person.

VALOGNES 50700, Manche

Map 3B
20 km SE of Cherbourg
Market: Fri.

Valognes clings to its old title 'The Versailles of Normandy' but that's pushing it a bit. The events of 1944 destroyed for ever most of the dignified 18C houses that hitherto lined the quiet streets. The one or two that were spared, like the Hôtel de Beaumont or the Hôtel de Granvol-Caligny, only emphasise the contrast between what was and what is now, in the concrete reincarnation. However it is still an important market town for the surrounding agricultural area, with a huge market filling the square on Fridays. Because of its position it would make a useful overnight stop, if only there were any recommendable hotels.

The restaurant scene is not much better in the town itself. In the square by the church is La Galetière, a pizzeria approved of by readers, and Le Versailles Normand, a useful brasserie. But there is a new possibility just outside the town on the Carentan road:

Beaurepaire ☒ M
    tel: (0)233.40.20.30
    closed: Sun. p.m.; Mon.

Opened in 1994 but still looking a bit raw, although old stone has been used to renovate and extend the old farm-house. The garden needs to fill out too and then it will all be very pretty and colourful.

Inside the restaurant is elegant and soothing, with a high gallery for extra seating. Cooking is said to be very superior, easily the best in the town. The 22€ menu yielded scrambled eggs and oysters, noisettes d'agneau aux herbs poivrées, cheese and dessert - good value in view of the high standard of surroundings and covers.

More reports most welcome.

LE VAL ST. MARTIN 27700 Le Thuit, Eure

Map 3H
3 km N of Les Andelys on D313

The best way to approach Les Andelys is to follow the river. There are pastures between the road and the river (and sometimes it must be said, ugly camping sites) and to the left the chalk escarpment is carved into bizarre shapes, towering high. Just pootle gently along, past a few scattered houses and in no time you will be in Les Andelys, with no traffic fret.

Le Manoir de Clairval 🛏 ⌧ M

> 2 r. de Seine
> **tel:** (0)232.54.37.17
> **fax:** (0)232.54.37.45
> **Restaurant closed:** Tues. and Wed.

A new enterprise which I think might prove very useful. The Manoir is a dignified white building overlooking the river (with a few caravans in between) which has recently been turned into a hotel. The grounds are scruffy, the taste inside the lovely rooms is dubious, but look at the price – 47€ for a spacious double room with shower, or 56€ with bath. Ceilings are high, windows down to the ground; one might wish the furniture were antique rather than job lot, but for this sum, so near the delectable Les Andelys, that would be asking too much.

   This would be a good kid-stop, with a big untamed garden, and no main roads to worry about. It would also be a very peaceful halt for these with a long journey ahead of them but I have a feeling that conferences and 'reunions' will be important. There is a restaurant, with menus from 15.5€, about which I know nothing. Reports welcome.

VARENGEVILLE 76119, Seine-Mar

Map 1G
11 km W of Dieppe

The coast road westwards from Dieppe, the D75, reveals a very different Seine Maritime from the acres of flat farmland that form the greater part of the landscape. There are gorgeous views of the spectacular chalk cuffs that painters have loved to portray for generations; far below the foam of the rollers and the curve of the bays are further temptations to stop the car and get out the camera. Pourville-sur-Mer and Quiberville are now caravanned blots on the landscape but the fishing boats still pull up on to the cobbled shores and these are good stops for a lunch of a dozen oysters and a glass of Chablis.

Buffeted by the sea breezes, graveyard running down to the very edge of the high cliffs, stands the ancient church where Braque is buried. Inside his Tree of Jesse, burning blue, attracts a steady stream of visitors. On the same lane is the Parc des Moustiers, a Gertrude Jekyll garden surrounding a rambling Lutyens house. The upper part is typical Jekyll - a series of 'rooms' approached via pergolas, with a good display of old shrub roses. Behind the house the grounds fall away dramatically and there are extensive walks through the woods and to the church.

Inland deep valleys carve their way through the wooded landscape down to the sea. Sheltering in one such is Vasterival, well-signed 3 km west

☆ **Hôtel de la Terrasse** 🛏 ⊠ M-S
   tel: (0)235.85.12.54
   fax: (0)235.85.11.70
   closed: 15/10-15/3

High above a lovely beach of sand, stones and rocks stands this popular little hotel, now in the hands of the fourth generation of the same family. The young Delafontaines are systematically brightening up the decorations, so that although the paint still peels a bit from the staircase, the bedrooms are painted in cheerful colours and some of them have views down to the sea.

It's a family hotel in every sense and booked up during the school holidays for months ahead. There's a cosy relaxed atmosphere about the place, which does not mean clutter and unruliness. Cooking is above average and readers have nothing but praise for the establishment and its owners. Menus from 15.5€. 22 rooms at 53€.

There are lovely walks from the hotel, to the lighthouse at Ailly and down to the beach; just one word of warning for the infirm, who might imagine that the sea is readily accessible. In fact it is a steep ten minutes away.

Starred for position, owners and good value.

{ Le SAUMON - Verneuil.

Les Pucheux ⊠ S
1 r. du Dr. Pierre Girard
tel: (0)235.97.19.28

Basically a crêperie, but a good one, with simple grills too. Pleasantly beamed and cosy, in the main street.

Les Tourelles ⊠ S
13 r. du Dr. Pierre Girard
tel: (0)235.57.18.56
closed: Tues. o.o.s.

Another pleasant little restaurant in the main street, claiming `etude de menus adaptés & à tous les budgets'. Certainly you could have just one dish here - say a sole for 11.5€, or the menu for 9.4€. Good charcuterie, to eat here or take away.

VERNEUIL SUR AVRE 27130, Eure

Map 5G
50 km S of Rouen
Market: Sat.

On Normandy's border, defined by the river Avre, and subsequently fortified in the 11C to hold the frontier against France. Several splendid old houses in the area between the Tour Grise, the drum tower, and the 15C church of La Madeleine, three storeys high, crowned by a double diadem of lantern and Flamboyant tower. The centre of the town, as it should be, is the wide market square, full of colour on Saturdays.

A good choice for a weekend or en route stop-off, with theramparts to explore, the river Avre nearby, and a trusty favourite in which to stay.

☆ Le Saumon 🛏 ☒ S-M
89 pl. de la Madeleine
tel: (0)232.32.02.36
fax: (0)232.37.55.80
closed: 15/12-15/1

Le Saumon is looking very smart these days, newly painted deep cream, proudly occupying the central position in the market square.

Inside the bedrooms too have been freshened up. 56€ buys a very nice twin bedded room overlooking the action in the square (don't worry, Verneuil goes to bed early). More modern ones are in the annexe at the rear, suitable for the handicapped, 38€.

The breakfast room has not changed - still the pretty blue and white iris pattern on the walls - and neither has the salon, with a faded flowery paper, the dining room has attractive green and yellow trellised walls;

M. Simon is chef and cooks very satisfactory meals on a 25€ menu terrine of langoustines, veal liver pan-fried in cider vinegar, salad or cheese and dessert. Mid-week, not veryhungry, broke? Go for the 14€ menu with plat du jour and crème caramel.

The star stays - the formula works well and readers have been very happy.

Hostellerie Le Clos 🛏 ☒ L
118 r. de la Ferté Vidame
tel: (0)232.32.21.81
fax: (0)232.32.21.36
closed: Mon. lunch; Tues. lunch; 12/12-20/1

When I compare the standard of luxury here with a similarly priced establishment in England, there is no doubt that Le Clos is the handsome winner. Outside it is an eccentric, turreted, lozenge-brick patterned Belle Époque manor house, on the outskirts of the town. Inside, the gates and the very air smells expensive. Nothing but the best, in dining room - china, silver, napery, flowers, antiques - and of course the cuisine; in bedrooms - not large but attractively decorated in light pastels, each with a Jacuzzi in the marble bathroom - and terrace - expensive recliners and flowers likewise. All this for 136€ for the room and from 29€ for dinner. Watch the wine bill and you've got a good deal. Readers have concurred.

At the other end of the scale, if you're looking to re-coup a little, there is a new wine bar in a pedestrianised alley off the main square. Les Moulettes in the rue Moulette will fix you up with an omelette/salad/cheese platter, with a glass of wine.

VERNON 27200, Eure

MAP 4H
63 km SE of Rouen
Market: Sat.

On the banks of the Seine. There are some attractive old houses near the 12C Notre Dame, and the Saturday morning market is a particularly good one, with all the bars surrounding the market square doing a thriving trade. Head here if you are looking for a sandwich lunch.

The other two local rivers, the Epte and the Eure, offer pleasant excursions and are good for picnic sites.

But Vernon's special interest for tourists is its proximity to Monet's garden in Giverny just across the river. It is therefore surprising and disappointing that there is little to recommend in the town to house the pilgrims. The two big hotels in the town centre were never great, and even one of those has now been demolished to make way for an apartment block. Look elsewhere I'm afraid. I did find two good restaurants, one an old favourite and one new:

La Poste

26 av. Gambetta
tel: (0)232.51.10.63
closed: Wed.; 3/8-23/8

Readers have been unanimously in favour of this one, in the town centre. Particularly busy on market days, but fewer stall holders now seem to be customers, perhaps because it's looking a bit too smart for them nowadays.

The prices are creeping up too, with the cheapest menu at 14.4€ (lunch) and 20€ (dinner) - timbale of foie gras, entrecôte, salad and dessert.

Les Fleurs ⊠ M

71 r. Carnot
tel: (0)232.51.16.80
closed: Sun. p.m.; Mon.; 1/8-28/8

The rue Carnot is probably Vernon's most attractive road, with some half-timbered houses and semi-pedestrianisation. It's the first turning to the left after you cross the Seine. Two comfortable little dining rooms are usually full. Good menus start at 21€.

VEULES-LES-ROSES 76980, Seine-Mar

Map 1F
26 km W of Dieppe
Market: Thurs.

I thought I knew Veules pretty well, having dined and rhapsodised many times about its famous, rosetted restaurant Les Galets. But I think I must have always arrived in the dark or just driven down to the beach, which is nothing much, and dismissed the claims that this is the prettiest village on the coast. This time I found I could agree with that. I started further back, parking by the church in order to visit the Thursday market which the Tourist Office had promised me. No market (July and August only), but that left the whole morning free to explore.

The Tourist Office's other recommendation proved altogether more worthwhile. It was to follow the signs for the Circuit de la

Veules, the little river, "le plus petit fleure de France" since its source and estuary are both in Veules-les-Roses. Utterly charming to zigzag across the main road and to discover little wooden bridges, water mills, cress fields, and some chocolate-box thatched cottages. We ate our picnic alongside one of these, and found a paddle in the fresh clear water irresistible. But there is more good news back in the town, which is undergoing a transformation from sleepy to buzzing.

☆ Douce France 🛏 M
   tel: (0)235.57.85.30
   closed: 18/11-3/12; 5/1-26/1

We journalists love nothing better than a scoop, so picture my glee on discovering this very special establishment only three weeks after it had opened. The conversion of some of the thirteen rooms contrived out of an old presbytery and stables set back from the main street were not even finished. The transformation has been thorough and tasteful. The typical but heavy Norman brown cross timbering of the facade around the courtyard has been muted to a soft sage green which gives an almost Scandinavian look. One of the most valuable bonuses, fully exploited, is that the little river Veules flows right through the property. A charming salon de thé has been established overlooking the rushing water and there are more basket chairs and tables in the courtyard for use whenever the weather allows. Some of the rooms have a private terrace with the same soothing aspect. The accommodation (from 67€) takes the form of small apartments, fitted with a smart kitchenette, fridge, microwave, cutlery and china; the opportunity to prepare one's own breakfast and snacks could knock pounds off the bill. The rooms vary and some in the roof are a bit dark, but most have little sitting areas, and luxury bath/shower rooms and are decorated with cheerful modern fabrics and expensive tiled floors.

For this standard you might expect a price at least double of the reality, which is from 57€. Go for the 64€ version if you can which will give you another bedroom (so you could sleep four) and much more space.

The restaurant is good news too, featuring Les Assiettes: Poissons Marinés (7.2€), Maraîchère (4.6€), Jambon de Parme (7.2€), platters of salads, with 13 different accompaniments, hot and cold. Or you could have just lobster bisque for 4.8€ or a platter of local cheeses for 5.6€. Leave room for super desserts, around 4€ extra. Wine by the glass - hooray! A real find. Go soon before the rest of the world discovers the bargain.

Starred of course.

VILLEDIEU-LES-POÊLES 50800, Manche

Map 5B
34 km S of St. Lô
Market: Tues.

It's not hard to discern what is Villedieu's speciality. The wide main street is lined with shops selling the copper pans which gave the town its name (poêle = frying pan). They have been made here since the 12C and the giant copper milk vats (cannes) to be found not so long ago outside every Norman farm came from here.

Today the craftsmen concentrate on rather less bucolic items like industrial boilers, or, increasingly, the tourist gew-gaws that are on sale in the shops. The Villedieu part of the name was bestowed on the town by the Knights of Malta; every four years since 1655 there is a great procession, known as the Grand Sacre, recalling the town's early history. The first Commandery of the Knights of St John of Jerusalem was established here in the 12C by Henry Beauclerk, successor to William the Conqueror.

The Knights of St. John also founded a bell foundry here and you can visit this unique workshop, which still produces bells for churches and ships world-wide. You can also visit the copper workshop where the history of copper-making in Villedieu is demonstrated, and the Museum of Copperware and the Lacemakers House, which displays specimens of old lace-making frames and bobbins as well as the lace itself.

So, all in all, its an interesting old town, with quiet inner courtyards like the Cour des Trois Rois and the Cour aux Lys, and a Flamboyant Gothic church built on the site of an earlier church erected by the Knights. Copper features even here, in the shape of vases flanking the 18C tabernacle. The Tuesday market which overflows from the main street is well worth a visit.

Le Fruitier 🛏 ☒ M

pl. des Costils
tel: (o)233.90.51.00
fax: (o)233.90.51.01
closed: Christmas; New Year's Day

Almost unrecognisable nowadays from the simple back-street hotel that readers alerted me to some fifteen years ago as an alternative to the then dominating Hôtel de France in the main street. Blonde Madame Lebargy has worked hard to achieve this transformation into an increasingly up-market proposition, facing onto the car-park square (but there is a private car park too). It's all very glossy nowadays, especially in the new reception area, which boasts a fountain. It's also very pink, extending to the pink leather seating, the pink bar and even a pink lift. Not necessarily what one might think appropriate for a small country town, but undoubtedly upwardly mobile.

The 38 rooms are really very comfortable and well-equipped, with good bathrooms, and the cooking is accomplished and generous, served in an elegant dining room decorated with trellis trompe l'oeil. In fact the whole deal is excellent value. Rooms 48€ , menus from 13.6€ (and you can happily stick with the cheapest one).

'As good as ever but one wishes one could get a smile out of the very efficient Mme Lebargy. Though only classified as two-star we think this hotel is definitely superior to many three-stars but apparently Mme L. doesn't wish to upgrade. Excellent accommodation, beautifully prepared food and a fantastic breakfast by French hotel standards - self service choice including fruit juices, cereals, eggs, croissants.' Roger Lushington.

VILLEQUIER 76490, Seine-Mar

Map 2F
45 km E of Le Havre

From Caudebec take the D81, following the Seine and 3 km further on is the village infamous for the fact that Victor Hugo's daughter drowned there. There is a pleasant walk along the riverbank but otherwise the village is spoiled by heavy traffic.

Auberge du Val au Cesne
Yvetot

Grand Sapin 🛏 ☒ M-S
tel: (0)235.56.78.73
fax: (0)235.95.69.27
closed: Tues. p.m. and Wed. (except in Jul. and Aug.); last 15 days of Nov.; 15/11-1/12.

An old-fashioned long-established restaurant with five bedrooms overlooking the river. Readers have been happy to overlook the fading decor and concentrate on the view from their rooms and from the long terrace. The restaurant is very popular at weekends and for celebrations. Twice we have been turned away because it was taken over entirely for a party, so don't rely on getting a table without booking. Five Rooms 41-51€, menus from 11.2€ weekdays, up to 32€.

VILLERS BOCAGE 14310 Calvados 1

13 km from Cherbourg
On the main N175 between Caen and Vire.

Les Trois Rois 🛏 (S)RM

tel: 02.31.77.00.32
fax: 03.21.77.93.25
closed: Sun p.m. and Mon; Jan, 25-30-Jun

If there were prizes for an archetypal French restaurant-with-rooms, Les Trois Rois would win hands-down. It is a solid bourgeois establishment, with solid bourgeois food. Excellent food and lots of it, served in an elegant and serious dining room. Menus are splendid value at 20€ upwards and there are thirteen adequate rooms to fall into afterwards at 32-64€.

YVETOT 76190, Seine-Mar

Map 2F
51 km NE of Le Havre by N15, 36 km NW of Rouen by A15

A largish market town in the centre of the farming territory of the Caux plateau. Its modern concrete buildings lack eye appeal and it is hard to believe that from the 14C to the Revolution the town was an independent territory with its own king. It was also famous as the legendary capital of an imaginary kingdom in a song by Béranger. The Max Ingrand glass in the hard-to-miss free-standing belfry is now easily the town's most interesting feature.

I personally would not choose to stay here, with the delightful alternative described below as an option, but I do have good reports of the Hotel Havre in the main Place Belges (tel: 35.95.16.77, rooms 35-56€; at Val-au-Cesne, 4 km SE by D5). Really pretty countryside, with steep green valleys running down to the Seine,

☆ Auberge du Val-au-Cesne 🛏 ⊠ M

tel: (0)235.56.63.06
fax: (0)235.56.92.78
closed: Mon.; Tues.; 20/8-3/9

I vowed that I would not overwork the word idyllic in this book, but I have no option but to squander it here. The old black-and-white timbered auberge set in a flowery garden is pure picture book, inside as well as out. Beams galore, guinea fowl pecking happily

Wines and spirits by John Doxat

Bonne cuisine et bons vins, c'est le paradis sur terre.
(Good cooking and good wines, that is earthly paradise.)
King Henri IV

OUTLINE OF FRENCH WINE REGIONS

Bordeaux

Divided into a score of districts, and sub-divided into very many communes (parishes). The big district names are Médoc, St Emilion, Pomerol, Graves and Sauternes. Prices for the great reds (châteaux Pétrus, Mouton-Rothschild, etc.) or the finest sweet whites (especially the miraculous Yquem) have become stratospheric. Yet 'château' in itself means little and the classification of various rankings of châteaux is not easily understood. Some tiny vineyards are entitled to be called château, which has led to disputes about what have been dubbed 'phantom châteaux'. Visitors are advised, unless wine-wise, to stick to the simpler designations.

Bourgogne (Burgundy)

Topographically a large region, stretching from Chablis (on the east end of the Loire), noted for its steely dry whites, to Lyons. It is particularly associated with fairly powerful red wines and very dry whites, which tend to acidity except for the costlier styles. Almost to Bordeaux excesses, the prices for really top Burgundies have gone through the roof. For value, stick to simpler local wines.

Technically Burgundies, but often separately listed, are the Beaujolais wines. The young red Beaujolais (not necessarily the over-publicised nouveau) are delicious when mildly chilled. There are several rather neglected Beaujolais wines (Moulin-à-Vent, Morgon, St Amour, for instance) that improve for several years: they represent good value as a rule. The Mâconnais and Chalonnais also produce sound Burgundies (red and white) that are usually priced within reason.

Rhône

Continuation south of Burgundy. The Rhône is particularly associated with very robust reds, notably Châteauneuf-du-Pape; also Tavel, to my mind the finest of all still rosé wines. Lirac rosé is nearly as good. Hermitage and Gigondas are names to respect for reds, whites and rosés. Rhône has well earned its modern reputation - no longer Burgundy's poorer brother. From the extreme south comes the newly 'smart' dessert vin doux naturel, ultrasweet Muscat des Beaumes-de-Venise, once despised by British wine-drinkers. There are fashions in wine just like anything else.

Alsace

Producer of attractive, light white wines, mostly medium-dry, widely used as carafe wines in middle-range French restaurants. Alsace wines are not greatly appreciated overseas and thus remain comparatively inexpensive for their quality; they are well placed to compete with popular German varieties. Alsace wines are designated by grape - principally Sylvaner for lightest styles, the widespread and reliable Riesling for a large part of the total, and Gerwürztztraminer for slightly fruitier wines.

Loire

Prolific producer of very reliable, if rarely great, white wines, notably Muscadet, Sancerre, Anjou (its rosé is famous), Vouvray (sparkling and semi-sparkling), and Saumur (particularly its 'champagne styles'). Touraine makes excellent whites and also reds of some distinction - Bourgueil and Chinon. It used to be widely believed - a rumour put out by rivals? - that Loire wines 'did not travel': nonsense. They are a successful export.

Champagne

So important is Champagne that, alone of French wines, it carries no AC: its name is sufficient guarantee. (It shares this distinction with the brandies Cognac and Armagnac.) Vintage Champagnes from the grandes marques - a limited number of 'great brands' - tend to be as expensive in France as in Britain. You can find unknown brands of high quality (often off-shoots of grandes marques) at attractive prices, especially in the Champagne country itself. However, you need information to discover these, and there are true Champagnes for the home market that are doux (sweet) or demi-sec (medium sweet) that are pleasing to few non-French tastes. Champagne is very closely controlled as to region, quantities, grape types, and is made only by secondary fermentation in the bottle. From 1993, it is prohibited (under EU law) to state that other wines are made by the 'champagne method' - even if they are.

Minor regions (very briefly)

Jura - Virtually unknown outside France. Try local speciality wines such as vin jaune if in the region.

Jurançon - Remote area; sound, unimportant white wines, sweet styles being the better.

Cahors - Noted for its powerful vin de pays 'black wine', darkest red made.

Gaillac - Little known; once celebrated for dessert wines.

Savoy - Good enough table wines for local consumption. Best product of the region is delicious Chambéry vermouth: as an aperitif, do try the well distributed Chambéryzette, a unique vermouth with a hint of wild strawberries.

Bergerac - Attractive basic reds; also sweet Monbazillac, relished in France but not easily obtained outside: aged examples can be superb.

Provence- Large wine region of immense antiquity. Many and varied vins de pays of little distinction. Best known for rosé, usually on the sweet side; all inexpensive and totally drinkable.

Midi - Stretches from Marseilles to the Spanish border. Outstandingly prolific contributor to the 'EU wine lake' and producer of some 80 per cent of French vins de table, white and red. Sweet whites dominate, and there is major production of vins doux naturels (fortified sugary wines).

Corsica - Roughish wines of more antiquity than breeding, but by all means drink local reds - and try the wine-based aperitif Cap Corse - if visiting this remarkable island.

Paris -Yes, there is a vineyard - in Montmartre! Don't ask for a bottle: the tiny production is sold by auction, for charity, to rich collectors of curiosities.

HINTS ON SPIRITS

The great French spirit is brandy. Cognac, commercially the leader, must come from the closely controlled region of that name. Of various quality designations, the commonest is VSOP (very special old pale): it will be a cognac worth drinking neat. Remember, champagne in a cognac connotation has absolutely no connection with the wine. It is a topographical term, grande champagne being the most prestigious cognac area: fine champagne is a blend of brandy from the two top cognac sub-divisions. Armagnac has become better known lately outside France, and rightly so. As a brandy it has a much longer history than cognac: some connoisseurs rate old armagnac (the quality designations are roughly similar) above cognac.

Be cautious of French brandy without a cognac or armagnac title, regardless of how many meaningless 'stars' the label carries or even the magic word 'Napoleon' (which has no legal significance).

Little appreciated in Britain is the splendid 'apple brandy', Calvados, mainly associated with Normandy but also made in Brittany and the Marne. The best is Calvados du Pays d'Auge. Do taste well-aged Calvados, but avoid any suspiciously cheap.

Contrary to popular belief, true Calvados is not distilled from cider - but an inferior imitation is: French cider (cidre) is excellent.

Though most French proprietary aperitifs, like Dubonnet, are fairly low in alcohol, the extremely popular Pernod/Ricard pastis-style brands are highly spirituous. Eau-de-vie is the generic term for all spirits, but colloquially tends to refer to local, often rough, distillates. Exceptions are the better alcools blancs (white spirits), which are not inexpensive, made from fresh fruits and not sweetened as crèmes are.

Bringing Back Those Bottles

When thinking of what to bring back from France in the way of wines and spirits, apart from considerations of weight and bulk, there are a few other matters to bear in mind. Within the theoretically unlimited import for personal consumption of products which have paid any national taxes in the country of origin, there are manifest practical as well as some semi-official restrictions.

Wine: to choose sensibly is not inevitably to go for the least expensive. Unless you envisage having to entertain a lot of relatives, beware the very cheapest of French table wines! Though France produces many of the world's greatest, her prolific vineyards also make wines to which no British supermarket would allocate shelf-space. Quality does count along with value. Primarily what you are saving by purchasing in France is the comparatively high excise duties imposed in Britain against the minimal ones in France.

However, the British tax is just the same on a bottle of the most ordinary vin ordinaire as on the rarest of vintage claret. When it comes to the latter, buying fine vintage wines in France does not automatically mean obtaining a bargain, unless you are an expert. There are not that many specialist wine merchants in France, a commerce in which Britain excels.

To summarise: it is undoubtedly sound, middle range wines that are the most sensible buy.

If you like those famous liqueurs, such as Bénédictine, Chartreuse, the versatile Cointreau, which are so expensive in Britain, shop around for them: prices seem to vary markedly.

I have briefly dealt elsewhere with French spirits. If you are buying Scotch whisky, gin or vodka, you may find unfamiliar names and labels offering apparent bargains. None will harm you but some may have low, even unpleasant, taste characteristics. It is worth paying a trifle more for well-known brands, especially de-luxe styles. Though they are little sold in Britain, former French colonies distill several excellent types of rum (rhum).

I deem it a good idea to make an outline list of intended purchases, after deciding what you can carry and how much you wish to spend. As to wines, do you want mainly red, or only white, or what proportion of both types? Can you afford champagne? Best to buy that in visiting the region where you should have the opportunity to taste and possibly find a bargain. What about other sparklers? What do you require in dessert wines, vermouths, liqueurs, spirits? Does your list work out at more cases (12 bottles) than you can easily transport? A conspicuously overloaded vehicle may be stopped by police as a traffic hazard. Now you have a list of sorts. What about cost? For essential comparisons, I would put against each item the maximum (per bottle) I would be prepared to pay in Britain.

Basic glossary of French wine terms

Alsace - See Wine Regions (page 266)

Abricotine - Generic apricot liqueur: look for known brands.

Alcool blanc- Spirit distilled from various fruits (not wine); not fruit-flavoured cordials.

Aligoté - Light dry Burgundy.

Anis - Aniseed, much favoured in pastis (Ricard/Pernod) type aperitifs.

Anjou - See Loire, Wine Regions (page 266)

Aperitif - Literally 'opener': any drink taken as an appetiser.

Appellation (d'origine) Contrôllée - or AC wine, whose label will give you a good deal of information, will usually be costlier - but not necessarily better - than one that is a VDQS 'designated (regional) wine of superior quality'. A newer, marginally lesser category is VQPRD: 'quality wine from a specified district'. Hundreds of wines bear AC descriptions: you require knowledge and/or a wine guide to find your way around. The intention of the AC laws was to protect consumers and ensure wine was not falsely labelled - and also to prevent over-production. Only wines of reasonable standards should achieve AC status: new ones (some rather suspect) are being regularly admitted to the list.

Armagnac - See Hints on Spirits (page 267)

Barsac - Very sweet Sauternes of varying quality.

Basserau - A bit of an oddity: sparkling red Burgundy.

Beaumes-de-Venise - Well-known vin doux naturel; see Provence, Minor Regions (page 267)

Beaune - Famed red Burgundy; costly.

Bergerac - Sound red wine from south-west France.

Blanc de Blancs - White wine from white grapes alone. Sometimes confers extra quality but by no means always. White wine made from black grapes (the skins removed before fermentation) is Blanc de Noirs - Carries no special quality connotation in itself.

Bordeaux - See Wine Regions (page 265).

Bourgeuil - Reliable red Loire wine.

Bourgogne - Burgundy; see Wine Regions (page 265).

Brut - Very dry; description particularly applicable to best sparkling wines.

Brut Sauvage - Dry to the point of displeasing acidness to most palates; very rare though a few good wines carry the description.

Cabernet - Noble grape, especially Cabernet-Sauvignon for excellent, if not absolutely top grade, red wines.

Cacao - Cocoa; basis of a popular crème.

Calvados - See Hints on Spirits (page 267).

Cassis - Blackcurrant; notably in crème de cassis (see Kir).

Cave - Cellar.

Cépage - Indicates grape variety; e.g. Cépage Cabernet-Sauvignon.

Chablis - See Burgundy, Wine Regions (page 265). Fine Chablis are expensive.

Chai - Ground-level storehouse, wholly employed in Cognac and sometimes in Bordeaux and other districts.

Champagne - See Wine Regions (page 266). Also specialty note Méthode Traditionelle below.

Château(x) - See Wine Regions, Bordeaux (page 265).

Châteauneuf-du-Pape- Best known of powerful Rhône red wines.

Chenin-blanc - Grape variety associated with many fine Loire wines.

Clairet - Unimportant Bordeaux wine, its distinction being probable origin of English word Claret.

Clos - Mainly a Burgundian term for a vineyard formerly (rarely now) enclosed by a wall.

Cognac - See Hints on Spirits (page 267).

Corbières - Usually a sound south of France red wine.

Côte - Indicates vineyard on a hillside; no quality connotation necessarily.

Côteau(x) - Much the same as above.

Crème - Many sweet, sometimes sickly, mildly alcoholic cordials with many local specialities. Nearer to true liqueurs are top makes of crème de menthe and crème de Grand Marnier (q.v.). Crème de Cassis is mixed with white wine to produce kir or a sparkling white wine to produce kir royale.

Crémant - Sparkling wine with strong but rather brief effervescence.

Cru - Literally 'growth'; somewhat complicated and occasionally misleading term: e.g. grand cru may be only grower's estimation; cru classé just means the wine is officially recognised, but grand cru classé is most likely to be something special.

Cuve close- Literally 'sealed vat'. Describes production of sparkling wines by bulk as opposed to individual bottle fermentation. Can produce satisfactory wines and certainly much superior to cheap carbonated styles.

Cuvée - Should mean unblended wine from single vat, but cuvée spéciale may not be particularly special: only taste will tell.

Demi-sec - Linguistically misleading, as it does not mean 'half-dry' but 'medium sweet'.

Domaine - Broadly, Burgundian equivalent to Bordeaux château.

Doux - Very sweet.

Eau-de-vie - Generic term for all distilled spirits but usually only applied in practice to roughish marc (q.v.) and the like.

Entre-deux-Mers - Undistinguished but fairly popular white Bordeaux.

Frappé - Drink served with crushed ice; viz. crème de menthe frappée.

Fleurie - One of several superior Beaujolais wines.

Glacé - Drink chilled by immersion of bottle in ice or in refrigerator, as distinct from frappé above.

Goût - Taste; also colloquial term in some regions for local eau-de-vie (q.v.).

Grand Marnier - Distinguished orange-flavoured liqueur. See also crème.

Haut - 'High'. It indicates upper part of wine district, not necessarily the best, though Haut-Médoc produces much better wines than other areas.

Hermitage - Several excellent Rhône red wines carry this title.

Izarra - Ancient Armagnac-based liqueur much favoured by its Basque originators.

Juliénas- Notable Beaujolais wine.

Kir - Well-chilled dry white wine (should be Bourgogne Aligoté) plus a teaspoon of crème de cassis (q.v.). Made with champagne (or good dry sparkling wine) it is Kir Royal.

Liqueur - From old liqueur de dessert, denoting postprandial digestive. Always very sweet. 'Liqueur' has become misused as indication of superior quality: to speak of 'liqueur cognac' is contradictory - yet some very fine true liqueurs are based on cognac.

Loire - See Wine Regions (page 204).

Méthode Traditionnelle- Most widely-used description of superior sparkling wine made as is champagne, by fermentation in bottle, now that any labelling association such as 'champagne method' is banned.

Marc - Mostly coarse distillations from wine residue with strong local popularity. A few marcs ('mar') - de Champagne, de Bourgogne especially - have achieved a certain cult status.

Marque - Brand or company name.

Meurseult - Splendid white Burgundy for those who can afford it.

Minervoise - Respectable southern red wine: can be good value as are many such.

Mise - As in mise en bouteilles au château ('château-bottled'), or ... dans nos caves ('in our cellars') and variations.

Montrachet - Very fine white Burgundy.

Moulin-à-Vent - One of the rather special Beaujolais wines.

Muscadet - Arguably the most popular light dry Loire white wine.

Muscat - Though used for some dry whites, this grape is mainly associated with succulent dessert-style wines.

Nouveau - New wine, for drinking fresh; particularly associated with now tiring vogue for Beaujolais Nouveau.

Pastis - General term for powerful anis/liquorice aperitifs originally evolved to replace banned absinthe and particularly associated with Marseilles area through the great firm of Ricard.

Pétillant - Gently, naturally effervescent.

Pineau - Unfermented grape juice lightly fortified with grape spirit; attractive aperitif widely made in France and under-appreciated abroad.

Pouilly-Fuissé - Dry white Burgundy (Macon); sometimes over-valued.

Pouilly-Fumé - Easily confused with above; a very dry fine Loire white.

Porto - Port wine: usually lighter in France than the type preferred in Britain and popular, chilled, as an aperitif.

Primeur - More or less the same as nouveau, but more often used for fine vintage wine sold en primeur for laying down to mature.

Rosé - 'Pink wine', best made by allowing temporary contact of juice and black grapes during fermentation; also by mixing red and white wine.

Sauvignon - Notable white grape; see also Cabernet.

Sec - 'Dry', but a wine so marked will be sweetish, even very sweet. Extra Sec may actually mean on the dry side.

Sirop - Syrup; e.g. sugar-syrup used in mixed drinks, also some flavoured proprietary non-alcoholic cordials.

Supérieur(e) - Much the same as Haut (q.v.) except in VDQS.

VQRPD. - See AC above.

Vin de Xeres - Sherry ('vin de 'ereth').

Glossary of cooking terms and dishes

This basic glossary provides an introduction to the terms you are most likely to encounter. For a more complete guide, see the companion pocket-sized book *French Entrée Menu Companion* that provides a comprehensive bilingual menu dictionary together with all the useful phrases that will help you make the most of French food and restaurants.

Aigre-doux	bittersweet	Beurre blanc	sauce from Nantes, with butter, reduction of shallot-flavoured vinegar or wine
Aiguillette	thin slice (*aiguille* - needle)		
Aile	wing		
Aioli	garlic mayonnaise		
Allemande (à l')	German style, i.e.: with sausages and sauerkraut	Beurre noir	browned butter
		Bigarade	with Seville oranges
		Billy By	mussel soup
Amuse-gueules	appetisers	Bisque	creamy shellfish soup
Andouille	large uncooked sausage, served cold after boiling	Blanquette	stew with thick, white creamy sauce, usually veal
Andouillettes	(as per Andouille) but made from smaller intestines, usually served hot after grilling	Boeuf à la mode	braised beef
		Bombe	ice-cream mould
		Bonne femme	with root vegetables
Anglaise (à l')	plain boiled. *Crème Anglaise* - egg and cream sauce	Bordelais	Bordeaux-style, with red or white wine, marrowbone fat
Anis	aniseed	Bouchée	mouthful, *e.g.* vol-au-vent
Argenteuil	with asparagus		
Assiette Anglaise	plate of cold meats	Boudin	sausage, white or black
Baba au rhum	yeast-based sponge macerated in rum	Bourride	thick fish-soup
		Braisé	braised
Baguette	long, thin loaf	Brandade (de morue)	dried salt-cod pounded into mousse
Ballotine	boned, stuffed and rolled meat or poultry, usually cold		
		Broche	Spit
		Brochette	skewer
Béarnaise	sauce made from egg yolks, butter, tarragon, wine, shallots	Brouillade	stew, using oil
		Brouillé	scrambled
		Brûlé	burnt, e.g. *crème brûlée*
Béchamel	white sauce flavoured with infusion of herbs		
Beignets	fritters	Campagne	country style
Bercy	sauce with white wine and shallots	Cannelle	cinnamon
		Carbonnade	braised in beer

Cardinal	red-coloured sauce, e.g. with lobster, or in *pâtisserie* with redcurrants
Cassolette or cassoulette	small pan
Cassoulet	rich stew with goose, pork and haricot beans
Cervelas	pork garlic sausage
Cervelles	brains
Chantilly	whipped sweetened cream
Charcuterie	cold pork-butcher's meats
Charlotte	mould, as dessert lined with sponge-fingers, as savoury lined with vegetables
Chasseur	with mushrooms, shallots, wine
Chausson	pastry turnover
Chemise	covering, i.e. pastry
Chiffonnade	thinly-cut, e.g. lettuce
Choron	tomato Béarnaise
Choucroute	Alsatian stew with sauerkraut and sausages
Civet	stew
Clafoutis	batter dessert, usually with cherries
Clamart	with peas
Cocotte	covered casserole
Compôte	cooked fruit
Concassé	e.g. *tomates concassées*-skinned, chopped, juice extracted
Confit	preserved
Confiture	jam
Consommé	clear soup
Coque (à la)	e.g. *oeufs* - boiled eggs
Cou	neck
Coulis	juice, purée (of vegetables or fruit)
Court-bouillon	aromatic liquor for cooking meat, fish, vegetables
Couscous	N. African dish with boiled grains of millet, served with chicken or vegetables
Crapaudine	involving fowl, particularly pigeon, trussed
Crécy	with carrots
Crème pâtissière	thick custard filling
Crêpe	pancake
Crépinette	little flat sausage, encased in caul
Croque-Monsieur	toasted cheese-and-ham sandwich
Croustade	pastry or baked bread shell
Croûte	pastry crust
Croûton	cube of fried or toasted bread
Cru	raw
Crudités	raw vegetables
Demi-glâce	basic brown sauce
Doria	with cucumber
Émincé	thinly sliced
Entremets	sweets
Étuvé	stewed, e.g. vegetables in butter
Farci	stuffed
Feuilleté	leaves of flaky pastry
Fines herbes	parsley, thyme, bayleaf
Flamande	Flemish style, with beer
Flambé	flamed in spirit
Flamiche	flan
Florentine	with spinach
Flûte	thinnest bread loaf
Foie gras	goose liver
Fond (d'artichaut)	heart (of artichoke)
Fondu	melted
Forestière	with mushrooms, bacon and potatoes
Four (au)	baked in the oven
Fourré	stuffed, usually sweets
Frais, fraîche	fresh and cool
Frangipane	almond-cream *pâtisserie*

271

GLOSSARY OF COOKING TERMS AND DISHES

Fricadelle	Swedish meat ball	Hors-d'oeuvre	assorted starters
Fricandeau	veal, usually topside	Huile	oil
Fricassé	stew (usually of veal) in creamy sauce	Île flottante	floating island - soft meringue on egg-custard sauce
Frit	fried	Indienne	Indian, i.e. with hot spices
Frites	chips		
Friture	assorted small fish, fried in batter		
Froid	cold	Jambon	ham
Fumé	smoked	Jardinière	from the garden, i.e. with vegetables
Galantine	loaf-shaped chopped meat, fish or vegetable, set in natural jelly	Jarret	shin, e.g. *jarret de veau*
		Julienne	matchstick vegetables
Galette	Breton pancake, flat cake	Jus	natural juice
Garbure	thick country soup	Lait	milk
Garni	garnished, usually with vegetables	Langue	tongue
		Lard	bacon
Gaufre	waffle	Longe	loin
Gelée	aspic		
Gésier	gizzard	Macédoine	diced fruits or vegetables
Gibier	game		
Gigot	leg	Madeleine	small sponge cake
Glacé	iced	Magret	breast (of duck)
Gougère	choux pastry, large base	Maïs	sweetcom
		Maître d'hôtel	sauce with butter, lemon, parsley
Goujons	fried strips, usually of fish	Marchand de vin	sauce with red wine, shallots
Graine	seed		
Gratin	baked dish of vegetables cooked in cream and eggs	Marengo	sauce with tomatoes, olive oil, white wine
Gratinée	browned under grill	Marinière	seamens' style e.g. *moules marinière* (mussels in white wine)
Grecque (à la)	cold vegetables served in oil		
Grenadin	nugget of meat, usually of veal		
Grenouilles	frogs: *cuisses de grenouille* – frogs' legs	Marmite	deep casserole
		Matelote	fish stew, e.g. of eel
		Médaillon	round slice
		Mélange	mixture
Grillé	grilled	Meunière	sauce with butter, lemon
Gros sel	coarse salt		
		Miel	honey
		Mille-feuille	flaky pastry, (lit. 1,000 leaves)
Hachis	minced or chopped		
Haricot	slow cooked stew	Mirepoix	cubed carrot, onion etc. used for sauces
Haricots	beans		
Hochepot	hotpot	Moëlle	beef marrow
Hollandaise	sauce with egg, butter, lemon	Mornay	cheese sauce
		Mouclade	mussel stew
Hongroise	Hungarian, i.e. spiced with paprika		

Mousseline	Hollandaise sauce, lightened with egg whites
Moutarde	mustard
Nage (à la)	poached in flavoured liquor (fish)
Nature	plain
Navarin (d'agneau)	stew of lamb with spring vegetables
Noisette	nut-brown, burned butter
Noix de veau	nut (leg) of veal
Normande	Normandy style, i.e. with cream, apple, cider, Calvados
Nouilles	noodles
Onglet	beef cut from flank
Os	bone
Paillettes	straws (of pastry)
Panaché	mixed
Panade	flour crust
Papillote (en)	cooked in paper case
Parmentier	with potatoes
Pâté	paste, of meat or fish
Pâte	pastry
Pâte brisée	rich short-crust pastry
Pâtisserie	pastries
Paupiettes	paper-thin slice
Pavé	thick slice
Paysan	country style
Périgueux	with truffles
Persillade	chopped parsley and garlic topping
Petit pain	bread roll
Petits fours	tiny cakes, sweetmeats
Piperade	peppers, onions, tomatoes in scrambled egg
Poché	poached
Poêlé	fried
Poitrine	breast
Poivre	pepper
Pommade	paste
Potage	thick soup

Pot-au-four	broth with meat and vegetables
Potée	country soup with cabbage
Pralines	caramelised almonds
Primeurs	young veg
Printanier (printanière)	garnished with early vegatables
Profiteroles	choux pastry balls
Provençale	with garlic, tomatoes, olive oil, peppers
Pureé	mashed and sieved
Quenelle	pounded fish or meat bound with egg, poached
Queue	tail
Quiche	pastry flan, e.g. *quiche Lorraine* - egg, bacon, cream
Râble	saddle, e.g. *râble de lièvre*
Ragoût	tew
Ramequin	little pot
Râpé	grated
Ratatouille	Provençale stew of onions, garlic, peppers, tomatoes
Ravigote	highly seasoned white sauce
Rémoulade	mayonnaise with gherkins, capers, herbs and shallots
Rillettes	potted shredded meat, usually fat pork or goose
Riz	rice
Robert	sauce with mustard, vinegar, onion
Roquefort	ewe's milk blue cheese
Rossini	garnished with foie gras and truffle
Rôti	roast
Rouelle	nugget
Rouille	hot garlicky sauce for *soupe de poisson*
Roulade	roll
Roux	sauce base -flour and butter

GLOSSARY OF COOKING TERMS AND DISHES

Sabayon	sweet fluffy sauce, with eggs and wine
Safran	saffron
Sagou	sago
Salade niçoise	salad with tuna-fish, anchovies, tomatoes, beans, black olives
Salé	salted
Salmis	dish of game or fowl, with red wine
Salpicon	meat, fowl, vegetables, chopped fine, bound with sauce and used as fillings
Sang	blood
Santé	lit. healthy, i.e. with spinach and potato
Saucisse	fresh sausage
Saucisson	dried sausage
Sauté	cooked in fat in open pan
Sauvage	wild
Savarin	ring of yeast-sponge, soaked in syrup and liquor
Sel	salt
Selle	saddle
Selon	according to, e.g. *selon grosseur* (according to size)
Smitane	with sour cream, white wine, onion
Soissons	with dried white beans
Sorbet	water ice
Soubise	with creamed onions
Soufflé	puffed, i.e. mixed with egg-white and baked
St-Germain	with peas
Sucre	sugar (*sucré* - sugared)
Suprême	fillet of poultry breast or fish
Tartare (sauce)	mayonnaise with capers, herbs, onions

Tartare	raw minced beef, flavoured with onions etc. and bound with raw egg
Tarte Tatin	upside down (apple) pie
Terrine	pottery dish/baked minced, chopped meat, veg., chicken, fish or fruit
Thé	tea
Tiède	luke warm
Timbale	steamed mould
Tisane	infusion
Tourte	pie
Tranche	thick slice
Truffes	truffles
Tuile	tile, i.e. thin biscuit
Vacherin	meringue confection
Vallée d'Auge	with cream, apple, Calvados
Vapeur (au)	steamed
Velouté	white sauce, bouillon-flavoured
Véronique	with grapes
Vert(e)	green, e.g. *sauce verte*, with herbs
Vessie	pig's bladder
Vichysoisse	chilled creamy leek and potato soup
Vierge	prime (virgin) olive oil
Vinaigre	vinegar (lit. bitter wine)
Vinaigrette dressing	wine vinegar and oil
Volaille	poultry
Vol-au-vent	puff-pastry case
Xérès	sherry
Yaourt	yoghurt

FISH - Les Poissons, SHELLFISH - Les Coquillages

Alose	shad
Anchois	anchovy
Anguille	eel
Araignée de mer	spider crab
Bar	sea bass
Barbue	brill
Baudroie	monkfish, anglerfish
Belon	flat-shelled oyster
Bigomeau	winkle
Blanchaille	whitebait
Brochet	pike
Cabillaud	cod
Calamar	squid
Carpe	carp
Carrelet	plaice
Chapon de mer	scorpion fish
Claire	oyster
Coquille St-Jacques	scallop
Crabe	crab
Crevette grise	shrimp
Crevette rose	prawn
Daurade	sea bream
Écrevisse	crayfish
Éperlan	smelt
Espadon	swordfish
Étrille	baby crab
Favouille	spider crab
Flétan	halibut
Fruits de mer	seafood
Grondin	red gurnet
Hareng	herring
Homard	lobster
Huître	oyster
Julienne	ling
Laitance	soft herring-roe
Lamproie	lamprey
Langouste	Dublin Bay prawn
Lieu	ling
Limande	lemon sole

Lotte de mer	monkfish
Loup de mer	sea bass
Maquereau	mackerel
Merlan	whiting
Morue	salt cod
Moule	mussel
Mulet	grey mullet
Ombre	grayling
Oursin	sea urchin
Palourde	clam
Pétoncle	small scallop
Plie	plaice
Portugaise	oyster
Poulpe	octopus
Praire	large clam
Raie	skate
Rascasse	scorpion-fish
Rouget	red mullet
Sandre	zander
Saumon	salmon
Saumonette	rock salmon
Seiche	squid
Sole	sole
Soupion	inkfish
St-Pierre	John Dory
Thon	tuna/tunny
Tourteau	large crab
Tortue	turtle
Truite	trout
Turbot	turbot
Turbotin	chicken turbot

FRUITS - Les Fruits, VEGETABLES - Les Légumes, NUTS - Les Noix, HERBS - Les Herbes, SPICES - Les Épices

Abricot	apricot
Ail	garlic
Algue	seaweed
Amande	almond
Ananas	pineapple
Aneth	dill
Arachide	peanut
Artichaut	globe artichoke

GLOSSARY OF COOKING TERMS AND DISHES

Asperge	asparagus	Haricot	dried white bean
Avocat	avocado	Haricot vert	French bean
Banane	banana	Laitue	lettuce
Basilic	basil	Mandarine	tangerine, mandarin
Betterave	beetroot		
Blette	Swiss chard	Mangetout	sugar pea
Brugnon	nectarine	Marron	chestnut
		Menthe	mint
Cassis	blackcurrant	Mirabelle	tiny gold plum
Céléri	celery	Morille	dark brown crinkly edible fungus
Céléri-rave	celeriac		
Cêpe	edible fungus		
Cerfeuil	chervil	Mûre	blackberry
Cerise	cherry	Muscade	nutmeg
Champignon	mushroom	Myrtille	bilberry, blueberry
Chanterelle	edible fungus		
Châtaigne	chestnut		
Chicorée	endive	Navet	turnip
Chou	cabbage	Noisette	hazelnut
Chou-fleur	cauliflower		
Choux de Bruxelles	Brussels sprouts	Oignon	onion
Ciboulette	chive	Oseille	sorrel
Citron	lemon		
Citron vert	lime	Palmier	palm
Coing	quince	Pamplemousse	grapefruit
Concombre	cucumber	Panais	parsnip
Coriandre	coriander	Passe-Pierre	seaweed
Cornichon	gherkin	Pastèque	water melon
Courge	pumpkin	Pêche	peach
Courgette	courgette	Persil	parsley
Cresson	watercress	Petit pois	pea
		Piment doux	sweet pepper
Échalote	shallot	Pissenlit	dandelion
Endive	chicory	Pistache	pistachio
Épinard	spinach	Pleurote	edible fungi
Escarole	salad leaves	Poire	pear
Estragon	tarragon	Poireau	leek
		Poivre	pepper
Fenouil	fennel	Poivron	green, red and yellow peppers
Fève	broad bean		
Flageolet	dried bean	Pomme	apple
Fraise	strawberry	Pomme de terre	potato
Framboise	raspberry	Prune	plum
		Pruneau	prune
Genièvre	juniper		
Gingembre	ginger	Quetsch	small dark plum
Girofle	clove		
Girolle	edible fungus	Radis	radish
Grenade	pomegranate	Raifort	horseradish
Griotte	bitter red cherry	Raisin	grape
Groseille	gooseberry	Reine Claude	greengage
Groseille noire	blackcurrant	Romarin	rosemary
Groseille rouge	redcurrant		

GLOSSARY OF COOKING TERMS AND DISHES

Safran	saffron	Foie	liver
Salsifis	salsify	Foie gras	goose liver
Thym	thyme	Cervelles	brains
Tilleul	lime blossom	Langue	tongue
Tomate	tomato	Ris	sweetbreads
Topinambour	Jerusalem artichoke	Rognons	kidneys
Truffe	truffle	Tripes	tripe

MEAT - Les Viandes

POULTRY - Volaille, GAME - Gibier

Le Boeuf	Beef	Abatis	giblets
Charolais	is the best	Bécasse	woodcock
Chateaubriand	double fillet steak	Bécassine	snipe
Contrefilet	sirloin	Caille	quail
Entrecôte	rib steak	Canard	duck
Faux Filet	sirloin steak	Caneton	duckling
Filet	fillet	Chapon	capon
		Chevreuil	roe deer
L'Agneau	Lamb	Dinde	young hen turkey
Pré-Salé	is the best	Dindon	turkey
Carré	neck cutlets	Dindonneau	young turkey
Côte	chump chop	Faisan	pheasant
Epaule	shoulder	Grive	thrush
Gigot	leg	Lièvre	hare
		Oie	goose
Le Porc	Pork	Perdreau	partridge
Jambon	ham	Pigeon	pigeon
Jambon cru	raw smoked ham	Pintade	guineafowl
Porcelet	suckling pig	Pluvier	plover
		Poularde	chicken (boiling)
Le Veau	Veal	Poulet	chicken (roasting)
Escalope	thin slice cut from fillet	Poussin	spring chicken
		Sanglier	wild boar
Les Abats	Offal	Sarcelle	teal
		Venaison	venison

French Entrée Series

A range of independent guides to the best restaurants, hotels and B&Bs in regions of France. Each guide is written in a personal style and is totally independent - we accept no paid entries so you read the honest and accurate views of the author as they visit the towns and villages in each area. Each guide includes travel information, contact details and chapters on local specialities.

French Entrée Guides to:

Bed & Breakfast in France	1-904012-04-3
Brittany	1-904012-03-5
Calais, Bolougne, North	1-904012-00-0
Normandy	1-904012-02-7
French Food & Drink	1-904012-05-1

All titles are new, revised and updated editions.